Modelling software with pictures.

UML diagramming for real-time embedded systems

Jim Cooling

Published by Lindentree Associates © 2018

From the Lindentree series 'The engineering of real-time embedded systems'

Modelling software with pictures

For Pauline

Mo shíorghrá

And to thank her for all her help and support over these many many years. Without that I would have achieved much less in my life.

CONTENTS

Glossary of terms

Preface

Chapter 1
Modelling - What and why.

1.1 Why bother to model in the first place?   1
1.2 What we can learn from modelling.   5
1.3 Modelling the qualities of systems.   7
    1.3.1 Introduction.   7
    1.3.2 Structure.   7
    1.3.3 Processing.   10
    1.3.4 Interactions.   10
    1.3.5 Dynamic behaviour.   13
    1.3.6 Usage.   14
1.4 The modelling of software - key aspects.   17
    1.4.1 The software machine and object-oriented techniques.   17
    1.4.2 Modelling OO software with UML diagrams - a broad perspective.   18
1.5 Review.   20

Chapter 2
Diagramming techniques: the world in pictures.

2.1 Diagrams – why?   23
    2.1.1 Introduction.   23
    2.1.2 Reality, modelling and diagrams.   25
    2.1.3 Diagrams as a design tool.   29
    2.1.4 Diagrams for design documentation.   30
    2.1.5 Diagrams for maintenance.   32
    2.1.6 Diagrams for communication.   33
2.2 The essentials of software diagrams.   35
    2.2.1 Fundamentals.   35
    2.2.2 Basic qualities.   36
2.3 Review.   39

Chapter 3
Diagramming and UML: a broad perspective.

3.1 Setting the groundwork. 41
3.2 Software diagramming - a historical prelude. 41
    3.2.1 The evolution of software diagramming - the embedded world. 42
    3.2.2 The evolution of software diagramming - the MIS world. 43
    3.2.3 Enter UML. 43
3.3 UML - a simple overview. 44
3.4 UML – assumptions, issues and remedies. 45
    3.4.1 Underlying assumptions of the UML specification. 45
    3.4.2 UML issues. 47
    3.4.3 UML and domain-specific issues. 47
    3.4.4 Employing UML in real-time systems. 49
3.5 Review. 50

Chapter 4
The structural design model.

4.1 Some important preliminaries. 51
4.2 Objects and their classes - the 'simple' model of OO design. 52
4.3 Collaborating objects. 59
    4.3.1 The design models. 59
    4.3.2 Coding aspects of associations - C++ examples. 65
4.4 Modular objects. 71
4.5 Software reuse - inheritance. 78
    4.5.1 General aspects. 78
    4.5.2 Implementation inheritance (subclassing) 78
    4.5.3 Interface inheritance (subtyping). 83
    4.5.4 Interface inheritance - flexibility aspects. 85
4.6 Building connectable structures. 87
    4.6.1 Setting the scene. 87
    4.6.2 The composite structure - why? 88
    4.6.3 Wiring objects together using Ports. 91
4.7 Building larger modular structures - components. 97
    4.7.1 Some background. 97
    4.7.2 Components - constructs and notation. 98
    4.7.3 Practical aspects of using components. 101
4.8 Packages, artifacts and deployments. 103
    4.8.1 Why things need to be organized. 103
    4.8.2 Packages and package diagrams. 103
    4.8.3 Artifacts. 107
    4.8.4 Deployment diagrams and nodes. 109
4.9 Review. 109

Chapter 5
The behavioural interactions model

5.1 Object types and their interactions.   113
5.2 Modelling interactions - the basics of sequence diagrams.   116
    5.2.1 Introduction.   116
    5.2.2 Basics of UML sequence diagrams.   116
    5.2.3 CASE tool issues.   121
    5.2.4 Some lesser-used constructs.   123
5.3 Modelling interactions - efficiently handling sequence diagrams. 124
    5.3.1 Brief introduction.   124
    5.3.2 Diagram maintenance.   124
    5.3.3 Diagram navigation.   124
    5.3.4 Diagram comprehension.   128
5.4 Modelling the timing of interactions.   133
5.5 The communication diagram.   138
5.6 Review.   142

Chapter 6
The behavioural dynamics model

6.1 Introduction to dynamical modelling.   145
    6.1.1 The basics of state modelling.   145
    6.1.2 State machine fundamentals.   146
6.2 Transition-related behaviour.   150
6.3 State-related behaviour.   154
6.4 Combining state-related and transition-related behaviours.   156
6.5 States and substates - composite states.   157
    6.5.1 Composite states and sequential state machines. 157
    6.5.2 Concurrent state machines.   160
6.6 Minor topics - diagram simplification and decluttering.   164
    6.6.1 History pseudostate.   164
    6.6.2 Junction and choice pseudostates.   166
6.7 Code-related aspects.   168
6.8 Review.   170

Chapter 7
The processing model

7.1 Introduction to process modelling.   173
7.2 Basics of UML process modelling - activity diagrams.   177
    7.2.1 Introduction to activity diagrams.   177
    7.2.2 Using signals.   180
    7.2.3 Important but lesser-used constructs.   182
7.3 Why program structure diagrams?   183
7.4 Structuring and decomposing activity diagrams.   187
7.5 Applying activity diagram symbols to interaction overview diagrams.   189
7.6 Code-related aspects of program design.   190
7.7 Review.   192

Chapter 8
The usage model

8.1 Introduction to usage modelling - use case analysis.   195
8.2 Describing, structuring and packaging use cases.   199
8.3 Review.   205

Chapter 9
Practical diagramming issues

9.1 Setting the scene.   207
9.2 Building well-structured embedded software.   208
9.3 Using the right diagrams - 1.   210
    9.3.1 General comment.   210
    9.3.2 Usage.   210
    9.3.3 Structure.   211
    9.3.4 Behaviour and interactions.   213
    9.3.5 Behaviour and dynamics.   213
    9.3.6 Processing.   213
9.4 Using the right diagrams - 2.   214
9.5 Review.   216

Chapter 10
Outline guide to UML notation

10.1. Overview of the diagram set.   219
10.2. Activity diagrams.   220
10.3. Artifacts.   222
10.4. Class diagrams.   224
10.5. Component diagrams   225
10.6. Deployment diagrams.   226
10.7. Interaction diagrams.   228
10.8. Object diagrams.   232
10.9. Composite structure diagrams.   233
10.10. Package diagrams.   234
10.11. State diagrams.   235
10.12. Use case diagrams.   242

References, further reading and bibliography   245

Index   247

Glossary of terms

AADL   Architecture Analysis and Design Language
ADC   Analogue to Digital Converter

CAN   Controller Area Network
CASE   Computer Aided Software Engineering
COM   Component Object Model
CORBA   Common Object Request Broker Architecture
COTS   Commercial Off The Shelf

DAC   Digital to Analogue Converter
DCOM   Distributed COM

EA   Enterprise Architect
EJB   Enterprise JavaBeans

FSM   Finite State Machine

HMI   Human-Machine Interface

IDE   Integrated Development Environment
IDL   Interface Definition Language
LIN   Local Interconnect Network

MARTE   Modelling and Analysis of Real-Time and Embedded Systems
MDA   Model-Driven Architecture
MIS   Management Information Systems

.NET   A programming framework developed by Microsoft

OMG   Object Management Group
OO   Object Orientation
OOD   Object Oriented Design
OOP   Object Oriented Programming
OS   Operating System

PSM   Platform-Specific Model

RTES   Real-Time Embedded System
RTOS   Real-Time Operating System
RUP   Rational Unified Process

SAE   Society of Automotive Engineers
SysML   Systems Modeling Language

UML   Unified Modeling Language

Preface

Another book in the series 'The engineering of real-time embedded systems'.

What is this book about?

The aim here is to show embedded software engineers how to model their designs using diagrams and descriptive text in an effective, clear and useful way. *The term 'diagramming', as used in this text, implicitly means 'modelling'.*

A key aspect in all of this is the *sensible* application of a set of diagrams defined within the Unified Modelling Language (UML) standard.

What is this book series about?

These books set out to provide a firm foundation in the knowledge and skills needed to develop and produce real-time embedded systems. They fall into two categories.

- Those providing a solid grounding in the fundamentals of the subject.
- Those showing the application of specific design and development techniques.

Engineers from the well-established professions (electronic, mechanical, aeronautical, etc.) fully understand the distinction between these two aspects. Moreover, experienced engineers recognize that to effectively apply your skills you must truly have a good grasp of fundamentals. Regrettably, this view is sadly lacking in the area of Software Engineering.

Please note two small points. First, I have used 'he' as shorthand for 'he/she', for simplicity and ease of reading. Second, when I express opinions supported by my professional colleagues, I use the term 'we'. If comments are made based on my own purely personal views then I use 'I'.

Who is this book written for?

Those designing - or who intend to design - software for real-time embedded systems (RTESs).

Why is there a need for a book like this one?

There are two particular reasons for producing this book. First, many embedded systems developers need to be convinced that modeling and diagramming are not only useful; they also help us to produce reliable software that is delivered on time and at the right price. Second, to show that it's not enough just to produce diagrams; it is essential that they be used in an organized, professional and rigorous manner.

Why is diagramming so important?

No matter what activity you're engaged in, be it sports, hobbies or work, you should always have a clear idea of:

1. What you're doing and
2. Why you're doing it.

You will soon, we hope, see how powerful and useful diagramming is as an aid to answer these questions. But be careful when you begin to use diagramming; it's all too easy to get enmeshed in detail and lose sight of the bigger picture. To use a cliché, we can't see the wood for the trees.

So what is the 'wood' here? Quite simply, it's **why** we use diagrams in the design and development process? In essence they help us to:

- Analyze and evaluate something that already exists.
- Analyze and evaluate something that's proposed.
- Develop design solutions to meet particular objectives.
- Specify what is to be designed.
- Specify what is to be built.

Now, does this mean that each activity uses a unique set of diagrams? Not so. For example, the sequence diagram (which you will meet later in the book) can be used in numerous phases of a development project

To be effective as a designer it's not enough to know what a diagram does; it's also important to know how to use it simply and effectively. And to do that you really need to understand the fundamentals of diagramming and diagramming techniques.

Why has diagramming been such a neglected topic?

In the early days of computers, diagramming didn't figure as an important topic in the design process. Further, the only pictorial method used was that of the flow chart. At that time there was little distinction between programming and design (nor, for that matter, between programmers and designers). The design and development process usually went something as follows:

- Programmers thought about the problem to be solved.
- They wrote lines of code to solve it.

- The code was tested and modified until it was correct (or appeared to be so).
- This source code was released as the system documentation.

Sometimes, in a token gesture to appease senior management (or the customer), a system flow chart was produced. Whether it represented what went on in the program is another matter. And the sad fact is that this describes the ethos that still pervades many parts of the embedded world.

Fortunately, in recent years a revolution has taken place concerning the use of diagramming for software. In the IT world the major driving force for this has been the widespread adoption of UML. As a result, practically all modern software tools use diagrams as an integral part of the design and development process.

Alternatives to this book?

Or to put it another way, are there cheaper or no-cost ways of getting the information contained here? The answer, as far as UML is concerned, is mainly 'yes'. Generally there are three options open to you:

- First, you could download a copy of the UML specification document from the Object Management Group (OMG) website.
- Second, you could trawl across the internet, seeking out articles, tutorials and the like relating to UML.
- Third, if you have a UML computer-aided software engineering (CASE) tool, use the documentation supplied with it.

These options aren't, of course, mutually exclusive.

Well, this is fine as far as it goes. Because, in reality, there are drawbacks with all three methods. More will be said in a moment about UML; but if you check out the specification using DrivelDefence (from the Plain English Campaign, www.plainenglish.co.uk) you'll get some idea of what you're faced with.

There is a great deal of useful information to be found on the Internet. Unfortunately there is also a lot of dross. A further problem is that even the good web postings tend to deal with individual diagramming aspects; there is a lack of a 'joined-up' process. And regrettably, the amount of material dealing directly with embedded design aspects is quite small indeed.

CASE tool material can be extremely useful. But, be careful. There *may* be tools that support all the features of UML, but we just haven't found them yet. In general you will be limited by the tool facilities. Moreover, most tools provide vendor-specific extensions to, and variations on, the UML specification. Lastly, with the high-end embedded tools you get a tool-specific design process as well as a design notation (and these are inseparable). This often results in designers ending up with a rather narrow, parochial, view of software design principles and practices. It's easy to end up knowing *what* to do but not *why* you're doing it.

UML; the answer to a maiden's prayer?

At this point I want to inject a personal note into the book. It's important for you to realize that the presentation here of UML is essentially *my* view of the topic. I have rarely modified the defined syntax of the specification; rather it's a case of emphasizing a subset of the full range of diagrams. This includes:

- Selecting the diagrams most useful for RTESs work.
- Specifying where these diagrams may, or should, be used.
- Showing, where possible, how to use these diagrams in an integrated fashion.

In the years after UML arrived it was promoted in an almost evangelical manner. All sorts of claims were made concerning its power, effectiveness and 'richness' (a dreadfully over-used word). The first release, at version 0.8, left me distinctly underwhelmed. From my experience of using software diagrams in embedded systems design for many years, I found that it didn't:

- Offer a great deal to the embedded world and
- Give much idea on how to effectively use the diagrams and
- Promote simplicity of design and directness of communication.

So, many years later, how do things fare? Well, UML does provide us with a good range of useful diagrams, though there are still a few gaps (UML enthusiasts insist that you can fill these gaps by adapting standard diagrams; myself, I'd rather use standard notation where possible). Tool support is extensive, ranging from very low-cost drawing packages through low-cost CASE tools to very expensive integrated development environments (IDEs). And it is, by far, the most widely-used non-propriety software diagramming technique. All in all, good reasons to consider using UML in your projects.

   Well, that's fine as far as it goes. But embedded developers new to the topic still have to overcome three major hurdles:

- What diagrams to use.
- When to use them and
- How to use them effectively, both singly and together.

This book aims to answer these questions, providing sensible, useful and logical guidance for the reader. If it fails to do this, the fault is entirely mine.

A brief look-ahead.

The content of this book falls into two quite distinct categories. The first, covered by chapters 1 to 3, is a 'selling' mission, to try to make you understand why it really is a good idea to use modelling methods in your designs. The rest of the book shows how to put these ideas into practice when designing software.

Chapter 1 sets out to show just how much can be achieved by using modelling in your projects. It discusses this in the broader engineering sense, identifies the key model types and shows how these can be applied to software projects.

Chapter 2, *Diagramming techniques*, is complementary to the modelling chapter. It revisits some of the material discussed in that chapter, but now emphasizes the diagramming aspects. It discusses a whole range of issues, showing just what a powerful tool diagramming is.

The aim of chapter 3 is to provide you with a very broad overview of UML: its history, the rationale for its development and, most important, some of its limitations and weaknesses. But its real purpose is to give you the confidence to use UML diagrams in a considered, selective and effective way: not just blindly doing things 'because they're in the manual'.

The next set of chapters is organized on a model-by-model basis, following the grouping defined in chapter 1. The diagrams described are those that we have found to be especially useful in the development of RTESs. This isn't limited to just the syntax and semantic aspects (such information is widely available) but also tries to show *how* and *why* such diagrams are used. Rounding things off is chapter 9, 'Practical diagramming issues'. This is especially important as it provides practical guidance on using UML diagrams for the design and development of real-time systems.

Acknowledgments.

The inspiration for this book was the work of Martin Fowler and his book 'UML Distilled' (ISBN 0-321-19368-7). The book itself is excellent, something I myself would have been quite proud of. What really grabbed my attention was his statement 'My intention is to find that fraction of the UML that is most useful and tell you just that'. In the context of the monster UML 2.0, this was a brave position.

Whilst the book is a first-class one it has, from the view of the embedded world, a key weakness; it is written more with the general software market (e.g. IT, databases, web working) in mind. I hope to fill that gap.

Good reading, ladies and gentlemen. I wish you well.

Jim Cooling
Markfield, 2018

Chapter 1

Modelling - What and why.

The objectives of this chapter are to:

• Define what, in general, we mean by the modelling of real systems.
• Explain what prompts us to model systems in the first place.
• Show why, to fully describe real systems, a variety of models is needed.
• Illustrate the fundamentals of these models, showing how and why we use them.
• Describe how software-specific modelling aspects relate to these general principles and practices.

1.1 Why bother to model in the first place?

The 'meat' of this book is all to do with UML diagrams and diagramming. Yet it's a mistake to treat the production of these diagrams as an end in itself (though that seems to be the case with some organizations). No, they are the *means* to an end: the modelling of software systems.

   One of life's great truisms: doing pointless things is a total waste of time, energy, effort and, frequently, money. So, why bother to spend our precious resources on the modelling of systems? Good question. However, to answer that, we first need to be clear what we mean by models and modelling.

   A model, in our view, is a 'representation of reality'. Though that sounds pretty abstract (and not especially helpful) it actually gets to the heart of the matter. Now, let's make it more meaningful by looking at some tangible items. First, figure 1.1 gives an example of one reality, a Spitfire aircraft.

Figure 1.1
Spitfire aircraft

By contrast, figure 1.2 depicts a physical model of the Spitfire, a specific representation of the real thing.   That, for example, represents things from the point of view of aircraft operators, maintainers, etc.

Figure 1.2 Spitfire aircraft - model

Of course, if we were aeromodellers, the model itself would be our 'reality', one representation of this being the 'construction plan' of figure 1.3.

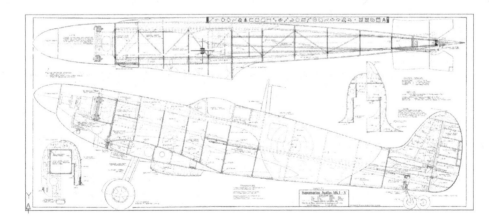

Figure 1.3 Spitfire model construction plan

   To summarize; what all this shows is that the 'reality' of interest depends on the nature of our work; the representation used depends on what aspect of this reality that we wish to show. And as for 'modelling'? It's nothing more than the work involved in producing a model.

   To see why modelling can be a valuable tool, let's look at some examples of its use.

(a) In the late 1990's aviation experts identified loss-of-control as a major factor in the fatal accident rate of aircraft. As a result a study was launched to investigate the aerodynamic characteristics of large airplanes at upset flight conditions. This involved the use of extensive wind tunnel testing of models that were representative of modern transport aircraft, figure 1.4

Figure 1.4 Wind tunnel test of an aircraft model

This is an excellent illustration of using physical modelling to evaluate the behaviour of an existing system: **analysis**.

(b) Something familiar to all of us: the weather forecast. Yet this is another example of modelling, as the forecast is really the output of a weather model, figure 1.5. What we have here is a second important use of modelling: **prediction**. One of the most important aspects of prediction modelling is that it often throws up unexpected and (and possibly worrying) results.

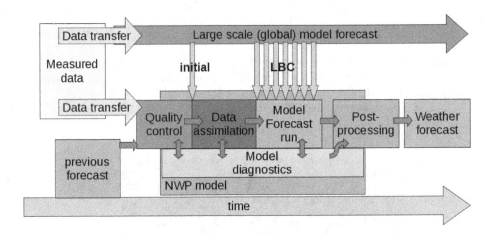

Figure 1.5 Weather model

(c) The MS Tûranor PlanetSolar is the largest solar-powered boat in the world, which in 2012 became the first solar electric vehicle to circumnavigate the globe. Shown here (figure 1.6) is a large-scale model of the vessel, used for proof-of-concept work. This work evaluates, amongst other things, **_performance improvement_**.

Figure 1.6 Model of autonomous semi-robotic test boat

(d) It's well known that auto manufacturers produce clay models (figure 1.7) of vehicles to evaluate, mainly, their styling ('styling sells cars' is an old saying of the car industry).

Figure 1.7 Modelling a car with clay

This is not a cheap process, yet it's very widely used in that industry, even in these days of computer-aided design. Why? Because, according to Alan Biggs a design-modelling manager for Ford, 'No one is willing to sign off a production car looking at a picture'.

   Once styling decisions have been finalized the clay model can be used to define what is to be built. For example, it can be scanned for dimensional information that can then be used to produce the bodywork for production cars. This is a further example of the application of modelling: **specification**.

   These modelling applications are not necessarily mutually exclusive. And in some situations we may find ourselves using all four as part of a project. For example we may start off by analyzing the aerodynamic behaviour of an aircraft to set a baseline of knowledge. If improvements are needed then the model may be modified until its behaviour and performance match our aims. Finally this information can be used to generate an engineering specification for future manufacturing purposes.

   Thus to summarize; four major uses of modelling are analysis, prediction, performance improvement and specification. And something really important: modelling needs to produce relevant, tangible and easily understood results if it's to be useful.

1.2 What we can learn from modelling.

Let us assume you're now convinced that modelling could actually be helpful. Then your next step is to try to pin down clearly:

- The reasons for using the models and
- The benefits that will result from this.

To answer these questions consider the example shown in figure 1.8, a brief description of its operation being given below.

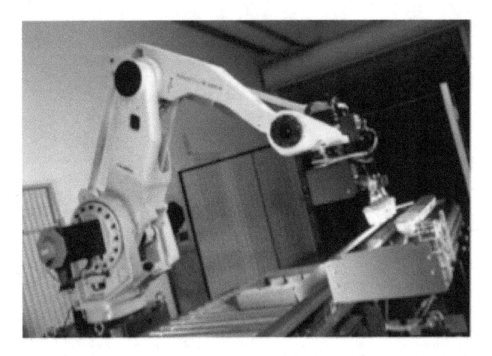

Figure 1.8 Automated materials handling

This shows an automated materials handling device that uses two robots: a pallet transport robot and a materials loader/unloader (palletizer) robot. The transport robot's function is to move the pallets about the factory, while the palletizer function is to unload and/or load items onto the pallets (palletizing). All operations are controlled by software, in particular a transport task and a palletizing task. Most important; before material can be transferred to/from the pallet both robots must be in their correct position.

Now let's consider the sort of detailed information that we, as designers, users, maintainers, etc., would like to know about this system. It's very likely to include the answers to the following questions (in no particular order):

1. How are the individual parts constructed/manufactured?
2. How do the individual parts work (i.e. what is their operation and behaviour)?
3. How do these parts fit together to build a specific robot unit?
4. What exactly is the purpose of each part in the complete unit (what do they do)?
5. How does each complete robot work?
6. How does the combination of robots work?
7. How do the robots communicate with each other?
8. When and why do they communicate?
9. What is the structure of the complete robotic system including, where relevant, its human-machine interfaces (HMIs)?

10. What happens when things fail (e.g. malfunction of an individual robot, loss of communication, etc.)?
11. How are failures to be detected and what are the desired responses to such failures?

From this we can see that the qualities of systems can generally be described using five categories, figure 1.9.   These descriptions should include initialization aspects, normal operations and abnormal (failure) conditions.

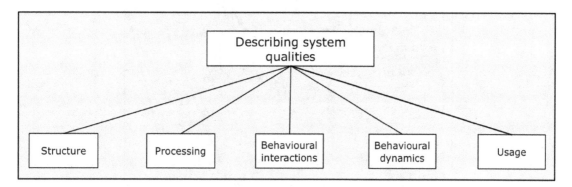

Figure 1.9 Describing system qualities

1.3 Modelling the qualities of systems.

1.3.1 Introduction.

What each category listed in figure 1.9 does is provide us with a 'view' of specific system qualities.   The precise descriptions and details depend very much on the needs of individual applications, industries and users. But a common aim in all areas is to present information so that it is accessible, understandable and correct.   And one of the most effective ways to do that is to use models, each model giving us a specific view of the system.   This sounds somewhat abstract, so to flesh things out some concrete examples are given in the following sections.

1.3.2 Structure.

What do we mean by 'structure'?   Well, it just depends!   We may, for instance, be interested in the overall physical composition and layout of a system (loosely, 'deployment'), figure 1.10.

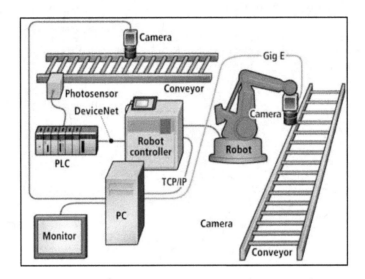

Figure 1.10 System physical layout (deployment)

A second item of interest is the makeup of individual items, one example being that shown in figure 1.11.

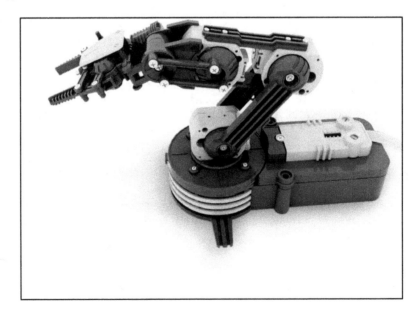

Figure 1.11 Structure of a specific item - robot arm

If our primary interest relates to the electronic structure of the system the model of figure 1.12 would be very meaningful.

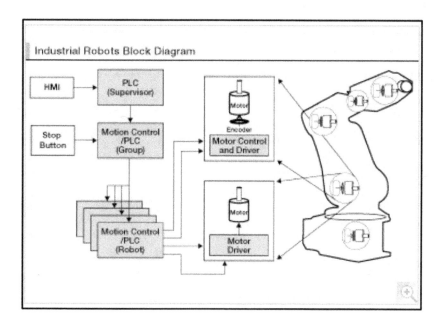

Figure 1.12 Electronic system structure

What these last three examples have in common is that they represent things ('entities') that actually do something. However these entities have to be made in the first place, so we need to show how they are actually constructed, figure 1.13.

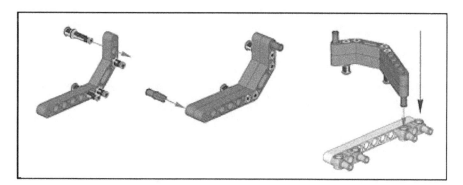

Figure 1.13 Construction plan

1.3.3 Processing.

'Processing' defines the detailed work that the entity performs, as, for example:

1. The robot loads up the correct sized drill.
2. It then rotates into position, and waits until the workpiece arrives.
3. When the workpiece is ready it drills the defined set of holes.
4. etc. etc. etc.

Text descriptions like this are fine to describe simple or relatively short operations. However, for more complex actions they really aren't the best medium; a much better technique is to use pictorial descriptions as, for instance, the flow chart of figure 1.14.

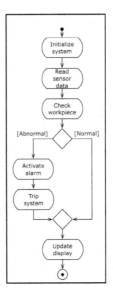

Figure 1.14 Flowchart description of a processing operation

1.3.4 Interactions.

Interactions between the various component parts of a system can be shown in a number of ways. Three particular aspects are especially important:

- What interactions take place.
- Why these occur.
- When these happen.

Figure 1.15 shows how the 'what' question can be answered. It shows the component parts of the system (essentially its structure) and their interconnections. But it extends the structure diagram by adding to it a list of interactions between the parts. These interactions, typically called signals, commands or data (for brevity, signals), highlight the communication aspects of the system. Thus a meaningful name for this diagram is the communication model.

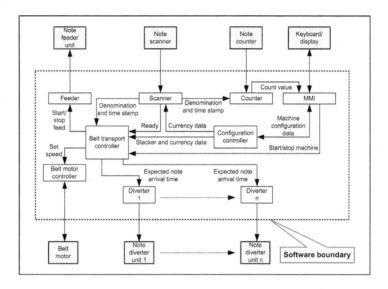

Figure 1.15 System components and their interactions - a communication viewpoint.

If it's important to know why these interactions occur (and what they're intended to achieve), this should be described in text documents. An additional useful feature is to provide hyperlinks between communication diagrams and the relevant text material.

In engineering, diagrams like this are very much 'bread and butter' items, which shows just how useful they are. But they don't answer the 'when' aspect; it could, for example, be the case that all signals are continually present. On the other hand certain signals might arrive only at specific times or when invoked by specific operations. Notation has been developed to add such information to communication diagrams; generally this have been fine in theory but useless in practice. We need something better.

Electronic developers will instantly recognize that figure 1.16 is a logic timing diagram for bus interactions within a processor system. It consists of:

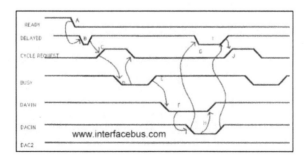

Figure 1.16 Processor system - logic timing diagram

- A set of 'items' (e.g. the ready, busy and DAC2 lines).
- The signalling that takes place between the various items.
- The event (or events) provoked by this signalling.

Here time implicitly flows from left to right. If we are primarily interested in the sequence of events then there is no need to include a time scale. However, where timing is critical, the scale would have to be included.

What we have here is a model of one set of interactions, one that occurs under specific circumstances. However, in most real applications many different types of interactions take place. Hence to fully model time-related operations (e.g. reading, writing, DMA accesses, interrupts, etc.) sets of individual diagrams are needed. These operations we will call scenarios. Thus there is one scenario that depicts reading, another for writing, and so on. Note that during system operation many, if not most, scenarios occur multiple times. But in each case the scenario interactions are identical, thus one diagram only is needed. Where scenarios are similar but not identical (compare reading the output of a peripheral device with that of reading from memory) each one needs its own diagram.

An alternative to the format of figure 1.16 is that of the sequence diagram, figure 1.17. Here time or sequence of events runs from top to bottom; the rest of the diagram should be self-explanatory.

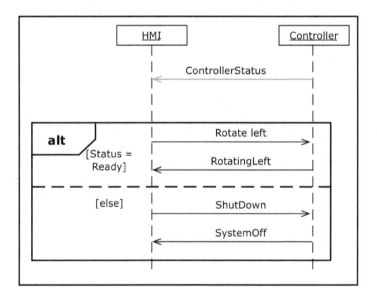

Figure 1.17 Sequence diagram representation of interactions

These examples also make the point that specific model properties can be shown in different ways. The practical, sensible approach is pick the one that's easiest to produce, understand and use. For modelling interactions a good general rule is to use the sequence diagram as the default approach (augmenting it with timing diagrams if and when needed).

1.3.5 Dynamic behaviour.

When we describe dynamic behaviour, the words 'condition', 'mode' and 'state' are frequently used. In fact, according to the Free Dictionary, they are synonymous:

Mode
  A manner or way of doing, acting, or existing.
  A designated condition or status, as for performing a task or responding to a problem.
State
  A condition or mode of being.

Dynamic modelling is used when we are primarily interested in:

- The various states (conditions, modes) that a system can be in.
- Why a system finds itself in these states.
- Why a system leaves a state.
- The relationship between the states.

We can, if we wish, use a text 'model' to describe system dynamics, as in the following example.

A robotic system, when powered up, has a number of possible operational states:

- Stopped
- Retracting
- Extending
- Rotating left
- Rotating right.
-

Note that, as described here, it can be in one state only at any instant in time; the states are mutually exclusive.

When it is first powered up it enters the Stopped state. From here it can be put into any of the other states by making appropriate command selections on a touch screen. For instance, to extend the robot arm Extend is selected, which starts the extension action. This continues until Stop is selected, at which point the robot instantly stops. The other available commands are Retract, Rotate left and Rotate right. The system must be in the Stopped state before it will respond to these commands.

To repeat a point made earlier, text descriptions are fine for modelling simple applications. But as things become more complex so too does the text, becoming increasingly difficult to understand. Once again 'pictures' can make things much easier for us to see what is going on, as with the state diagram of figure 1.18. This simplified diagram shows the possible system states, commands that cause changes of state and the routes taken between the states.

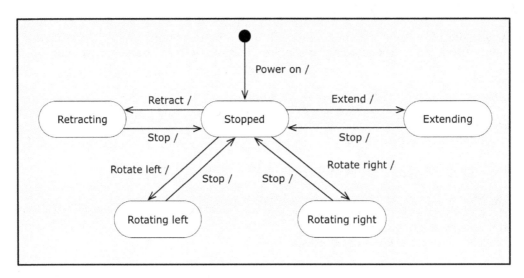

Figure 1.18 State diagram model of system dynamical behaviour

1.3.6 Usage.

It's only when a system interacts in some way with external 'things' (such as people or other systems) that we need to model usage. Now, some 'deep' embedded systems are totally self-contained; they don't interact with external bodies. But many, perhaps the majority, do interface to humans and/or other systems. As a result we frequently need to answer the following questions concerning the various interactions:

- Why interact with the system?
- What interactions take place?
- When do they take place?
- How, precisely, are they carried out?

We can show the answers to these in a usage model.

Now, the key question is the first one: 'why'. Everything else follows from this. The answer to that, together with those for the next two questions, can be perfectly well described using text (though we may choose to augment this with diagrams). Moreover, text is often used to describe the details of interactions. Unfortunately as the detail becomes more complex it naturally increases the complexity of the text description itself. We may well find ourselves struggling to understand and correctly implement the interactions. It's now that models and modelling can be really useful or, in some cases, essential. Let's have a look at some examples of techniques that have been used in practice, starting with a training simulator, figure 1.19. Its purpose is to train operators to be able to control a variety of marine systems such as dynamic positioning, vessel stability and position mooring.

Figure 1.19 Operator training simulator
        http://www.km.kongsberg.com
        Photo courtesy: Harald Nordbakken

A second example is the need to provide diagnostic information for the testing and maintenance of existing systems. In practice, one if the most effective methods is that of the diagnostic flow chart, figure 1.20. We can also use this as a specification technique; for instance it could be the defining document for a computer-based diagnostic tool.
    Flow charts can also be used to describe or specify details of specific interactions, as shown in figure 1.21. This also illustrates the use of solution prototyping techniques, an extremely powerful method to describe precisely and unambiguously:

- What should be done.
- When it is to be done.
- How to deal with illegal or undesired inputs.
- Details of HMI inputs and outputs.

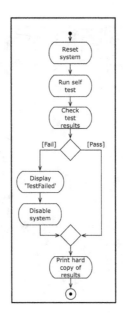

Figure 1.20 Diagnostic flowchart

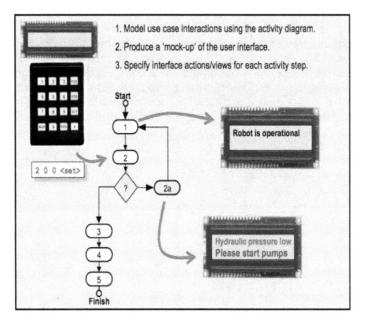

Figure 1.21 Flow chart description of operator interactions

In other circumstances our primary concern is to describe the various interactions and their time-ordering that occur during a specific scenario. One of the best ways to do this is to use a sequence diagram, as for example, figure 1.22.

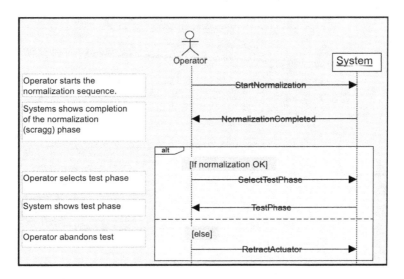

Figure 1.22 Sequence diagram description of interactions

This, like the previous diagrams, can be used for two purposes: to describe what happens in an existing system or to specify what should happen in a new system.

1.4 The modelling of software - key aspects.

1.4.1 The software machine and object-oriented techniques.

The central plank of modern software design is that software systems are built as sets of cooperating, communicating software machines. Please note; we're not talking about program design, although this is a part of the overall development process.

Precise details of both system and individual machine construction methods vary, as do their cooperation and communication features. But the fundamentals are exactly the same across all design techniques. A software machine (figure 1.23):

- Is a self-contained unit.
- Carries out a defined processing function.
- Can be used without knowing the details its internals.
- May be implemented in various ways; e.g. a function, an object, a component.
- Communicates with other machines using messages.
- Cooperates with other machines on either a peer-to-peer or master-slave (also called client-server) basis.

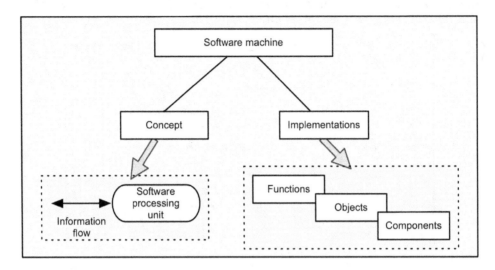

Figure 1.23 Software machines - concept and implementation

Put simply, software machines are the building blocks of software. And regrettably, if you don't believe in using this approach, then much of what UML has to offer is irrelevant.

For simplicity, conciseness and personal choice, we'll call the software machine an object. Another reason for doing this is that UML was developed originally as a notational method for object-oriented systems. And in those early days the 'things' that actually did the work during program execution were called objects. The alternative is to use words like instances, instantiations or representations.

1.4.2 Modelling OO software with UML diagrams - a broad perspective.

Object Orientation has one simple, central feature. It is that software designs may be structured as sets of intercommunicating, collaborating objects. These can be described using three models:

1. The *structural* model: provides the construction and design plans of the software.
2. The *behavioural* model: describes the behaviour of the software, including interactions, communication, dynamics and timing.
3. The *functional* model: describes the processing (or 'algorithmic') features of the software.

Now there are two quite different ways to view such object-based designs, figure 1.24. First there is the external - system oriented - view. Then there is the internal or object level view. The external view emphasises the:

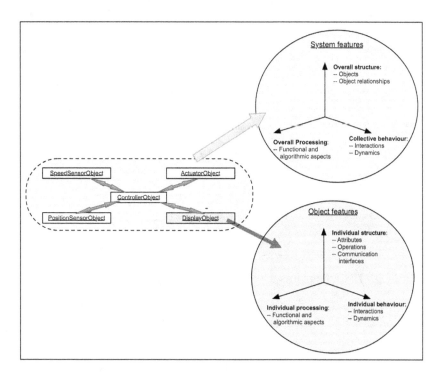

Figure 1.24 System and object features

- Overall system function.
- Role of objects within a system.
- Object relationships.
- Object interactions.
- Communication between objects.

In contrast, the internal view focuses on the qualities of individual objects. Each one is required to carry out some particular function; to do this it must:

- Be correctly structured.
- Behave in a predefined manner, and
- Provide communication interfaces.

Our modelling, given the nature of this book, will be implemented using UML diagrams. But it is obvious that not all the models described earlier can be built using diagramming; we are limited in what we can do. The message here for developers is that employing UML doesn't negate the use of techniques such as animation, simulation, rapid prototyping, etc. You should always look to model your systems in the best possible way, using whatever methods are appropriate.

In order to develop our models we will use the set of UML diagrams shown in figure 1.25 (compare this with figure 1.9).

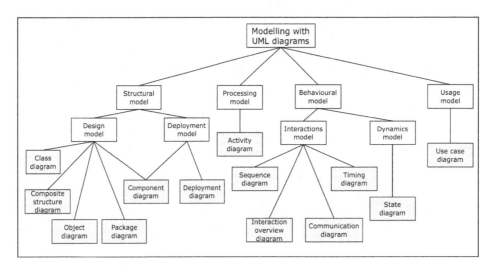

Figure 1.25 Modelling with UML diagrams

These are described in detail in later chapters. For now treat this diagram as a route map, giving you an indication of what diagrams we use, why they're used and how they relate to our modelling needs.

One small point needs to be mentioned: the inclusion of the Usage aspects. Strictly speaking this is not one of the OO models. It's primary purpose is to analyse system requirements and, from this, to generate the software specifications.

1.5 Review.

You should now:

- Understand that models are representations of reality, usually depicting simplified or limited versions of the reality.
- Appreciate that modelling is an immensely powerful (and often essential) aspect in the development of real systems.
- Recognize that modelling can used for analysis, prediction, performance improvement and specification purposes.
- Realize that the reason we use diagrams is to develop and represent models. Diagramming is a means to an end, not an end in itself.
- Understand what the following models are, why we produce them and what they can tell us: structural, processing, interactional, dynamical and usage.
- Appreciate that such models can be produced in a variety of ways and using different media: simulation and simulators, physical devices, text descriptions and diagramming.
- Recognize that, to fully represent the qualities of systems, a variety of models is needed.
- Realize that the number and type of models we need to develop depends entirely on the job being tackled.
- Recognize that using text to model complex systems has its problems.

- See how diagrams can overcome many of the limitations of text.
- Appreciate that software modelling is a specific application of general modelling techniques.
- Know what a software machine is, what its qualities are and why it's such an important building block of modern software systems.
- Know which models are used to describe the features of object-oriented designs.
- Understand that (usually) there is a need to model OO designs from both a system and an individual object perspective.
- Know what information is contained in the system and object models.
- Know which UML diagrams may be used for the modelling of software systems.

END OF CHAPTER

Chapter 2

Diagramming techniques: the world in pictures.

The objectives of this chapter are to:

- Explain why diagrams and diagramming play key roles in our work.
- Show why diagrams are used as part of the modern software toolset.
- Describe, in general terms, what they achieve.
- Define the requirements and attributes of software diagrams.

2.1 Diagrams – why?

2.1.1 Introduction.

Diagrams are an intrinsic part of our everyday life. We use them for countless reasons, for all sorts of applications. Just a few:

- Showing the various displays produced on a TV screen when setting up a PVR.
- Illustrating foot positions when dancing the Tango.
- Showing family trees.
- Providing guidance for filling in forms.

Why use diagrams for this?   Because the alternative, text, is a very poor option. Experience has shown that diagrams are much more effective for conveying information (just try putting together self-assembly furniture using only written instructions).   Even so, diagrams by themselves aren't always enough; adding text can really help our understanding.

   Now, here is the great conundrum. We're happy to use diagrams all the time in our everyday life.   We couldn't imagine civil, mechanical or electrical engineers working without diagrams.   Yet things are quite different in the world of software. We ourselves have found from our software engineering courses that, where diagramming is concerned, there are fundamentally three groups of people:

(a) Those who don't see the need for diagrams and who use expressions like 'the code is my design' (frequently made by those producing write-only C++ programs).

(b)   Those who, because of the influence of UML, see that diagramming is 'good', but appear to have little understanding of its effective use.

(c)   Those who truly understand the value of diagramming, practise it and attempt to integrate it within their design processes (the smallest group, it must be said).

There has also been a sea-change in attitude with UML becoming the de-facto standard for OO-based designs.
    To understand why diagramming is so powerful, we need to start with its psychological aspects.   Our experiences show that pictures convey information in a different way from words: and in a way which is clearer and easier to understand. T. R. G. Green says much about this in his paper *Pictures of programs and other processes, or how to do things with lines.* In it he describes issues in terms of temporal processes, dealing with many aspects of the problem, including:

- Recognition – is the process familiar?
- Modularity – what chunks can the description be broken into?
- Tractability – how can a modification be made?
- Sequence – in what order do the events happen?
- Circumstance – if such-and-such happens, what does it mean?

So, assuming that pictures really do help us, where can we sensibly use them in the software world?   There are four main areas in which diagramming can be applied (figure 2.1).

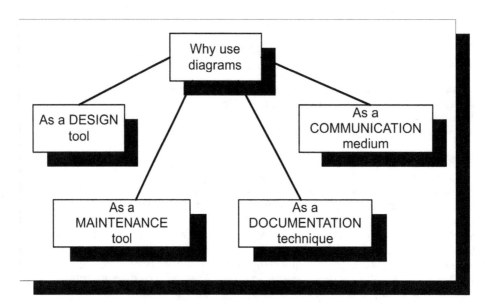

Figure 2.1 The role of diagrams in software development

In the following sections these are discussed in general terms; specific techniques are covered in part 2. But note that here we are mainly concerned with the **effects** produced by using diagrams, not **how** they are used in detail.

2.1.2 Reality, modelling and diagrams.

Before looking at how diagrams fit into the development process, consider three basic questions:

- What do diagrams actually do?
- Are the correct diagrams being used?
- Are the diagrams really usable?

Let's take these questions in turn.

Show the circuit symbol in figure 2.2 to an electronic engineer and ask him what it is. He'll probably reply 'Oh, that's a capacitor'. Well, of course, it's nothing of the sort; it's merely marks on a piece of paper. What the engineer really means is that it 'represents' a capacitor in his mind. Not that it has a particular shape and size, etc., but that it has the electrical properties defined as capacitance.

Now, at this point you may feel that this has become a pretty irrelevant discussion. Not so! What we have here is an extremely important issue; it demonstrates our ability to take an abstract view of reality. The diagram itself is not the reality of an actual capacitor; it is an abstract, conceptual view of that reality (abstract view: expressing a quality or characteristic apart from any specific object or instance).

Figure 2.2 Reality, abstraction and symbols

This abstraction process is, in engineering, often called 'modelling'. Thus a diagram allows us to model reality using pictures. Other modelling methods, such as mathematical equations or computer algorithms, can, of course, be used wherever suitable. But please, always bear in mind that the resulting models only approximate to the real thing.

Dealing with abstract ideas affects the way in which we interact with the real world. How, for instance, do we view the jet engine of an aircraft? To an aircraft designer it is a power unit, the driving force of the vehicle (figure 2.3). To the company accountant it is a profit centre (we hope), existing only on the balance books. And yet we're talking about the same physical device.

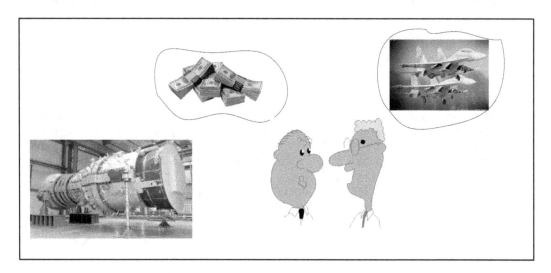

Figure 2.3 Reality, abstraction, domains and viewpoints

Now let us put this in the context of diagramming in order to answer the second question - *are the correct diagrams being used?.* This essentially is about the matching of diagrams to what they represent (rather grandiosely, their domain of application). This point is very well demonstrated in figure 2.4 giving two views of part of an auto electrical system. Figure 2.4a represents the system from the point of the repair mechanic (the maintenance domain). In contrast, figure 2.4b shows its electrical structure (the design domain). Same system, different views. What the diagrams have done is to abstract reality from a particular domain into a model. The models are quite different, true, but is this a problem? Absolutely not - provided the right one is used.

An amusing yet instructive tale of bungling caused by not using the correct model for the domain (in this case a navigation chart) is as follows:

Amateur sailor's island confusion - Thursday April 29, 2010
A man who thought he was sailing around the British coastline was surprised to learn he had in fact been circling the Isle of Sheppey. He had set out from Gillingham for Southampton but kept on sailing around the small island, off the coast of Kent, all day and night. He was using a road map to navigate. Rescuer Tom Ware said: "Because he had no chart, his general principle was to keep the land on his right, except he didn't realise Sheppey was an Island."

And it should be no surprise to find that many software problems are due to misuse of models.

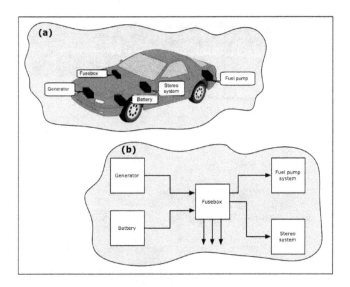

Figure 2.4 Domain specific views

The third question is concerned with how much information a diagram should contain. Put simply, just how complex can a diagram be before it becomes unusable? This issue was investigated as a psychological problem in the 1950's by George Miller. His paper, *The Magical Number Seven, Plus or Minus Two,* is a landmark one - I recommend it to you. The conclusions are clear. Too much information (especially the complex variety) is counter-productive. It merely confuses rather than enlightens. The reason is that people can effectively handle only a small amount of information at any one time. Thus simplicity is the order of the day.

Perhaps you can now begin to see the difficulty we face when using diagrams. On one hand there is a need to keep them simple and clear. On the other the systems we deal with may well be complex. Clearly, a single type of diagram cannot satisfy both needs. So, what to do?

The only sensible way to deal with this mismatch is to use *sets* of diagrams. Those produced first aim to give a large-scale (high-level) view of the system; later ones provide detailed (low-level) information. In many cases these later diagrams are 'exploded' versions of earlier ones, as, for example, the maps of figure 2.5. There are, though, two crucial factors here: first, complete consistency across levels, and second, design/diagram traceability. It's important to understand why these are such important features; they *should* have a big impact on your choice and use of diagrams. So often with real designs we find ourselves asking the question 'how and why did we ever get here?'. Good consistency and traceability give us a fighting chance to answer that question. They help us to work through the diagrams from start to finish ('forward navigation') without too many problems. Now that's fine if you know where you started from.

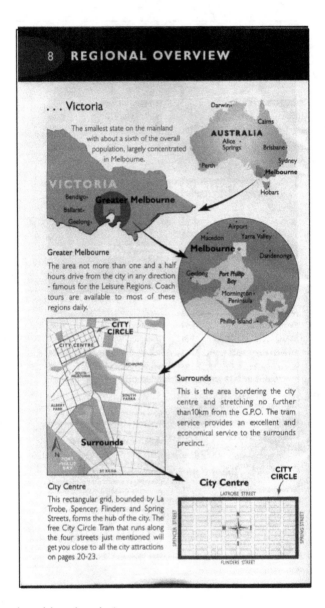

Figure 2.5 High-level and low-level views

 Unfortunately, in many cases you know where you are but have little idea as to how you got there (especially with legacy designs). What we need now is to be able to reverse navigate, from solution to specification. And the only way to do that is to have a diagram set that has excellent traceability.

2.1.3 Diagrams as a design tool.

Consider an electronic engineer carrying out power-circuit design. One of the first things he does is to sketch the circuit diagram (figure 2.6).

Figure 2.6 Initial design

Very quickly this is followed up by a series of calculations to verify the performance of the design. It **would** be possible to describe the design using words only. In one sense this is how computer-aided printed circuit board layout design tools work. Yet no engineer would adopt such an approach at the initial design stage. Why not?

First, the exercise of producing the diagram requires an explicit action. Implicit relationships cannot exist. Thus, even to draw a diagram requires a clear understanding of the problem. But when we just think about designs we often carry implicit information in our minds.

Next, if we work to an agreed set of drawing rules we introduce formality and design rigour into the process (figure 2.7). This means that it is possible for others to view, assess and discuss the design. It also eliminates ambiguity and ambivalence.

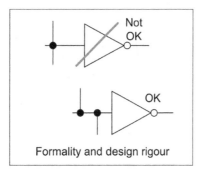

Figure 2.7 Drawing rules

For instance, in Figure 2.7, a dot indicates a connection; but why is one arrangement satisfactory and the other not so? Because in one format there is no confusion between crossing lines and connecting lines should the draftsman omit a dot.

Finally, the design as a whole can be reviewed and analysed, and the performance assessed. At this stage many incorrect or illogical design features may well come to light (figure 2.8).

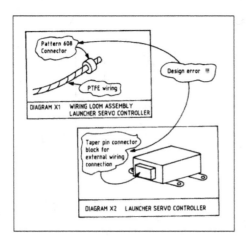

Figure 2.8 Design review

These can be corrected at a very early stage, saving time, effort and money (and embarrassment for the designer).

All of this is directly applicable to software. After all, at this stage of the design we are still working with concepts and ideas, so it should work for software as well as hardware.

2.1.4 Diagrams for design documentation.

Diagrams are a powerful means of documenting the design task (preferable to a mass of source code listings). But a moment's thought shows that a single type of drawing is very unlikely to meet all our needs. Two groups of diagrams are needed (figure 2.9). The first gives us a high-level view of the problem, showing what we've set out to do. The second, low-level one, concentrates on how we're going about solving the design problem. Each one is oriented towards a different aspect of the same problem. For any particular system, high-level diagrams:

- Are task (job) oriented.
- Show the overall system structure together with its major sub-systems.
- Describe the overall functioning of the design.

- Show the interaction of the system with its environment.
- Describe the functions and interactions of the various sub-systems.

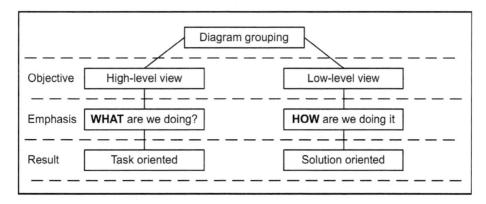

Figure 2.9 Diagrams for documentation

Low-level diagrams:

- Are solution oriented.
- Concentrate on detail.
- Emphasize system internal information.

Consider the attributes of such diagrams when applied, at a functional block level, to a mythical weapon control system (figure 2.10).

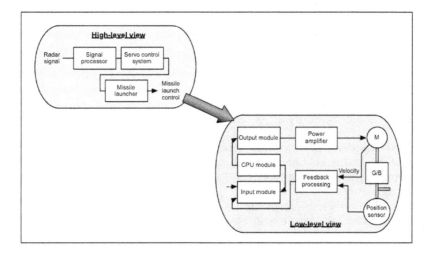

Figure 2.10 High-level vs low-level views

The high-level view concentrates on the overall task, its purpose being to ensure that we tackle the right problem. We can see from this figure how the main building blocks of the system fit together. Questions like 'Is the launcher compatible with the servo controller? Will the servo be powerful enough? Should we use hydraulics instead of electrics?' are considered at this level. In contrast, the low-level diagram tells us how the design task has been solved. It gives much information about the system internals, together with the interaction of such internals. It deals with questions like 'What's the best type of power amplifier?'

Good high-level diagrams are simple and clear, bringing out the essential major features of a system. Using these it is relatively easy to see the effects on system behaviour when making modifications. On the other hand, low-level diagrams tend to be detailed and complex. This is inherent in their nature; it isn't a criticism of such drawings. But, although their structure helps us to answer the question 'are we doing the job correctly?' they aren't very good when we ask 'are we doing the correct job?'.

These ideas can be directly translated to software engineering. We gain all the benefits outlined above by using pictures in the design process. What it also shows is that whatever diagramming method is used, it must be able to give both high-level and low-level views.

2.1.5 Diagrams for maintenance.

Post-design maintenance is done for two reasons; either to correct faults or to upgrade equipment. Ideally, this would be done by the original designers. But, in reality, once some years have passed, few of the original designers are still around. So, software maintenance is usually carried out by workers who:

- Weren't involved in the development in the first place.
- Have only a limited understanding of the overall task.
- Have to learn a lot very quickly to perform even small design changes.
- Wouldn't have done the job like that in any case.

It is not surprising that maintenance is unpopular. It may be an obscure and difficult job but somebody has to do it. And the better the original documentation the easier it can be. Therefore, design information must support the maintenance process by being complete, correct, clear and consistent (figure 2.11).

System documentation needs to give both an overview as well as detailed information. It is very easy to be swamped by an excess of paper, typified by many technical manuals. An example of such overkill is described by Rothon in his paper *Design structure diagrams: a new standard in flow diagrams*. He stated that 'the recent specification for the software for an American fighter plane occupied more than 26 thick volumes of text. It is hardly surprising that developers faced with such bulky documentation are unable to perceive the nature of the software ....'.

However, by using overview information it *is* much easier to see the overall picture. For instance, questions such as 'where and how can changes be made? What are the knock-on effects of these on the complete program?' can be much more easily answered. We still, though, need detailed information, relating specifically to the source code itself. Once again there is a clear need for a two-level documentation system.

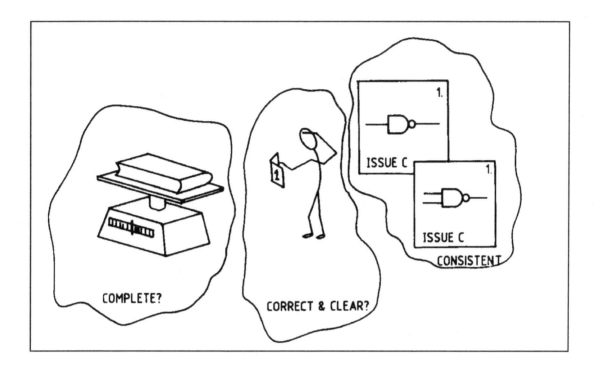

Figure 2.11 Document requirements

2.1.6 Diagrams for communication.

It's already been shown that written and spoken words can be ambiguous, ambivalent or even totally confusing. We've also seen that by using sketches, pictures, etc., many such problems are eliminated. Therefore, design diagrams can be used to help communications between members of the software and system project teams.

Who are likely to be the main users of such diagrams? They are: the system users (or procurement agency), the system designers and the post-design support group (maintainers). Figure 2.12 shows the general lines of communication between these groups. It also shows at which periods of the design these take place.

What questions do diagrams aim to answer? Consider first the user-designer interaction, figure 2.13. Read through this and see how there are two matching aspects ('two sides of a coin') of each individual question.

Let's now turn to designer-designer communication. Even in a small job involving only one designer there are still 'chiefs' to be talked to (figure 2.14). Ideally, such discussions should be clear, understandable and not open to individual interpretation. Pictures can help considerably in such cases.

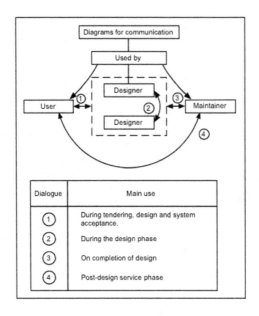

Figure 2.12 Communication aspects of diagrams

User	*Designer*
Does he understand what I want?	Has the job been properly specified in the first place?
Am I getting what I want?	Am I doing the right job?
How is the job going?	How is the job going?

Figure 2.13 User-designer dialogue

Chief Designer	*Designer*
This is the overall plan.	I understand the task.
This is how the job is split up.	Here is the detailed design response.
These are **your** responsibilities.	I know what I'm responsible for.
This is the development plan.	Here is my work plan document.
These are the time scales.	Here are the project milestones.
I want a record of progress.	Here is a record of the design.

Figure 2.14 Designer-designer interaction

In the post-design phase the requirements of the user tend to reduce in quantity. Unfortunately for the maintainer, these requirements are usually highly demanding ones (figure 2.15).

User	Maintainer
Fix my problem (now!).	Can this problem even be fixed?
How much to fix my problem?	Need to assess work effort. Lots!
What happens if .... ?	How does the system really work?
Modify my system.	Can it be modified successfully?
How much for modifications?	Need to assess work effort. Lots!
How long?	This is what it entails.

Figure 2.15 User-maintainer interaction

2.2 The essentials of software diagrams.

2.2.1 Fundamentals.

What is the fundamental purpose of software design diagrams? In a very simple way they can be seen as a way to bridge the gap between what is wanted (the problem) and what is provided (the solution), figure 2.16. Think of it as if the 'bridge' is actually built from a set of design diagrams.   At the leftmost we have diagrams that deal with customer requirements and specification.   The rightmost ones, the final in the set, specify the implementation (the 'build') aspects of the design. These, for software systems, specify the program and code aspects of the design. Hence we can navigate from a problem specification to its code solution by working our way across the bridge. In fact, the total design process can be viewed as a two-stage activity, figure 2.17.

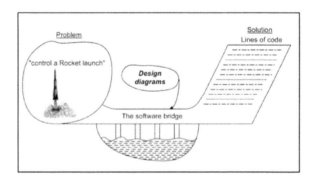

Figure 2.16 Bridging the gap

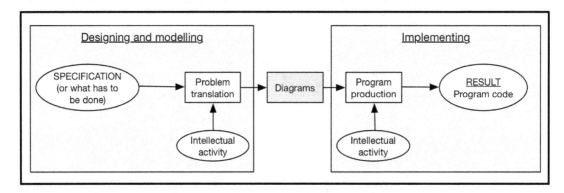

Figure 2.17 The two-stage design process

The diagrams sit in the middle of this, serving two groups of people. From the point of view of problem translation, diagrams **must** meet the needs of the user. That is, the design approach must be stated in terms of the problem not its solution; the diagrams must be easy for the users to understand. In most cases they won't be software engineers, so there's not much point in sending them a pile of computer print-outs. Finally, it must be easy to produce and modify such diagrams to encourage their use in the translation stage.

The information shown by the diagram is then used as an input to the program production process. But unless diagramming methods support program design techniques (e.g. top-down design), programmers won't find them very helpful. In such cases all that happens is that yet another translation stage is used in the design process. It is also essential that diagramming methods relate strongly to modern program design methods. Ideally the diagram constructs should mirror those of the more widely-used programming languages.

2.2.2 Basic qualities.

Consider the assembly instruction diagram of figure 2.18. This has taken time and money to produce; yet its manufacturer considers this a worthwhile investment. This isn't done through a sense of altruism, it's just good business practice. It conveys considerable information to the user in a simple, direct way. But it succeeds in this only if it has key qualities (figure 2.19). Let's look at each point in turn, putting it in terms of software production.

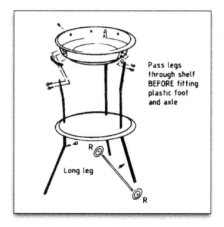

Figure 2.18 Kit assembly diagram

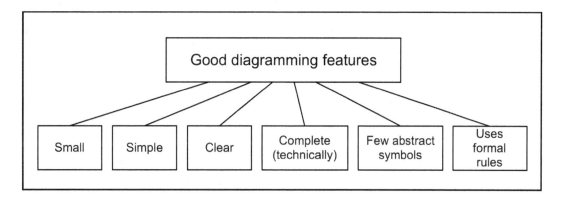

Figure 2.19 Diagrams – key qualities

(a) Small
Here, small means sizes between A2 and A4. One major reason for limiting diagram size is to avoid overloading the reader with information. Good pictorial methods use a top-down method in presenting such information, as in figure 2.20. There are, however, some mundane grounds for keeping to these sizes. In the first case they can be produced easily on low-cost plotters and printers. Moreover, these are usually widely available; there's no need to invest in expensive plotters. Second, such diagrams usually form part of a main design document; thus it must be easy to integrate these with the rest of the documentation. Large diagrams cause problems here.

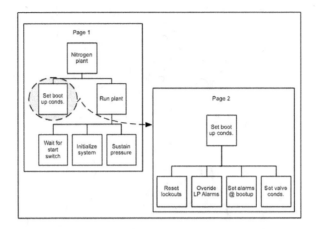

Figure 2.20 A top-down diagramming method

(b) Simple and clear

Diagrams are supposed to help our understanding, not act as intellectual puzzles. When diagrams are simple and clear they are quickly understood and assimilated. This may seem a statement of the obvious, yet many diagrams break these rules. The resulting consequences may be disastrous. Some years ago a military transport plane crashed on take-off, killing 50 passengers. The disaster was caused by the reverse fitting of a non-return fuel control valve. But the factor which led to this was a poor, ambiguous fitting diagram which didn't show clearly the flow direction through the valve.

An example of a diagram which breaks all the rules is given in figure 2.21 (taken from *Pictures of programs and other processes* by T.R.G. Green, reproduced by permission).

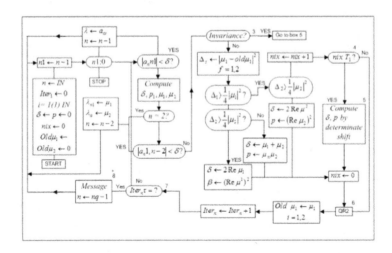

Figure 2.21 A confusing diagram

(c) Complete
This means that information should not be missing from the diagram. Now this shouldn't be confused with the use of extra pictures to show all the facts. That, for software documentation, is the rule rather than the exception. What it does mean that omissions of data which leave the information incomplete are taboo.

(d) Few abstract symbols
It is impossible to construct software design diagrams without using abstract symbols. Unfortunately, abstract symbols can be a problem in themselves, especially if complex constructs are used. In such cases it may be quite difficult to see what message the picture is trying to convey. So the fewer symbols used the better. And keep them simple.

(e) Uses formal rules
All notation used in diagramming should be done in accordance with a set of rules. These rules should be defined, clear and consistent. Without this we can never be sure that we understand what the diagrams mean.

2.3 Review.

Having completed this chapter you should:

- Appreciate the importance of diagramming as a core design tool.
- See how diagrams bring rigour, clarity and formality to the design process.
- Perceive the power of diagrams as an aid to communication.
- Understand that these objectives cannot be achieved unless the syntax and semantics of diagrams are well defined.
- Realize that diagrams are used for a variety of purposes: analysis, design, documentation and maintenance.
- See how diagrams fit into the overall software design process.
- Know what qualities to look for in diagrams and their associated methods.
- Recognize that many diagrams are needed to fully define large systems.
- Be able to define a basic range of diagrams that would support the development of real-time systems.

END OF CHAPTER

Chapter 3

Diagramming and UML: a broad perspective.

The objectives of this chapter are to:

- Look at the historical development of diagramming methods for real-time embedded systems.
- See where UML fits into this and how it evolved from its early form into the latest specification.
- Identify the major issues that cause problems for the specifiers, designers and implementers of software systems.
- See how we can avoid (or minimize) these problems.

3.1 Setting the groundwork.

I hope, by this time, that you truly appreciate that diagramming is an essential part of professional software development. I also hope that you fully understand what we set out to achieve by using diagrams. Well, before getting into the detail of UML, we need to do consider a very important question; just how well does UML fit the bill?

Now, this might seem to be a non-question if you believe the torrent of uncritical acclaim for UML. We are assured that by using UML we *will* significantly improve our software. Reality, unfortunately, is somewhat different. There has been success, true. But there have also been many failures along the way. Mostly these have been due to the uncritical use of UML by software developers. And compounding this is the failure of many developers to really understand *how* to use it.

To effectively use tools, techniques or processes, you *must* understand their weaknesses and limitations. This is especially true for UML because it does have some important (and usually unheralded) drawbacks. What we're going to do here is look at these issues and see how we can mitigate their effects. Once having done that we're in a good position to actually achieve many of the claimed benefits of using UML.

3.2 Software diagramming - a historical prelude.

Something philosophical for you to think about:
"Those who don't know history are doomed to repeat it." Edmund Burke.

3.2.1 The evolution of software diagramming - the embedded world.

Diagramming for software started life as a way to describe program structures. The pioneers were IBM who, in the 1950s, adapted the humble process flow chart of the mechanical engineer for just this purpose. Humble perhaps, but still going strong some 90 years after its first appearance.

Effective though the flow chart was, it did have limitations, some significant. To counter these a new diagram type was developed, the program structure chart. Many variations were produced, the best known perhaps being those of Jackson, Yourdon, Nassi-Shneidermann and Warnier-Orr. Each, naturally, came with its own particular syntax and semantics.

During the 1970s the international standards organisation CCITT, *Comité Consultatif International Téléphonique et Télégraphique* (also irreverently known as Coffee and Croissants Interspersed with Trivial Talk) defined a set of diagrams for modelling telecommunications software. Significantly, this set included means to model software concurrency ('tasks') and dynamics ('states') as well as program structures.

After this, mainly in the 1980s, a number of important real-time software development processes were defined. The most important were those of Yourdon/Ward-Mellor, Hatley-Pirbhai, Michael Jackson and David Harel. Each offering used various diagrams to support its particular process; unfortunately the syntax of the diagrams varied immensely (the semantics, though, were often similar). As a result it was virtually impossible to mix the techniques. From a practical point of view, the best thing to do was to pick one method and live with the consequences.

The difficulties were further compounded by the use of CASE tools. Many tools were produced to support these processes; unfortunately they usually had their own adaptations, limitations or extensions. It *was* possible to exchange some information between different tools using common interchange formats. But actually trying to use imported design information was a much more difficult job.

So what was the situation in the embedded world in the early 1990s vis-à-vis software design and development? First, the arrival of low-cost CASE tools had given a tremendous boost to the use of 'formal' design and diagramming methods. Second, the predominant design methodologies were those of Yourdon/Ward-Mellor and Hatley-Pirbhai; Jackson methods were much less widely used. Third, programming was almost always done using procedural languages: assembly, PL/M, Forth, real-time Basic, embedded Pascal, Coral66, Modula-2, Ada83 and C, for example. Fourth, hardly any of the CASE tools generated program code automatically from the modelling diagrams. As a result many, if not most, companies:

- Decided what design method most suited their work.
- Bought a CASE tool to support the chosen method (and their budgets).
- Integrated these into their software design and development processes.
- Manually translated the diagram information into source code.

For some organizations the problems of exchanging information between different tools was a source of difficulty. These, though, were mainly large companies having several software development teams, often in different locations. Most people accepted life as it was and got on with things. At that time, in the embedded world, the major challenge was to get developers to use professional tools, techniques and processes. There wasn't a burning desire to unify the various software design and diagramming techniques. Nor, for that matter, was there a drive to adopt object-oriented programming languages and techniques. The changes that came later weren't driven by deficiencies in the embedded world; they were a consequence of events in the world of management information systems (MIS).

Many designers of embedded systems found the OO 'paradigms', languages and techniques to be alien, immature and inappropriate. Others, though, were eager to adopt the new 'technology'. This led to a clear split in the technologies used by the embedded community. First, there are the direct descendants of the techniques of the early 1990s, to be found in tools such as Matlab/Simulink and Labview. These are extensively used in 'deep' embedded applications such as auto systems, robotics and control systems (i.e. mechatronics in general). Then there are the techniques that resulted from the ideas of the OO world. And central to these is UML.

3.2.2 The evolution of software diagramming - the MIS world.

The term MIS is used here to lump together anything that doesn't fall into the category of real-time embedded systems. Thus it includes algorithmic processing, an area that was the first to use software diagramming (the flow chart). So software diagramming has its roots in MIS.

During the period spanning the early 1960's to the beginning of the 1990's, innumerable MIS diagramming and design methods were produced. In particular, in the late 80's/early 90's, a whole new set arrived, the object-oriented graphical modelling languages. It's true that some OO-based modelling techniques were developed for real-time systems. It's also true that, at that time, they made relatively little impact on the embedded community.

Thus, in the early 90's, MIS developers could be forgiven for being totally confused by the plethora of modelling techniques and languages. What to use? When to use it? *How* to use it? How to sort out the competing claims? This, then, is the background to the emergence of UML.

3.2.3 Enter UML.

The Unified Modeling Language resulted from collaboration between Grady Booch and James Rumbaugh at Rational Software Corporation. What they set out to do is clearly summarised in their 1995 document (Unified Method for Object Oriented Development, version 0.8), as follows:

This series of documents describes the Unified Method, a method for specifying, visualizing, and documenting the artifacts of an object-oriented system under development. The Unified Method represents the unification of the Booch and OMT methods as well as the best ideas from a number of other methodologists. By unifying these two leading object-oriented methods, the Unified Method provides the basis for a defacto standard in the domain of object-oriented analysis and design founded on a wide base of user experience.

Over the following years the original specification was updated, the final version (UML 1.5) being issued in 2003.

Unfortunately UML 1.x didn't live up to expectations of its designers and so a the search began for its successor. The resulting UML 2.0 specification, issued in 2004, was very different from that of UML 1.x. The original specification was relatively focussed, readable and comprehensible. In contrast, UML 2.0 was like the 'Swiss army knife' tool of the software world: something for everybody. At present the specification is at version 2.5, consisting of two documents: Superstructure and Infrastructure. Roughly speaking, the Superstructure document is written for UML users while the Infrastructure one is aimed at tool developers. However, it must be understood that these are written for the general software community; aspects specific to real-time embedded systems are not dealt with in the Superstructure document. This is left to an extension document called MARTE (**M**odeling and **A**nalysis of **R**eal-**T**ime and **E**mbedded **S**ystems). More of that later.

For simplicity, here the words 'specification' and 'standard' have the same meaning.

3.3 UML - a simple overview.

So far in the discussion about UML, little has been said about what it actually is. More precisely, what does it offer the embedded systems developer? The original proposal was clear: *a method for specifying, visualizing, and documenting the artifacts of an object-oriented system under development.* Unfortunately, when you first come to UML, its sheer complexity and size can confuse rather than enlighten. So here, to give a concise, simple and perhaps narrow view of UML, I'm going to use an analogy: the building of a house.

What do you have to do to turn a requirement ('I need somewhere to live') into a product (the house)? Apart from the actual building work itself, three other factors are essential parts of the project. First, we have the actual construction technique to be used, the *how* of building the house. This isn't unique; it varies according to local circumstances (figure 3.1) such as building skills, materials and costs.

Figure 3.1 Some building techniques

Of course, we need to know *what* to build. This is where plans (aka diagram models) are essential, figure 3.2.

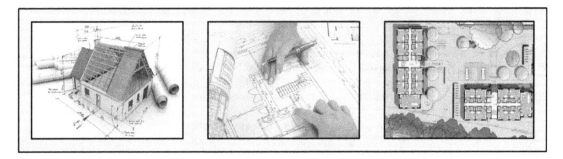

Figure 3.2 Building plans - various notations.

The final point is *when* to do things, in other words, the process to be followed during the project. A typical process for the actual construction phase is shown in figure 3.3.

Figure 3.3 The building process

So how does UML relate to this viewpoint? Some believe that it defines how software artifacts should be built. No, not true; it is *not* a technique. Others think that it specifies a process for the building of software. Also not true; it is *not* a process. This just leaves the plans. And that, for us, is exactly what UML is: a set of rules defining the syntax and semantics of software plans. In other words it defines the diagrams we can use and the way to use them.

3.4 UML – assumptions, issues and remedies.

3.4.1 Underlying assumptions of the UML specification.

The UML model was developed with several explicit assumptions in mind. It would:

- Support work in the analysis, design and implementation phases of a project.
- Represent the semantics, physical details and visualization of such work.
- Ensure that designs could be implemented by the major object-based and object-oriented programming languages.

But there are also implied assumptions made by individuals involved in the specification process. These, which are unstated, depend on factors such as the person's background, experience and work area. To our mind the _emphasis_ placed on many features of UML only make sense when viewed in the context of the commercial MIS world where:

- The basic computing model is that of a client/server system.
- Key constructs are related to the storage and handling of data and databases, including remote databases.
- The distributed computing model implicitly assumes the use of the internet and its protocols.
- The implied hardware platforms are those of desktop computers, workstations and mainframes, using industry-standard operating systems.
- Sufficient processor power and memory _will_ be available; resources aren't constrained.
- Software concurrency on a single processor _will_ be provided by the machine OS.
- The concurrency model is a threading one in the style of standard implementations such as Microsoft's COM (Component Object Model).
- Distributed computing support will be provided by middleware such as, for example, Microsoft's DCOM (Distributed COM).
- Interfacing to the real world is relatively simple.
- The interfacing devices used are few in type (e.g. printer, mouse, keyboard, etc.) and can be handled using standard pre-built driver software.
- A successful project is one that performs its required functions correctly; temporal factors are hardly considered.

Now contrast this with real-time embedded systems such as industrial automation, avionics, automobile applications and the like where:

- The computing model most generally used is the materials flow ('pipe-and–filter') one.
- Many different hardware platforms are used for embedded designs.
- In general, resources are inferior to those of desktop machines:
    - Processing power may be limited, especially where designs use 8-bit processors.
    - Clock rates, even with 32-bit machines, are much lower.
    - Much less memory, both RAM and ROM, is available.
- A real-time operating system (RTOS) is needed to provide multi-tasking operation.
- RTOSs vary considerably in terms of size, structure and tasking model.
- Communication support for distributed systems is sector-dependent (e.g. CAN and LIN for the auto industry, ARINC 653 for avionics, Profibus for marine systems, etc.).
- Real-world interfacing is a key factor in terms of both function and time.
- Projects must be functionally _and_ temporally correct.
- Systems are frequently required to operate continuously for long periods of time.
- Many applications must meet safety-critical requirements (e.g. railways, medical, avionics, etc.).

Thus it is no surprise that developers have struggled to effectively use 'plain vanilla' UML in embedded applications.

3.4.2 UML issues.

What we've seen above is merely the first hurdle to be overcome in trying to use UML. Because there are, in fact, further obstacles, the main issues being:

- The size and complexity of the standard.
- Problems in understanding the standard.
- Impreciseness of the semantics.
- Problems in choosing and using diagrams.
- Confusion between notation and process.
- Inadequate modelling of run-time software.

These, discussed below, are not trivial aspects but can cause developers real grief and angst (it might be a good idea to include a 'health warning' with UML documents, figure 3.4!).

Figure 3.4 Software health warning for the unwary

The aim of this book is to provide you, when you come to use UML, with sufficient guidance to turn these into non-problems. You can find a more detailed description of these aspects in the paper 'Why there are difficulties in using UML' at:
 http://lindentreeuk.co.uk/publications.html#Technical.

3.4.3 UML and domain-specific issues.

What's different about using UML in real-time systems compared with areas such as databases, management information systems (MIS), Internet search engines, etc? Is it more complex? Does it require specialized knowledge? Do you need special training? Well, the reality is that in terms of the diagram types, their syntax and their semantics, the answer is no. The difference, in fact, has little to do with the diagrams themselves but is driven by the following factors:

- The range of diagrams used.
- The emphasis placed on their use.
- The traceability between diagrams.
- The support for program design.

Moreover, the following three aspects heavily influence our selection and usage of diagrams:

- Design viewpoint.
- External (real-world) interfacing.
- Performance requirements

As shown in figure 3.5, there are two quite contrasting views of the role of software within complete systems: software-centric and system-centric. In many (perhaps most?)

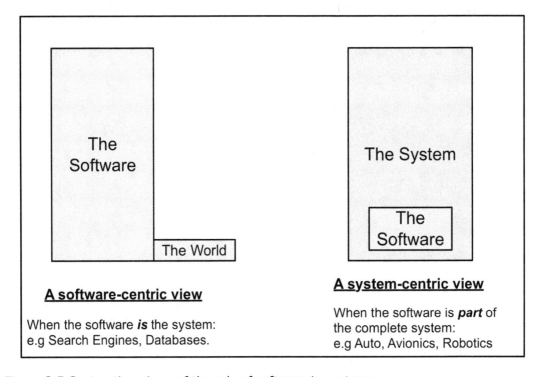

Figure 3.5 Contrasting views of the role of software in systems

desktop and mainframe applications, software aspects dominate all other factors. From that perspective the software really **is** the system, all other things being subordinate. Now, this is a reasonable approach when developing applications such as mathematical modelling, computer-based games, databases, etc. But when this same philosophy is applied to producing software for systems such as robotics, process control, health-treatment and the like, the outcomes can be disastrous. This is especially true of user interfaces and interfacing. In fact I have seen design guides implying that interface class design is somewhat simple, and implementation can be deferred to the final stages of a project. Some consequences of this are described by Paul Gruhn in his paper 'Human Machine Interface (HMI) Design: The Good, The Bad, and The Ugly (and what makes them so)':

Poor HMI designs have been identified as factors contributing to abnormal situations, billions of dollars of lost production, accidents, and fatalities. Many HMIs actually impede rather than assist operators.

So, why raise these points? It's because UML has its roots in software-centric systems, in particular from the Object Modelling Technology work of James Rumbaugh. Many things in the UML specification make sense only when seen from this point of view.

Now, in contrast to this, the software in embedded designs is merely one component within the complete system. Why it's needed, what it should do and how it should do it are dictated by system, not software, needs. And this is especially true for the interfacing and performance aspects. One very telling account is that given by Robyn Lutz in his paper 'Targeting Safety-Related Errors During Software Requirements Analysis'. The information given was based on examining 192 safety-related software errors documented during integration and system testing of two spacecraft, Voyager and Galileo. It showed that the most common causes of these errors were:

- Misunderstandings of the software's interfaces with the rest of the system, and
- Discrepancies between the documented requirements and those *actually* needed for correct functioning of the system.

Problem areas included:

- Out-of-range values.
- Timeouts.
- Unexpected arrivals of inputs.
- Data age (staleness).
- Arrival rates.
- Lost events.
- Delays in error responses.
- Effects of input signals arriving during non-operational mode (startup/offline/shutdown).

What this tells us is that, from the point of UML diagramming, we have to:

- First, identify the factors that are key to producing a safe and successful product.
- Second, establish which diagrams best model these properties.
- Third, define a cohesive and integrated way of using these diagrams through the design and development process.

3.4.4 Employing UML in real-time systems.

It's clear that the UML issues discussed so far are serious and need to be dealt with. But how? The answers to this lay the foundations for the selection and use of UML diagrams in real-time embedded systems.

The starting point is to once again emphasize that UML is *not* a process; it is a drawing language. You can produce a multitude of diagrams and still end up with a design that is incomplete, incorrect and incohesive. True, you should be able to understand that part of the design described by a specific diagram. Unfortunately the views provided by the *set* of diagrams may well be fragmented. Therefore what is essential is to use a good software design and development process supported by UML diagramming.

The second aspect is the choice of diagrams to be used. Be realistic. Decide what you really need. Use this as guidance in selecting a subset of the available UML diagrams. But is should also be clear from the discussion on MARTE that UML is deficient in the area of run-time modelling. What to use and what to do is really up to the individual designer; experience is very helpful here. So with a view to the future, consider what the Systems Modeling Language (SysML) and the SAE AADL Aerospace Standard (**S**ociety of **A**utomotive **E**ngineers **A**rchitecture **A**nalysis and **D**esign **L**anguage) have to offer.

Next, tackle the problems of actually using and understanding the diagrams. Make sure that the semantics of your chosen subset are clearly and explicitly stated. And avoid what I call the esoteric features; keep things simple if at all possible. Just because something *can* be done doesn't mean it *should* be.

What about CASE tools? Some provide no flexibility; what they have is what you get. Others allow you to adapt diagrams or even develop ones of your own choice. Whatever you do, make it a considered, professional decision. And make it clear why such choices are made.

Be pragmatic and parochial. Concentrate and what you and your team want to do, then do it. Make sure that everybody agrees on what has to be done and how to do it ('singing from the same hymn sheet', to use an old phrase). Don't try to save the world. You don't know what the future holds; get it right for now.

Finally, recognize that UML is a rigorous, not a formal, specification language. You cannot apply formal discharge proofs to the designs, so don't even try. Augment your diagrams with supporting explanatory text wherever you consider it necessary. This may upset the purists of the world of formal specification languages; just point out that engineers have successfully used that approach for a very long time.

3.5 Review.

At this stage you should:

- Understand, in broad terms, the evolution of software diagramming techniques.
- Appreciate that this evolution differed between the system-centric and software-centric worlds.
- Know that the development of UML was driven by the needs of the software-centric world.
- Be aware of the many assumptions, stated and unstated, which shaped the development of UML.
- Recognize that there is a great difference between the UML view of computing environments and those of embedded systems.
- Know what the major impediments are to the effective use of UML in system-centric systems.
- Understand the rationale for the advice given here on using UML in real-time systems.

END OF CHAPTER

Chapter 4

The structural design model.

The objectives of this chapter are to:

- Describe the fundamental aspects of objects, their structures and their attributes.
- Introduce the 'simple' class and define its relationship with the object.
- Show how systems may be structured as sets of collaborating objects having client-server and peer-to-peer relationships.
- Explain how objects can be used to implement modular structures.
- Describe the fundamental aspects of composite structures (class and object) and their associated attributes.
- Illustrate how composite objects may be used to implement 'plug and play' structures, with special reference to the 'pipe and filter' (materials flow) software processing model.
- Introduce component technology as a way of building large modular structures.
- Describe the reasons for, and advantages of, packaging software diagrams and show how this can be implemented.
- Introduce artifacts and describe their use.
- Show how the physical aspects of systems can be modelled using deployment diagrams.

4.1 Some important preliminaries.

Object Orientation has, in our view, one key concept. It is that designs may be structured as sets of interconnected, collaborating objects. Now, this seems to be a reasonable, non-contentious definition, given that the whole subject is called 'object oriented'. Yet this view is seen to be almost heretical by many in the 'traditional' OO world, where classes (or, more broadly, 'classifiers') are king.

Object diagrams were part and parcel of the UML suite, right from the very beginning. But even then they were seen as a somewhat inferior feature, having limited value. The seeds for confusion were set in the Unified Method v0.8 document, which had the following definition:

Class diagrams show generic descriptions of possible systems and object diagrams show particular instantiations of systems and their behavior. Class diagrams contain classes and object diagrams contain objects, but it is possible to mix classes and objects for various purposes, so the separation is not rigid.

Sparx Systems, the producers of the Enterprise Architect UML modelling tool, have produced a excellent set of tutorials (I recommend that you look these out at the Sparx Systems web site). However even their definition isn't especially helpful:

An object diagram may be considered a special case of a class diagram.

At least UML 1.x was more precise, stating:

An object diagram is a graph of instances, including objects and data values. A static object diagram is an instance of a class diagram; it shows a snapshot of the detailed state of a system at a point in time. **The use of object diagrams is fairly limited, mainly to show examples of data structures.**

Please note that final sentence; it shows absolutely clearly the mindset at work in the development of the UML specifications. Our experience in researching and implementing real-time OO designs, stretching over 20 years, is absolutely the opposite. And we are not alone. The account given by Steven Stolper in his paper 'Streamlined design approach lands Mars pathfinder', IEEE Software, Sept./Oct. 1999, is highly supportive of our approach:

Although many textbooks recommend defining classes an initial step in an OO approach, it was difficult for us to conceive abstract classes without concrete examples of objects that solved particular problems in the spacecraft domain.

Landing a spacecraft on Mars is much less defined than the example problems encountered in the textbooks.

It was more advantageous to enumerate objects and to extract possible classes than it was to fit classes to a problem we were defining as we explored the design space.

UML 2.x pretty much ignores the object diagram and its role, which has resulted in at least two problems. First, trying to describe everything in terms of classifier instantiations and the like has generated many mind-numbing, tortuous, impenetrable descriptions. Second, it has led to the need to produce a new diagram, the composite structured unit. More of this later.

4.2 Objects and their classes - the 'simple' model of OO design.

To recapitulate: an object is a software machine used as a basic building block for OO systems. From an external point of view it:

• Is seen as a single unit.
• Has a well-defined function or purpose (**what** it does).
• Encapsulates all resources required to achieve that purpose (**how** it does it).
• Has distinct separation of 'what' from 'how'.
• Hides implementation aspects from the outside world.
• Has a well-defined, clean interface which acts as the 'access window' of the object. Only this is visible to the outside world.

It is also important that the object should not produce side effects (which would negate many of the benefits of OO design). To achieve this, all interactions with the outside software world must go via the interface.

Note that the term 'simple' is an informal term. It is used to distinguish the OO model described here from the composite one which comes later. An object, in a UML object diagram, is shown as a simple named rectangle, figure 4.1. The name is the one chosen by you, the designer. Observe that it is underlined, indicating that it represents a software run-time unit (i.e. when the program executes it actually does something).

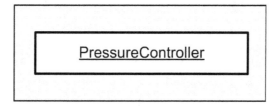

Figure 4.1 The basic object diagram

Let us suppose that our software design consists of one object only (fairly unlikely in reality). We can then show its context within the complete embedded system using the format of figure 4.2.

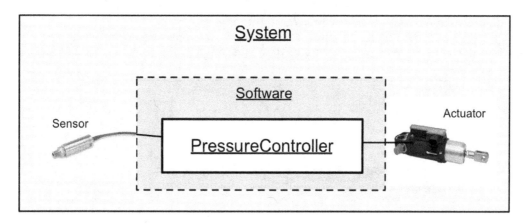

Figure 4.2 A single object software design - context diagram

This is *not* a standard UML diagram. However, in our experience, the context diagram is a key one in the design of real-time embedded systems; we have *never* done a real system design that hasn't included a context diagram.

One of the primary aims in object-oriented design is to hide as much information as possible. It's a variant on the 'need to know' principle; what you don't know about can't hurt you. We do this by separating an object into two parts: the visible and hidden sections, figure 4.3.

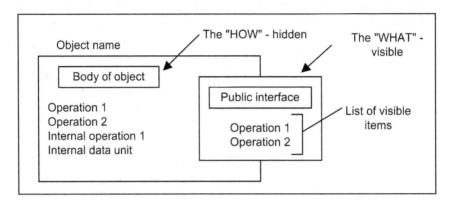

Figure 4.3 Global view of an object

The visible section (the interface) describes essentially the services it provides. In the outside world of *software* only the interface details can be seen. The body itself implements the required functions of the object. How these are achieved is hidden within the body, being of no concern to the user. In fact it is imperative that internal operations and data cannot be accessed directly by external objects. As shown here, for example, the object contains three operations and one unit of internal data. Operations 1 and 2 are made available for use by other objects (*clients*) as they are listed in the interface section. Hence they are considered to be public items. By contrast, the internal operation and the data unit remain hidden – they are private to the object.

   Now, this raises the question; how do we specify the operations and data items of an object? There are, in fact, two aspects to this, illustrated in figure 4.4. To build a product

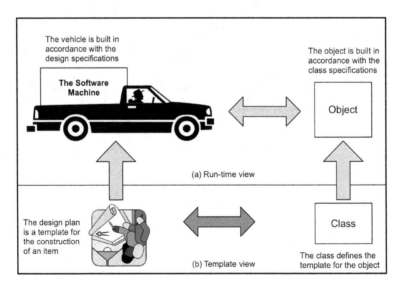

Figure 4.4 The software object and its template

such as a vehicle we need to work to a set of plans (templates); in building the vehicle we 'instantiate' these plans. The object itself can be considered to be the equivalent of the vehicle, its defining plan being the 'class'. The class defines *what* the attributes (qualities) of the object are, together with the object operations. Thus every object manufactured from this template has the same attributes and operations. However, the individual attribute *values* are defined at build time. Thus the class defines the form, content and behaviour of objects; in itself it is *not* a run-time item. Thus the class cannot do anything; it is merely a specification. Please note this most carefully, imprint it on your brain; it will help you deal with confusing descriptions regularly found in OO articles.

To make things more meaningful let's now move from this high-level view of things to something more concrete. Suppose that we *have* decided to implement a single object design as depicted in figure 4.2. After analysing the system requirements we arrive at the following specification for the *PressureController* object:

The purpose of the object is to control the pressure of the hydraulic system. It does this by measuring the actual pressure, comparing this with a preset value, and then adjusting the position of an actuator-driven valve to maintain the preset value.

The object will contain three internal software functions:
- *Read the sensor pressure.*
- *Compute the actuator signal.*
- *Set the actuator position.*

It also will have the following data items:
- *Measured pressure.*
- *Preset pressure (a constant value).*
- *Actuator control signal.*

It is set into execution by calling a 'run' function provided on its public interface.

The key software aspects can be represented informally as shown in figure 4.5.

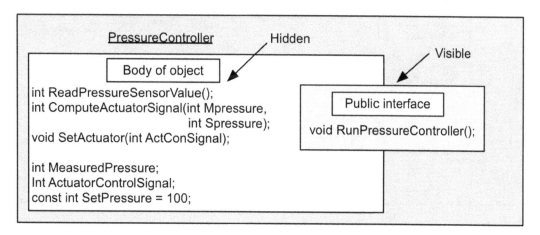

Figure 4.5 Informal view of the pressure controller object

The specification for these items is provided by the class using the diagram symbol of figure 4.6, a rectangular box having three compartments.

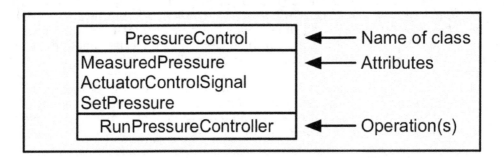

Figure 4.6 Class symbol

The name of the class is shown in the first (upper) section. Its attributes (qualities) are listed in the middle section, whilst its *visible* operations appear in the bottom section. By comparing this with figure 4.5 it can be seen that attributes become data items; operations are implemented by subprograms (procedures or functions). Variations of this class symbol can be used legally in UML; however this particular format is widely used.

Figure 4.7 shows the relationship between classes, objects, attributes and attribute values.

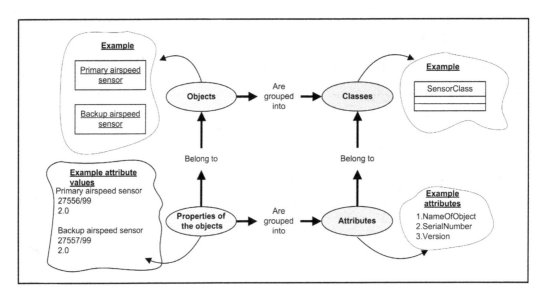

Figure 4.7 Class and object inter-relationship

Objects can be represented in a number of ways, as set out in figure 4.8.

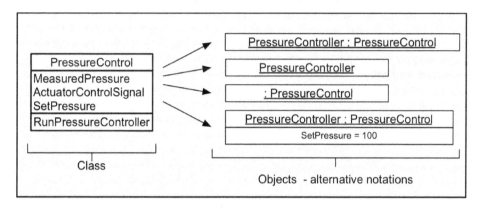

Figure 4.8 Example class and object notation

The first three forms should be self-explanatory. The fourth one can be used if we wish to denote that an object has specific values (in this case the data item *SetPressure* has a value of 100). A point to note is that if you use a CASE tool you may be forced to use tool-defined formats.

The purpose of figure 4.9 is to reinforce the fact that, from a single class, we can produce as many objects as desired. It also highlights a really important aspect; the class diagram does *not* tell us how many objects exist in our system (there are work-rounds for this, but strictly aren't legal UML). Thus the mapping from class diagram to object diagram is not a unique one. In contrast, mapping from the object diagram to the class diagram *is* unique.

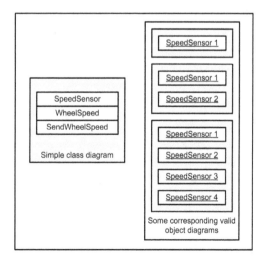

Figure 4.9 Simple class and some corresponding object diagrams

The class information of figure 4.9 can be regarded as a 'high-level' specification; it is independent of detailed code issues, including the programming language to be used to implement it. Now, if the translation from diagram to code is handled manually then this is sufficient; the program designer can fill in all code-level aspects.   However, if an autocode generator is used, things are quite different.   In order for the generator to produce correct source code it needs detailed information about *all* the class items.   An example of this can be seen in figure 4.10, produced using the Enterprise Architect CASE tool.

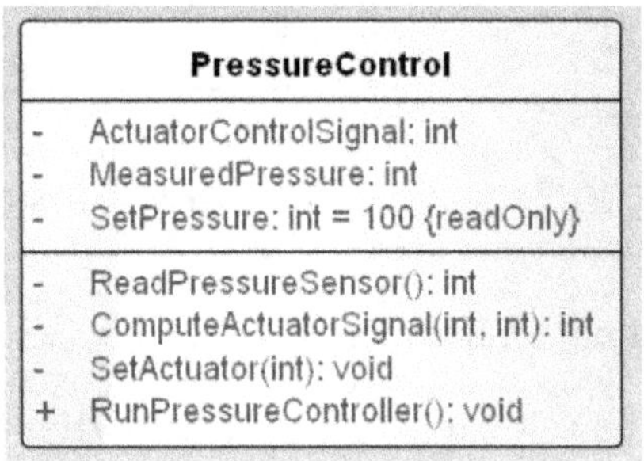

Figure 4.10 Simple class diagram - CASE tool version

Here the minus sign denotes private items, the plus being used for public ones.   This, together with information provided via a properties dialogue, allows the tool to generate the essential code of the class.   It was decided that the example would be coded in C++, resulting in the code structures of figures 4.11 and 4.12.

```
/////////////////////////////////////////////////
//  PressureControl.h
//  Implementation of the Class PressureControl
//  Created on:     29-Apr-2015 11:24:13
//  Original author: jamescooling
/////////////////////////////////////////////////

#if !defined(EA_E77A054A_C56A_4784_AE51_D86905DC7370__INCLUDED_)
#define EA_E77A054A_C56A_4784_AE51_D86905DC7370__INCLUDED_

class PressureControl
{

public:
        PressureControl();
        virtual ~PressureControl();

        void RunPressureController();

private:
        int ActuatorControlSignal;
        int MeasuredPressure;
        const int SetPressure;

        int ReadPressureSensor();
        int ComputeActuatorSignal(int Spressure, int Mpressure);
        void SetActuator(int ActConSignal);

};
#endif // !defined(EA_E77A054A_C56A_4784_AE51_D86905DC7370__INCLUDED_)
```

Figure 4.11 Autogenerated code - C++ .h file

```
/////////////////////////////////////////////////////
// PressureControl.cpp
// Implementation of the Class PressureControl
// Created on:      29-Apr-2015 11:24:13
// Original author: jamescoolIng
/////////////////////////////////////////////////////

#include "PressureControl.h"

PressureControl::PressureControl(){

}

PressureControl::~PressureControl(){

}

int PressureControl::ReadPressureSensor(){

        return 0;
}


int PressureControl::ComputeActuatorSignal(int Spressure, int Mpressure){

        return 0;
}


void PressureControl::SetActuator(int ActConSignal){

}

void PressureControl::RunPressureController(){

}
```

Figure 4.12 Autogenerated code - C++ .cpp file

Three very important points come out of this example. First, provided the class is correctly specified, then the autocoder guarantees that the code actually implements its specification. Second, there is still a great deal more work to be done before the code is complete. Third, you cannot glean any details of the executable aspects of the code from the class diagram.

4.3 Collaborating objects.

4.3.1 The design models.

As stated earlier, single object implementations are unlikely to be seen in practical work. Realistic designs usually consist of *sets* of co-operating objects which, acting together, provide the desired system function and behaviour. So let us revisit the pressure control system and change its design to a three-object one, figure 4.13.

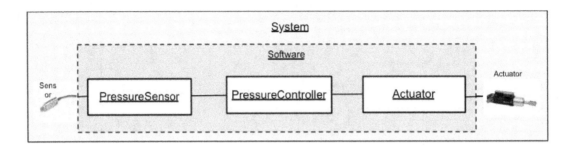

Figure 4.13 Revised design of the pressure control system - object diagram

This we'll call a 'flat-object' model as all objects co-exist at the same level. Good naming can make the design virtually self-explanatory, though clearly detailed design information must be provided somewhere.

   We've said that these objects co-operate, but exactly how do they do this? The answer is that they interact by sending messages to (communicating with) each other, this being fundamental to OO design (figure 4.14).

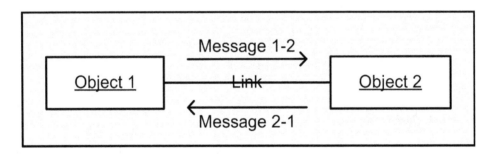

Figure 4.14 Object communication in OO designs

The connecting 'channel' between the objects is, in UML, called a link.

   Next we need to consider the nature of the relationship between these objects. Take, for example, the pressure sensor and pressure controller objects, figure 4.15. Figure 4.15a illustrates the fundamental ideas of a client-server relationship, where the client needs (requires) information and the server provides it. Here the controller object is the client with the sensor object being the server (though you wouldn't be able to deduce this from the object diagram).

   In figure 4.15b the design is extended to include the relevant messaging, this being an example of an object communication diagram. Observe that messages are denoted using arrowed lines. From the directions of the arrows we can deduce which objects are clients and which ones are servers.

   Normally we would transmit such information via object interfaces, the small rectangles of figure 4.15c. The notation here is informal, used merely to illustrate some aspects of provided and required interfaces. One very important point is that, for a standard C++ object, there is only one explicit interface, the provided one. This we've already met in the previous section. By contrast the required interface will be buried somewhere in the code implementation of the pressure controller object. Unfortunately, this structure is a major weaknesses of 'classical' OO client-server designs.

   In some cases the clients message requires a reply; information must be returned to the caller. Such replies can be shown by using dashed arrowed lines, figure 4.15c.

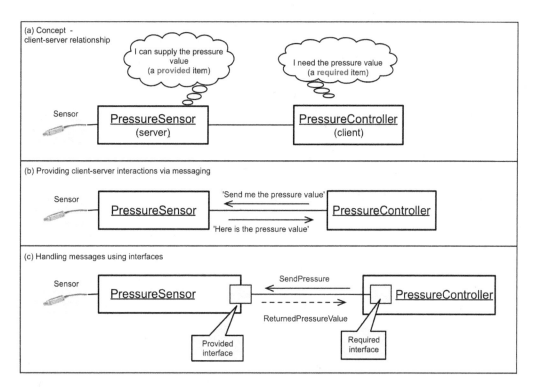

Figure 4.15 Object relationship - client-server (informal notation)

   So, looking across the design as a whole, figure 4.16, it can be seen that:

   • There is one client object - the pressure controller.
   • There are two server objects - the pressure sensor and the actuator.
   • Each server has one provided interface.
   • The client has two required interfaces.

A design decision is made that the pressure sensor class should have one attribute and one public operation, figure 4.17.

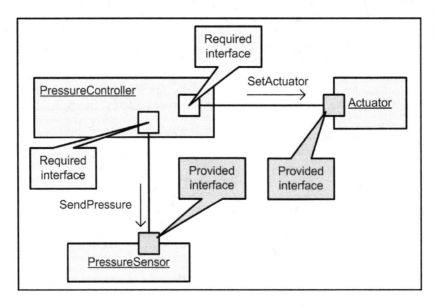

Figure 4.16 Required and provided interfaces

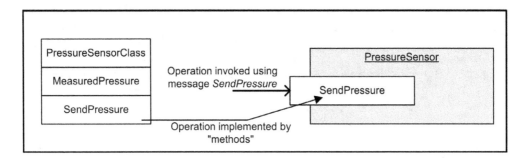

Figure 4.17 Concept - messages and methods

The implementation of the operation is called a method, which is then built using the appropriate language construct.   Operations are invoked by sending messages to methods; thus every message must have a corresponding method.

   A note for completeness; operations can also be defined as being abstract, i.e. ones that don't have associated methods.

   The final complete class diagram for the pressure control system is given in figure 4.18.

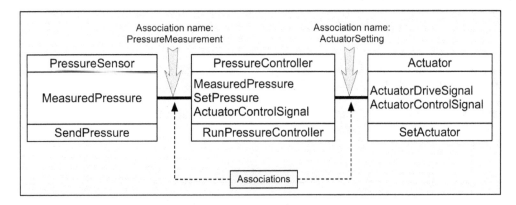

Figure 4.18 Class diagram for the revised pressure control system

When we work backwards from the object to the class design, one important rule must be followed; when objects are linked their corresponding classes are also connected ('associated'). These associations can, if you wish, be named. However, the naming should define the nature of the relationship between the classes; there isn't any concept of one class 'doing something' to another one.

A last point about this example; as the pressure controller class has a provided operation, doesn't this mean it also acts as a server? And if so, where does the message come from? Who's the client? Well, if we code this in C++ for example, we would have a function call *RunPressureController* in 'main'. This is the message, and main acts as a 'hidden' object.

So far we've been discussing what I've earlier called the 'classical' OO model. This is well-suited to designs that are fundamentally client-server in nature (such as databases and web servers). However, in real-time embedded systems, the most enduring model is one where object relationships are peer-to-peer, figure 4.19.

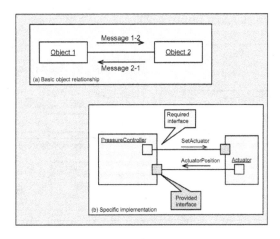

Figure 4.19 Object relationships - peer-to-peer

It is, of course, not unusual to find a mix of client-server and peer-to-peer models in embedded system designs. However, the peer-to-peer aspects normally predominate, with relatively small use of client-servers (e.g. data stores and the like). A key difference between the two is that:

- In a client-server relationship a client has to be able to 'see' the server but the server doesn't need to see the client. Thus the association can be implemented as a uni-directional one.
- In peer-to-peer operations objects have to be able to see their peers. To support this associations need to be bi-directional.

These points are illustrated in figure 4.20.

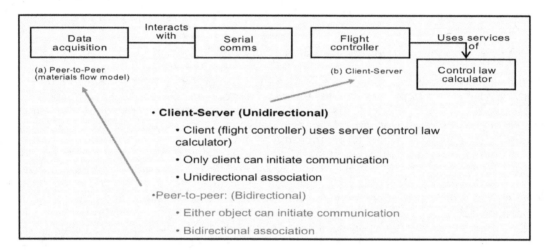

Figure 4.20 Brief comparison - uni and bi-directional associations

We'll now look at the some general aspects of class-object relationships where the design consists of multiple classes, figure 4.21

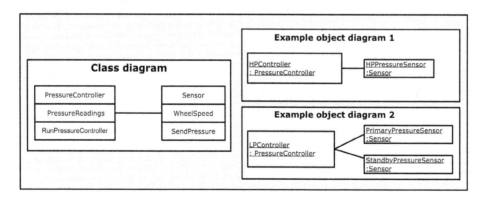

Figure 4.21 Example class and object diagrams - multiple classes

Both object diagrams 1 and 2 are valid instantiations of the class diagram; we could also have further ones having three, four, five etc. sensor objects. Clearly, when a class-first design process is used, we need to specify precisely what the object model should be. That is, define the number of objects involved in relationships, a 'multiplicity specification', figure 4.22. Details of the notation are given in this figure.

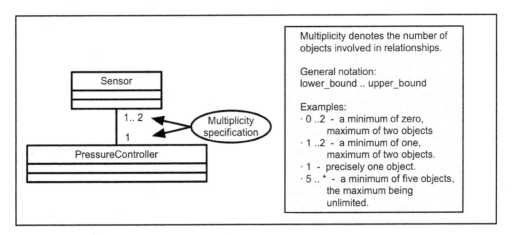

Figure 4.22 Associations and multiplicity

   As shown, the class diagram and its multiplicity has the following meaning:

- Each pressure controller object 'sees' one *or* two sensor objects.
- Each sensor object sees one pressure controller object only.

For some this can, at first, be slightly confusing because we're using the class model to describe object model relationships. You might also come to the conclusion that including multiplicity values makes the class-to-object mapping a unique one. Not so. We can, for instance, make multiple instantiations of the pressure controller class, with corresponding instantiations of the sensor class.

4.3.2 Coding aspects of associations - C++ examples.

What follows here is *not* a tutorial on how to implement class designs. That, in itself, would turn out to be rather extensive as we'd have to consider implementations involving:

- Sequential code structures.
- Multitasking structures.
- Multiprocessor, multicomputer and multicore designs.

Another point is that detailed language aspects are well beyond the scope of this book (and C++ may not be your language of choice). Even so, there is value in looking at some simple examples; they let us demonstrate concrete aspects of class implementation. It also gives an opportunity to show further uses (and limitations) of CASE tool technology for diagramming and code generation. As before, the examples have been produced using the Enterprise Architect tool. First we'll look at a client-server model, then a peer-to-peer one (but please feel free to skip this section if you consider it to be an irrelevance).

(a) Client-server relationships.
This exercise takes the class design first shown in figure 4.21 and then reproduces it using the CASE tool, figure 4.23

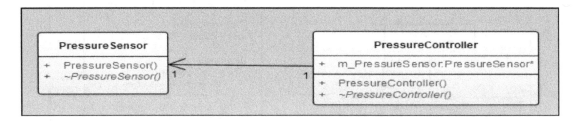

Figure 4.23 Client-server 1:1 association - initial design model

We have decided that the design should be implemented as a client-server relationship, the client being the pressure controller class. It is also decided that the object model will consist of two objects only. Thus the association can be a unidirectional one, having a multiplicity of one (1) at each end.

Figure 4.23 actually shows the state of the initial design model *after* the first run of the autocoder. The class names were entered manually into the design; all other items are tool-generated. Now, from this we can learn a bit more about the pro's and con's of automatic code generation:

- The *PressureSensor* class is shown here as having two compartments while the *PressureController* class is a three-compartment one. Both are legal UML, but the actual selection was (in this example) made by the CASE tool.
- The constructor and destructor methods were generated automatically.
- The controller class has a single attribute, *m_PressureSensor* this being a pointer to objects of class *PressureSensor*. This attribute was also generated automatically.

The corresponding auto-generated code (.h and .cpp files) for the controller class is presented in figures 4.24 and 4.25. These are interesting in that they show what the autocoder can do, what it can't do and what assumptions it makes.

First, it provides both constructor and destructor functions. Now, in most embedded designs we construct all objects during initialization (or something similar). However, as these are usually intended to exist as long as the software runs ('static'), the destructor isn't needed.

Second, the destructor is declared as being virtual, something needed only when using derived classes (inheritance, see later).

Lastly, it assumes that we'll use pointer methods to implement the associations (strictly to 'wire' the objects together). This, although a widely-used technique, is best suited to sequential (i.e. non-concurrent) implementations.

```
///////////////////////////////////////////
// PressureController.h
// Implementation of the Class PressureController
// Created on:     19-MAY-2015 12:13:38 PM
// Original author: jec
///////////////////////////////////////////

#if !defined(EA_46BC0CBC_8837_44b1_80A0_791DE93A7290__INCLUDED_)
#define EA_46BC0CBC_8837_44b1_80A0_791DE93A7290__INCLUDED_

#include "PressureSensor.h"

class PressureController
{

public:
        PressureController(PressureSensor* SensorObjectAddress);
        virtual ~PressureController();
        PressureSensor *m_PressureSensor;

};
#endif // !defined(EA_46BC0CBC_8837_44b1_80A0_791DE93A7290__INCLUDED_)
```

Figure 4.24 PressureController class initial code - .h file

```
/////////////////////////////////////////////////
// PressureController.cpp
// Implementation of the Class PressureController
// Created on:     19-May-2015 12:13:38 PM
// Original author: JEC
/////////////////////////////////////////////////

#include "PressureController.h"

PressureController(PressureSensor* SensorObjectAddress)
{

}

PressureController::~PressureController(){

}
```

Figure 4.25 PressureController class initial code - .cpp file

The final version of the model is given in figure 4.26 where all new attributes and methods are user-provided.

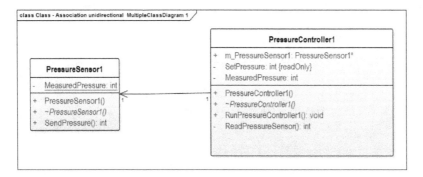

Figure 4.26 Client-server 1-1 uni-directional association - final design model

Using this information the autocoder generates the required .h and .cpp files, figures 4.27 and 4.28.

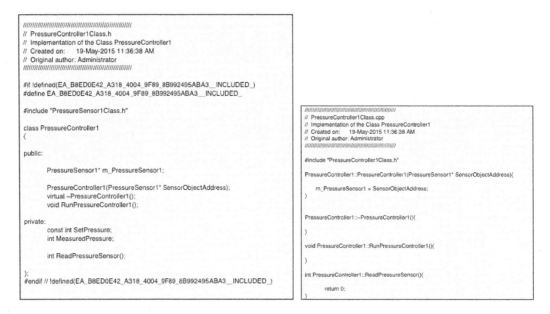

Figure 4.27 PressureController1 class: Final autogenerated code - .h file

Figure 4.28 PressureController1 class Final autogenerated code - .cpp file

Finally, using this code, we can produce the code of the pressure control system, one possible implementation being that of figure 4.29.   Observe how we wire the objects together at declaration time using the constructor mechanism.

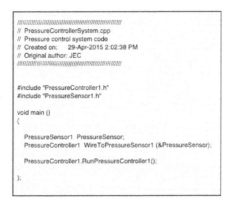

```
//////////////////////////////////////////////////
//  PressureControllerSystem.cpp
//  Pressure control system code
//  Created on:    29-Apr-2015 2:02:38 PM
//  Original author: JEC
//////////////////////////////////////////////////


#include "PressureController1.h"
#include "PressureSensor1.h"

void main ()
{

    PressureSensor1  PressureSensor;
    PressureController1  WireToPressureSensor1 (&PressureSensor);

    PressureController1.RunPressureController1();

};
```

Figure 4.29 Pressure control system code

Note also that this code design doesn't involve any concurrency; i.e. it's standard C++ sequential code.

(b) Peer-to-peer relationships.
Suppose that the design requirements are changed so that:

- A pressure controller object can ask a sensor object to send its current reading to it.
- The sending of data is to be done under the control of the sensor object.
- The sensor object may also update the controller object at any time.

To meet these needs we alter the design so that sensor and controller objects can 'talk' to each other on a peer-to-peer basis. Hence we denote the class association as being a bi-directional one, figure 4.30.

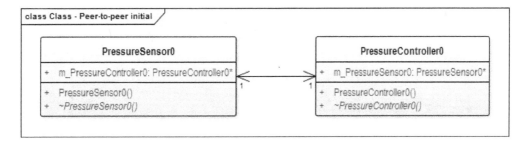

Figure 4.30 Peer-to-peer 1 -1 association EA diagram - initial

Also provided (figure 4.31) are code fragments to demonstrate:

- Means to set up addresses of objects so that they can be wired together (the constructors).
- Instantiation of the objects and their wiring together.

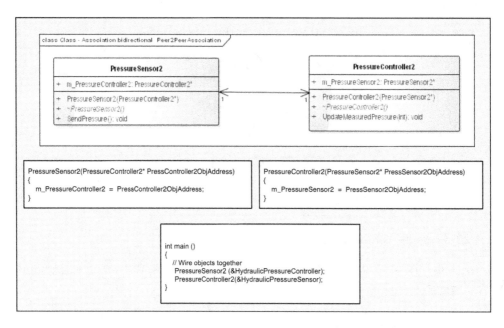

Figure 4.31 Peer-to-peer 1 -1 association extended

In practice you will find that the same results can be produced using a variety of programming methods. Also, where a design consists of many objects, it may simplify the code review process to have explicit wiring functions (as, for example, figure 4.32):

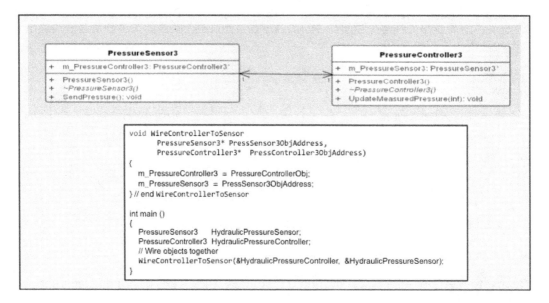

Figure 4.32 Peer-to-peer object wiring

Please note; this example, as with the earlier ones, assumes that we're using sequential code units.

4.4 Modular objects.

In general engineering terms a modular item is something that's constructed from a set of parts, as for example the pistol of figure 4.33.

Figure 4.33 Example of a modular item - pistol

A key point; there is no concept of making a pistol in one go. Instead the parts that make it up are built separately, then get assembled into a finished product. This, of course, is something that's been practiced by the auto industry for many, many years, figure 4.34.

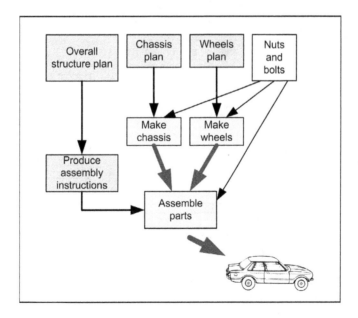

Figure 4.34 Modular build

Now, let's look at some of the properties of the pistol. It:

- Is seen by the user as a single unit.
- Has a well-defined purpose.
- Has simple, clear interfaces.
- Is easy to use.
- Hides its complexity - on the surface looks very simple.

Think of it as just one part of say a personal weapon system. So, at the system level we have a relatively small number of items, thus minimizing system complexity. Each item is produced separately, and then tested to ensure that it meets its operational requirements. We can also evaluate the quality, reliability, usability and cost aspects of individual items before integrating them into the overall system.   What we have here then is another example of the well-proven 'divide and conquer' approach to building systems. Now, how can we apply this to the software arena, specifically a UML-based method?

UML provides us with notation to define objects which themselves are made up of 'contained' objects. This is called 'composition', and such objects are often referred to as 'composite objects'. An example is given in figure 4.35 which depicts part of the software used to control a conveyor belt.

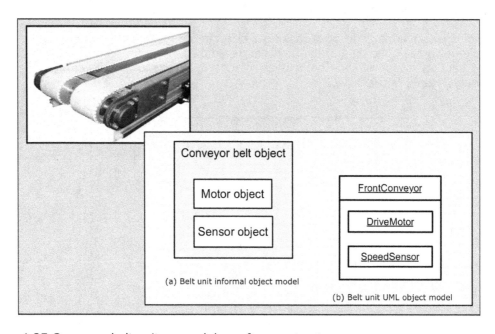

Figure 4.35 Conveyor belt unit - modular software structure

The general concept is shown in figure 4.35a, while that of 4.35b is a specific example using UML notation. Here *FrontConveyor* is the composite object, the contained objects being *DriveMotor* and *PositionSensor*. In UML-speak, *FrontConveyor* is called the 'whole', the others being 'parts'.

A critical aspect of composition is that when the whole object is created the parts are also created. Likewise, if the whole is destroyed the parts also get destroyed. In other words the parts do not have existence independent of the whole.

The class specification for this is presented in figure 4.36, this being called 'composite aggregation'.

A brief aside: UML says *Composite aggregation is a strong form of aggregation.* However you will find that some developers use the terms *composition* and *aggregation* to distinguish between the strong and 'weak' aggregation forms. Here, though, we aren't going to bother with 'weak' aggregation; our experience is that it isn't widely used in deep embedded systems.

The class diagram of figure 4.36 was produced using the Enterprise Architect CASE tool. All operations and attributes shown here were generated by its autocoding feature, the associated code for the conveyor belt class being that of figure 4.37.

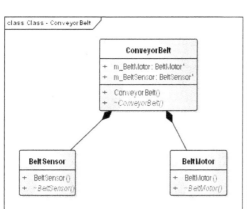

```
/////////////////////////////////////////////////////////
// ConveyorBelt.h
// Implementation of the Class ConveyorBelt
// Created on:     29-Apr-2015 5:19:27 PM
// Original author: JEC
/////////////////////////////////////////////////////////

#include "BeltMotor.h"
#include "BeltSensor.h"

class ConveyorBelt
{

public:
     BeltMotor* m_BeltMotor;
     BeltSensor* m_BeltSensor;

     ConveyorBelt();
     virtual ~ConveyorBelt();

};
#endif // !
```

Figure 4.36 Class diagram:
conveyor belt object - initial

Figure 4.37 Conveyor belt class - composite aggregation code (initial - outline structure)

The 'pointer to' objects *m_BeltSensor* and *m_BeltMotor* were, like earlier examples, generated automatically (as were the constructors and destructors).

The completed class design is depicted in figure 4.38, whilst the associated conveyor belt class code is given in figure 4.39 (note: during design it was decided not to use pointer methods to link the objects together).

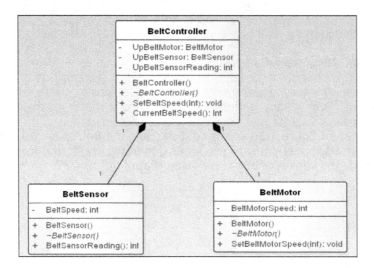

Figure 4.38 Class diagram for the conveyor belt object (final version)

```
/////////////////////////////////////////////////////////////
//  BeltController.h
/////////////////////////////////////////////////////////////
#include "BeltSensor.h"
#include "BeltMotor.h"

class BeltController
{
public:
     BeltController();
     void SetBeltSpeed(int BeltSpeed);
     int  CurrentBeltSpeed();

private:
     BeltSensor UpBeltSensor;
     BeltMotor  UpBeltMotor;
     int        UpBeltSensorReading;

}; // end class BeltController

/////////////////////////////////////////////////////////////
//  BeltController.cpp
/////////////////////////////////////////////////////////////

#include "BeltController.h"

void BeltController::SetBeltSpeed(int BeltSpeed)
{
     UpBeltMotor.SetBeltMotorSpeed(BeltSpeed);
} //end SetBeltSpeed


int BeltController::CurrentBeltSpeed()
{
int UpBeltSensorReading;

     UpBeltSensorReading = UpBeltSensor.BeltSensorReading();
     return UpBeltSensorReading;
} //end CurrentBeltSpeed
```

Figure 4.39 Conveyor belt class code - final (part)

You can see from this that the belt class has two private objects, *UpBeltMotor* and *UpBeltSensor*. These are, of course, the contained objects (parts) which are created when the belt class itself is instantiated. Note also that the all the work of the composite object (whole) is actually done by the parts; messages arriving on the whole are directed to the appropriate part. For instance, the public message *SetBeltSpeed* actually calls the function *SetBeltMotorSpeed* of the motor class; it does absolutely nothing else.

You don't have to do things this way but we highly recommend that you should; it keeps things very simple and clear, so streamlining the testing, debugging, integration and maintenance of code units.

Included for completeness is part code of the motor and sensor classes (figure 4.40). Also included is a simple example of the belt object in use, figure 4.41, together with associated code aspects, figures 4.42a, 4.42b and 4.42c.

```cpp
//////////////////////////////////////////////////////////////
//  BeltMotor.h
//////////////////////////////////////////////////////////////
class BeltMotor
{
private:
        int BeltMotorSpeed;
public:
        void SetBeltMotorSpeed(int Speed);
}; // end class BeltMotor

//////////////////////////////////////////////////////////////
//  BeltMotor.cpp
//////////////////////////////////////////////////////////////
#include "BeltMotor.h"

void BeltMotor::SetBeltMotorSpeed(int Speed)
{
        //Code that uses Speed to set the motor speed
} // end SetBeltMotorSpeed
```

```cpp
//////////////////////////////////////////////////////////////
//  BeltSensor.h
//////////////////////////////////////////////////////////////
class BeltSensor
{
private:
        int BeltSpeed;
public:
        BeltSensor();
        int BeltSensorReading();
}; // end class BeltSensor

//////////////////////////////////////////////////////////////
//  BeltSensor.cpp
//////////////////////////////////////////////////////////////

#include "BeltSensor.h"

int BeltSensor::BeltSensorReading()
{
int ActualBeltSpeed;

        // Code to measure the belt speed  - loaded into
        // ActualBeltSpeed
        return ActualBeltSpeed;
} // end BeltSensorReading
```

Figure 4.40 Motor and sensor classes code - final (part)

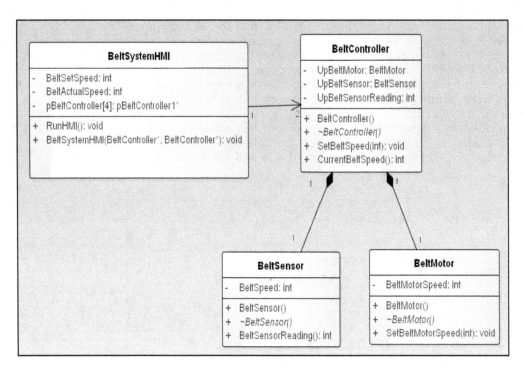

Figure 4.41 Example of belt object use in a small system

```
class BeltSystemHMI
{
private:
// Allow up to four belt controllers to be interfaced to the HMI
        BeltController* pBeltController[4];

        int                        BeltSetSpeed;
        int                        BeltActualSpeed;
public:
        BeltSystemHMI();
        BeltSystemHMI(BeltController* BeltControllerObjectAddress,
BeltController* BeltControllerObject2Address);
        void RunHMI();
}; // end class BeltSystemHMI
```

Figure 4.42a Code of BeltSystemHMI

```
//This is demonstration test code only to validate the design.
// Written for clarity, not compactness, of the source code.

void BeltSystemHMI::RunHMI()
        {
        int BeltSpeedTestValue = 0;
        BeltController BeltControllerObject1;
        BeltController BeltControllerObject2;

                BeltControllerObject1 = *pBeltController[1];
                BeltControllerObject1.SetBeltNumber(1);
                BeltControllerObject1.ShowBeltNumber();
                BeltControllerObject1.SetBeltSpeed(100);
                BeltSpeedTestValue = BeltControllerObject1.CurrentBeltSpeed();

                BeltControllerObject2 = *pBeltController[2];
                BeltControllerObject2.SetBeltNumber(2);
                BeltControllerObject2.ShowBeltNumber();
                BeltControllerObject2.SetBeltSpeed(50);
                BeltSpeedTestValue = BeltControllerObject2.CurrentBeltSpeed();
        } // end RunHMI
```

Figure 4.42b Code of function RunHMI

```
// Demonstration test code

void main()
{
int BeltSpeedTestValue;

        cout<<"Start of program"<<endl;
        system("pause"); cout<<endl;

        BeltController UpBeltController1;
        BeltController UpBeltController2;
        BeltSystemHMI TransportSystemHMI(&UpBeltController1, &UpBeltController2);

        cout<<"Ready to run the BeltController "<<endl;
        system("pause"); cout<<endl;

        TransportSystemHMI.RunHMI();
}// end main
```

Figure 4.42c Code of main (part)

4.5 Software reuse - inheritance.

4.5.1 General aspects.

We constantly strive to produce software that, when compared with current methods, is:

- Cheaper to produce and maintain.
- More reliable.
- More flexible.
- Less demanding on memory storage requirements (for resource-constrained systems).

Many years ago programmers realised that one method could really help here: the reuse of existing software. Traditionally this was based on the 'cut and paste' method, the copying of existing work. However, OO brought a new reusability technique to the software world: *inheritance*. More precisely there are two aspects to this. First there are methods to directly reuse software, sometimes called *Implementation Inheritance*. Second, there are methods to reuse the interfaces of software units, often called *Interface Inheritance*. We'll now look at these in some detail.

4.5.2 Implementation inheritance (subclassing).

Here our aim is to produce as little source code as possible. One way to achieve this goal is to minimize the number of classes in a system. How, though, can we do this? Assume we've come up with the object design of figure 4.43a. Our next step is to generate the

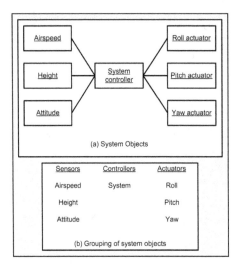

Figure 4.43 Classifying items - example design

class design for this. A very simple method would be to produce a class for each object, thus giving a six-class design.   Simple, yes, but, from a code point of view, not very efficient.   A much more sensible approach is to look for natural groupings of objects, then produce a class for each group.   One such grouping solution (a 'classification' of objects) is given in figure 4.43b, decisions being based on commonality of:

- Function
- Behaviour
- Qualities

As shown here there are three classes: *Sensors*, *Controllers* and *Actuators*.   In a perfect world all objects within each class would be identical; hence these could be produced from just one unit of source code.   As a result the system of figure 4.43 could be built using just three classes.

Unfortunately, reality is rarely so obliging.   It is likely that the initial classification exercise will collect together objects that are similar but not identical.   In our example it turns out that the actuator objects are identical but the various sensors are quite different at the detailed level.   Thus a *single* class cannot act as the template for all the sensor objects.

It might, at this point, seem that we are back to square one, needing a class for each object.   However, object-oriented programming offers us a way out of the problem: class extension using subclasses, figure 4.44.

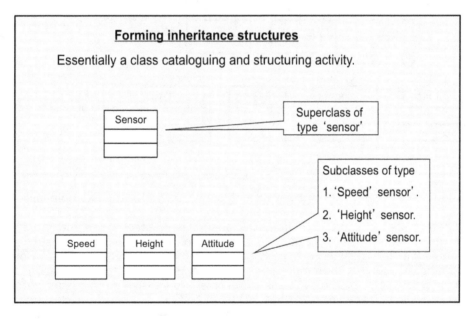

Figure 4.44 Extending classes with subclasses

This is essentially a class cataloguing and structuring activity, giving rise to what we call inheritance structures.   The class that appears at the highest level in the structure is defined to be the *superclass*, also know as a parent or base class.   This normally is the simplest class, where the information it contains applies to *all* the extended items, the *subclasses*. Subclasses 'tailor' the superclass by extending it to meet the needs of specific items; thus they add detail.

Let's return to our example of figure 4.43 and apply these ideas. We make a design decision that the actuator objects can be built from a single template: one class only is needed. And as there is only one controller object, classification is straightforward. However, to specify the requirements of the different sensor objects, we need to use class extension (inheritance) techniques. figure 4.45. On the class diagram extension is denoted using an association which has an open arrow at the superclass end. It can be seen from this that the classes are organized in a hierarchical manner. At the top there is the superclass *Sensor*. Below this are the three subclasses, *Speed*, *Height* and *Attitude* (and if we wish we can also subclass these, as shown).

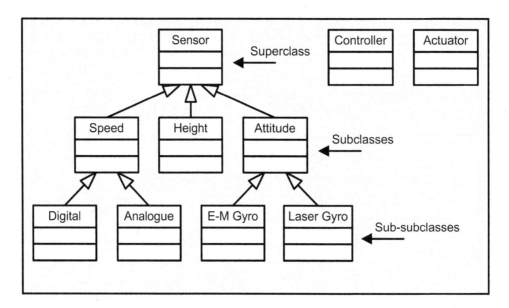

Figure 4.45 Class structuring - subclasses and superclasses for the example design

To reiterate some important points; the superclass *Sensor* gives the most abstract definition (in terms of attributes and/or operations) of a sensor object. A subclass adds detail to the superclass definition which is specific to that individual subclass. However, it also automatically acquires the properties of its parents, this being known as inheritance. Thus, moving down the hierarchy, classes become progressively more specialized. But now for a most important point. What we have here is essentially a class-cataloguing exercise; we aren't decomposing objects. Thus a *Laser Gyro* class is a specialized form of an *Attitude* class; in turn this is a specialized form of a *Sensor* class.

Producing such inheritance diagrams may be intellectually stimulating; but how does it help to raise software productivity? This is where the inheritance features of OO languages come in to play. Let us see what they can do for us by looking at the example of figure 4.46.

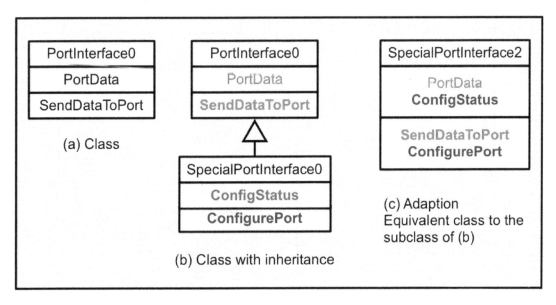

Figure 4.46 Inheritance vs adaption

First we define a class *PortInterface0*, figure 4.46a. It has an attribute *PortData* and an operation *SendDataToPort*. We later decide to produce a specialized version of this, *SpecialPortInterface0*, figure 4.46b. This adds another attribute, *ConfigStatus*, and another operation, *ConfigurePort*. As a result of inheritance, *SpecialPortInterface0* is equivalent to the class of figure 4.46c, *SpecialPortInterface2*. However, there is a significant difference between the two from a source code point of view. Without inheritance we would have to produce two separate classes. Each one has to be complete in its own right; thus there will be duplication of the source code of the *PortInterface0* class. But with inheritance, there is no need to reproduce the superclass material in the subclass. It is automatically inherited (and thus reused) by applying appropriate programming constructs.

   The autogenerated code for figure 4.46b is given in figure 4.47. It is clear from this which attributes and operations belong to the specific classes; also it is clear that, if we wish, we can create objects of both the super class *PortInterface0* and the subclass *SpecialPortInterface0*.

   The benefits obtained by using inheritance are quite limited in designs structured a la figure 4.46. However, if we now take figure 4.48, the reuse benefits are more obvious. The autogenerated code for the class *SpecialPortInterfaceB* is given in figure 4.49

   Another factor to take into account is how changes made to the parent class(es) affect the design. Such changes are, in fact, automatically propagated on code recompilation to their subclasses. This can profoundly improve productivity vis-à-vis maintenance efforts, software configuration control and program version control. But a word of warning concerning inheritance. You don't inherit only the good things; you also get the dross. Please; use inheritance carefully.

```
// PortInterface0.h                          // SpecialPortInterface0.h
// Implementation Class PortInterface0       // Implementation of the Class
                                             // SpecialPortInterface0
class PortInterface0
{                                            #include "PortInterface0.h"

  public:                                    class SpecialPortInterface0 : public
      PortInterface0();                      PortInterface0
      virtual ~PortInterface0();
      void UpdatePort();                     {
  private:                                     public:
      int Port0Data;                             SpecialPortInterface0();
};                                                virtual ~SpecialPortInterface0();
                                                  void ConfigurePort0();
/////////////////////////////////////         private:
// PortInterface0.cpp                               int ConfigurationStatus;
                                             };
#include "PortInterface0.h"                   #endif // !
                                             /////////////////////////////////////////
PortInterface0::PortInterface0()             // SpecialPortInterface0.cpp
{
                                             #include "SpecialPortInterface0.h"
}
PortInterface0::~PortInterface0()            SpecialPortInterface0::SpecialPortInterface0()
{                                            {

}                                            }
void PortInterface0::UpdatePort()            SpecialPortInterface0::~SpecialPortInterface0()
{                                            {

}                                            }
                                             void SpecialPortInterface0::ConfigurePort0()
                                             {

                                             }
```

Figure 4.47 Code example for figure 4.46b

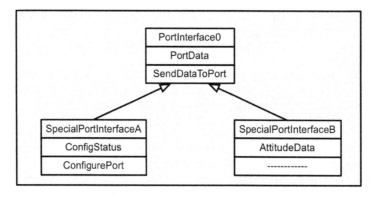

Figure 4.48 Inheritance - example 2

```
//  SpecialPortInterfaceB.h
//  Implementation of the Class SpecialPortInterfaceB

#include "PortInterface0.h"

class SpecialPortInterfaceB : public PortInterface0
{

  public:
      SpecialPortInterfaceB();
      virtual ~SpecialPortInterfaceB();
  private:
      int AttitudeData;

};

/////////////////////////////////////////////////
//  SpecialPortInterfaceB.cpp
//  Implementation of the Class SpecialPortInterfaceB

#include "SpecialPortInterfaceB.h"

SpecialPortInterfaceB::SpecialPortInterfaceB()
{

}
SpecialPortInterfaceB::~SpecialPortInterfaceB()
{

}
```

Figure 4.49 Code example for part fig.4.48

4.5.3 Interface inheritance (subtyping).

Let us now look at a second major use of inheritance, the provision and control of interfaces. Of course, it's helpful to understand why we'd want to do this in the first place. Take, for example, an avionic system that contains a variety of sensors, such as speed, height and attitude. Let us also assume that identical code is used for the reading of sensor values. What we want to do is to ensure that we use identical APIs when calling on the read operation. The reasons for this? First, interfaces usually become simpler and cleaner, making overall object testing simpler. Second, integration testing also becomes more straightforward as a result of the consistency and clarity of interfaces.
   So, how does this work in practice? Probably the most common approach is to start with a superclass that will never be instantiated. Take the example of figure 4.50, where the superclass *Sensor* has been marked as 'abstract'. This means that we never intend to build *Sensor* objects. Our aim is to create objects of the subclass types: *Speed*, *Height* and *Attitude* (hence these are termed 'concrete' classes).
   At first sight it may seem that the base class is used merely to define the root point in the inheritance structure (actually a commonplace application of abstract classes). In fact the key aspect here is the operation *ShowData.* Code is produced to implement this, and this is inherited by all subclasses. The result is that all objects generated using this template end up with identical interfaces. This approach, in effect, provides for reuse of

the interface. Hence, should we add a *Temperature* subclass, then its objects would also present the same *ShowData* interface.

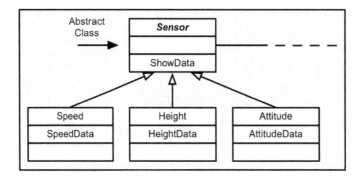

Figure 4.50 Inheritance as a specification technique - the abstract class

Figure 4.51 shows part of the autogenerated code for the class diagram of figure 4.50, for the abstract class *Sensor* and the concrete class *SpeedClass*.

```
//  SensorClass.h                          //  SpeedClass.h
//  Implementation of                      //  Implementation of
//  the Class SensorClass                  //  the Class SpeedClass

class SensorClass                          #include "SensorClass.h"
{
   public:                                 class SpeedClass : public
       SensorClass();                      SensorClass
       virtual ~SensorClass();             {

       int ShowData();                     public:
};                                             SpeedClass();
/////////////////////////////////           virtual ~SpeedClass();
//  SensorClass.cpp
//  Implementation of                      private:
//  the Class SensorClass                      static int SpeedData;

#include "SensorClass.h"                    };

SensorClass::SensorClass()                 /////////////////////////////////////////
{                                          //  SpeedClass.cpp
                                           //  Implementation of
}                                          //   the Class SpeedClass
SensorClass::~SensorClass()
{                                          #include "SpeedClass.h"

}                                          SpeedClass::SpeedClass()
int SensorClass::ShowData()                {
{
    return 0;                              }
}                                          SpeedClass::~SpeedClass()
                                           {

                                           }
```

Figure 4.51 Code example for fig.4.50 (part)

Please note that we could achieve the same aims *without* using an inheritance structure. So why use inheritance? Well, there are two particular advantages. To start with, it guarantees that as new subclasses are added their interfaces will, by default, be correct. The inheritance process takes care of that. Another way of looking at it is that policing of the interface standard is enforced automatically; it doesn't require manual checking (although never underestimate the creativity of programmers).

The second advantage is quite different, one related to flexibility issues.

4.5.4 Interface inheritance - flexibility aspects.

What we've done so far is fine provided that the *ShowData* function meets the needs of all subclasses.   There are, though, many cases when this isn't true; different functionality may be needed by the different subclasses, as illustrated in figure 4.52.

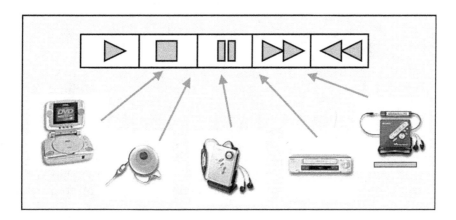

Figure 4.52 The HCIs of some consumer devices

It's taken quite some time for most manufacturers to agree on a common interface standard, but we're there now (mostly). So, whether we're using a PVR, a DVD player or an iPod for example, pressing the rectangle control stops the current play. The response, at a software level, is that the program invokes the 'stop' function for the device. Yet it's clear that the different code implementations are going to differ considerably; everything depends on the device being controlled. What we need is a mechanism that permits us to have common application programming interfaces (APIs) that invoke different implementations.

So let us return to a modified form of the sensor example, where the details of the read functions depend on the sensor type. We still wish to provide a common 'read' API but automatically invoke the correct code unit. We denote this by amending the class diagram as shown in figure 4.53 so that each subclass now includes an operation *ShowData*.

Thus our requirements are to:

- Provide a consistent interface for all objects – the operation *ShowData,* for example.
- Allow each subclass to provide its own specific implementation of *ShowData*.
- Call on this operation as and when required.

• Guarantee that the correct method is automatically executed (known as polymorphism).

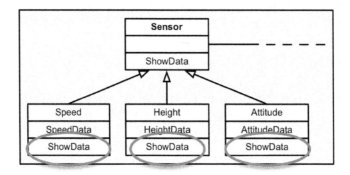

Figure 4.53 Subclass-specific operations

There are two further aspects to take into account. First, will the programmer define which method should be called? Or second, will it be left to the run-time code to select the appropriate method?

The first aspect, where decisions are made a-priori, is a case of *static* polymorphism. Here the programmer decisions are hard-coded, so the compiler knows which object code should be generated. A second approach, known as *dynamic* polymorphism, is one where the compiler *doesn't* select the required object code. Instead it offers all possible options; then the one actually required is chosen by the run-time code (a minor point; people commonly use the terms overloading and polymorphism instead of static and dynamic polymorphism.

Let us now create objects based on the class diagram of figure 4.53 as follows:

```
Speed     TrueAirspeed;
Height    RadarAltimeter;
Attitude  AngleOfAttack;
```

In the case of static polymorphism the following hard-coded message/operation relationships would be true (figure 4.54):

Message	Resulting operation
TrueAirspeed.ShowData	ShowData (from Speed class)
AngleOfAttack.ShowData	ShowData (from Attitude class)
RadarAltimeter.ShowData	ShowData (from Height class)

Figure 4.54 More on static polymorphism

However, when it comes to dynamic polymorphism a different approach is needed. Please bear in mind that the techniques used depend on your programming language.   In general, however, we'd use a source code construct that doesn't name a specific object, viz.:

SomeObject.ShowData();

As a result:

- Because of the way *SomeObject* is declared, the compiler knows that the actual object to be called at run-time is undefined.
- However, the compiler also knows that it must belong to one of the following classes: *Speed*, *Height* or *Attitude*.
- At some stage of program execution, *SomeObject* is replaced by the actual object identifier.

Thus, when the object code for *SomeObject.ShowData();* is reached, the run-time code works out which specific operation should be invoked (typically using a look-up table technique).

Two important points to note are:

- First, there is a run-time time overhead incurred in deciding which method to invoke and
- Second, it is impossible to statically verify the code (hence precluding the use of dynamic polymorphism in safety-critical systems).

4.6 Building connectable structures - composite structures, parts and ports.

4.6.1 Setting the scene.

The integrated circuit profoundly changed the way that electronic design, development and build was carried out. Designers working at the board and system level achieved their goals by:

- First, selecting ICs that met their needs and
- Second, connecting these together in specific ways.

Hence the overall functionality of a unit built like this depends on two factors: the function of each IC *and* how they are connected. A very simple example of this, using small scale ICs, is that of figure 4.55.

Another important point is that board-level designers don't need to know anything about the internal design of the ICs; we leave that to the specialists, the microelectronic designers. Moreover, the IC designers only have to concern themselves with producing the best possible IC; how it's going to be used is of little interest to them.

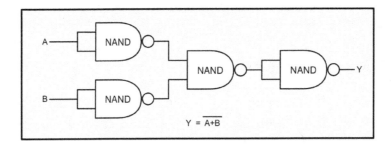

Figure 4.55 NOR function using NAND gates

There are real advantages in using these ideas in software design and development (by now they shouldn't need spelling out to you).   Even so we'll never reap all of the benefits they bring with them unless we can produce software units that have:

- Good modularity and
- Good interfaces (makes it easy to connect them together).

Earlier we had a look at modularity vis-a-vis composite aggregation, and seen how effective it can be.   Regrettably, the virtual absence of object modelling in UML is very much a hindrance to its use.

With regard to interfaces, the problems are different; they're essentially structural ones. In our electronic world, ICs are 'plugged together' using input and output interfaces. The equivalent plugging methods for our software machines are the interconnection of the required and provided interfaces. Now, as pointed out earlier, the explicit visible (public) interfaces are the provided ones; required aspects are buried within client code. This has a number of downsides, but two are especially important. First, it is quite difficult to track down the full route of inter-object messages in anything other than simple designs (not good for test, debug and maintenance in general). To get such information you have to go *into* the code of client objects and hunt around until you find what you want. Second, we don't have any simple mechanisms to 'wire' the objects together.

UML 2 brought with it new constructs to take care of these problems, important ones being composite structures and ports. In the following pages only a subset of all available constructs are shown; these are sufficient to build sensible embedded systems (for more information consult the UML superstructure document.   But, be prepared to end up in a near comatose state; mind-numbing is the kindest thing to say about it).

4.6.2 The composite structure - why?

Before looking into composite structures in detail, let's see why the class itself isn't really a rigorous specification mechanism. Let's assume that we've done an object-first design and come up with the composite object model of figure 4.56a. Classifying this leads to the class diagram of 4.56b. Well, all seems fine. Now, turn things around; consider that we've done a conventional class-first design, and figure 4.56b now acts as the specifier for

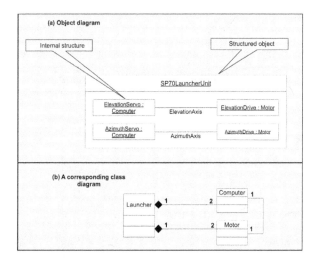

Figure 4.56 Example composite aggregation

the object model.   If we didn't understand the system (or were just incompetent) we could come up with the object design of figure 4.57.

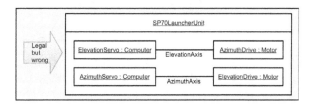

Fig. 4.57 Example composite aggregation - legal but wrong

As you can see it is perfectly legal; yet it is wrong as far as the system is concerned.

    We *could* add extra information to the class diagram to try to clarify things, but that's a somewhat sticking-plaster approach.   Further interesting examples are given by Conrad Bock (http://www.jot.fm/issues/issue_2004_11/column5/) and Steve Cook (http://blogs.msdn.com/b/stevecook/archive/2009/06/17/uml-structured-classes-part-1.aspx).   I suggest that, at the least, you have a look at these - don't just take my word for things. The problem stems from the fact that the class diagram only specifies the *general* relationship between the instantiated items, the objects. What we really need are means to define the interconnection between objects in *specific* situations.   And this is where composite diagrams come into play, the first one being the composite object diagram of figure 4.58.   This has exactly the same structure as the composite object diagram of figure 4.56a but now contains additional specification information, the *roles*. These define *why* the objects are used.   For example, the *ElevationServo* object is to be used for elevation control purposes.   Likewise, the *ElevationDrive* object is used to provide elevation servo drive functionality.

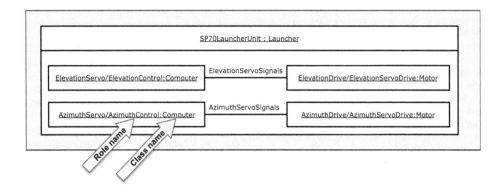

Figure 4.58 Composite object diagram showing roles

Now this raises an interesting question. If we take a class-first approach, how do we specify this information? The class diagram, as we've already seen, can't do this; it essentially deals with attributes and operations. A new diagram is needed, the UML 2.x solution being the 'composite structure diagram', figure 4.59. Here a new construct has appeared: the p*art*. A part represents a specification for instances (objects), specifically:

- The class template to be used for the construction of the objects and
- The role that each object is to play in the executable model.

Observe also that what were called associations on ordinary class diagrams are here called *connectors*.

From this it is clear that class diagrams and composite structure diagrams model different aspects of the software; thus they are *not* alternatives, but complement each other.

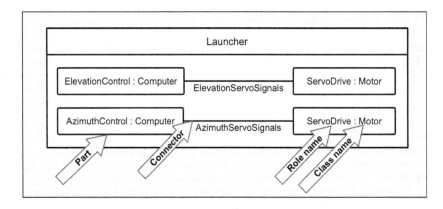

Figure 4.59   Specification for the composite object diagram of figure 4.58   -   the composite structure diagram

Two minor asides at this point:

- If you take an object-first design approach the composite structure diagram is irrelevant.
- Experience, especially in the embedded world, has shown that the class-first approach is woefully deficient.

Well, we've got our composite structure to allow us to build modular designs: now to see about connecting these structures together.

4.6.3 Wiring objects together using Ports.

To build systems using plug-connect methods we have to have defined interaction points between the insides of units and the outside world. Such points are defined to be *ports*, denoted as rectangles, and attached to the composite structure diagram as shown in figure 4.60. You can see the similarities between ports and parts. In this case the diagram defines that composite objects of class *Power* will have interface objects of class *Shaft*; all interactions to/from the power object go via the shaft object (for clarity the internal features of the composite unit, the parts, are omitted).

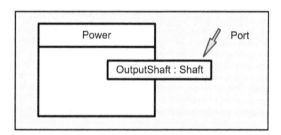

Figure 4.60 Composite structure diagrams and ports

Let's look at how such structures get connected together using the port construct, figure 4.61.

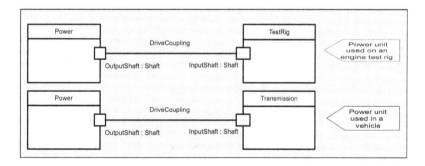

Figure 4.61 Ports as a connecting mechanism

91

The first example shows a port *OutputShaft* on one composite unit (type *Power*) is connected to a port *InputShaft* on another composite unit (type *TestRig*). This specification says that a power unit object is to be connected to a test rig object via the shaft objects. The second example is self-explanatory. Note that multiplicity information can be shown on the diagram if and when required.

Well, that's fine so far, and designs can (and have been) implemented using structured classifiers like this. However, we still need to provide interfaces for the ports. To reiterate; ports show <u>*where*</u> messages flow into and out of composite units. Interfaces are used to define <u>*what*</u> messages pass through the ports and the direction of such messages. One method to denote that ports have interfaces is the ball and socket notation of figure 4.62. As you can see a ball defines a provided interface, the socket being a required interface.

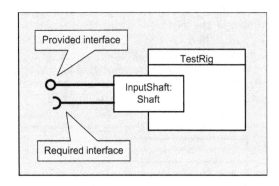

Figure 4.62 Interfaces on ports - ball and socket notation

Using these we can show how structures are 'wired' together, figure 4.63.

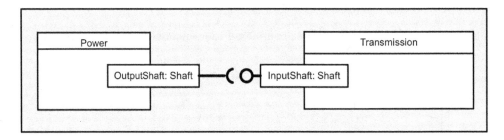

Figure 4.63 Wiring composite structures together

Note: this diagram was produced using the UML stencil of the Visio drawing package.

An individual port can have any number of interfaces, each one being shown (and labelled) on the structure diagram. One alternative is to use multiple ports, each one having a single interface. The choice is entirely yours.

So, what does this mean at the object diagram level? Unfortunately, the UML documents are masterpieces of obfuscation on this point, constantly treating specification and instantiation models as if they are the same thing. What we'll do is adapt the classifier diagram, clearly denoting that all structural units are objects, figure 4.64. While this is not legal UML it is at least clear in its intent (what most writers do is pussy-foot around this issue by treating classifier diagrams as depicting either classes or instances, depending on circumstances). You can see that port specifiers are implemented as port objects, these belonging to the composite objects (i.e., *EngineShaft* part of *Engine*, *PTShaft* part of *PowerTrain*). By contrast, the ball and socket are merely indicators that the ports offer interfaces.

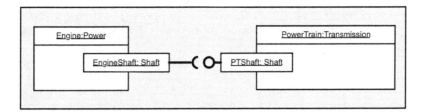

Figure 4.64 Wiring composite **<u>object</u>** structures together (non-UML diagram)

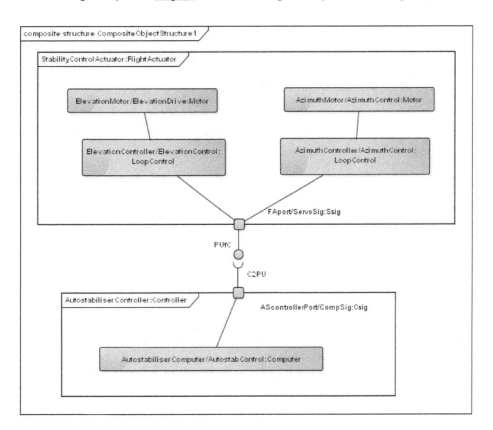

Figure 4.65 Example design using composite classes

Figure 4.65 provides a simple example design based on composite structures. By now its structure and content should be familiar, though some of the notation is slightly different to that of figure 4.64. The reason for this isn't anything fundamental; it's just that the diagram aspects were dictated by the EA CASE tool.

This example reinforces a very important fact; what you actually end up with depends on your diagram production methods (irrespective of the notation used in the UML documents).

Figure 4.66 presents an object diagram that complies with the composite structure diagram of figure 4.65. Here there are two composite objects, *FlightActuators* and *AutostabiliserController*. The *AutostabiliserController* contains two objects (port object *AScontrollerPort* and internal object *AutostabiliserComputer*) and has a required interface (denoted as C2FA). Similarly, *FlightActuator* contains five objects and has a provided interface FAfC.

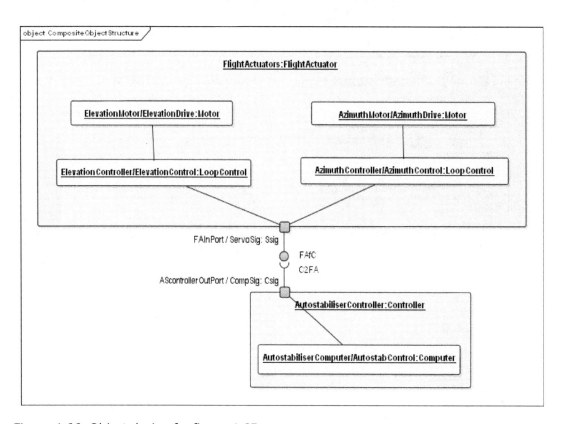

Figure 4.66 Object design for figure 4.65

Please note; all the diagrams covered in this section are *design specifications*, acting as inputs to the coding stage. Some CASE tools allow all such code to be generated automatically; they also have the ability to reverse-engineer code changes back into the design diagrams. If you don't have such luxuries, then it's a matter of doing things manually, especially true when implementing composite structures.   CASE Tool vendors face two significant problems.   First, UML gives little (if any) guidance relating to implementation.   Second, it is possible to code up the designs in a number of different ways, leading to debates about which one is 'correct'. So here is our take on the problem.

The first step is to produce a class design for the problem of figure 4.66, shown in figure 4.67a. In this design the *FlightActuators* and *AutostabiliserController* objects are treated as 'containers' for their internal objects. For simplicity these are treated as a 'whole-part' structure, resulting in the use of composite aggregation ('composition') construction.   To simplify the demonstration code all code units are located within a single compilable unit.

The code for the Controller class is shown in figure 4.67b (that for the FlightActuator class is similar).   In this role it also act as a scheduler or coordinator object, merely scheduling the execution of the contained objects, *AutostabiliserComputer* and *AScontrollerOutPort*.

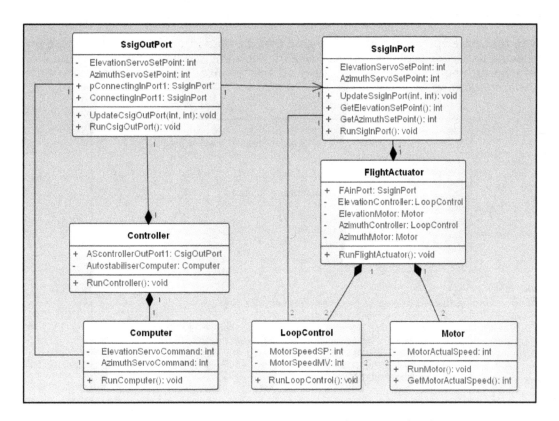

Figure 4.67a Class diagram for the composite structure (part complete)

```
class Controller
{
public:
          CsigOutPort AScontrollerOutPort1;  // OutPort object
          Computer AutostabiliserComputer; // Computer object
          void RunController();
}; // end class Controller
/////////////////////////////////////////////////////////////////
void Controller::RunController()
{
    AutostabiliserComputer.RunComputer(AScontrollerOutPort1, 1);
    AScontrollerOutPort.RunCsigOutPort();
} // end RunController
```

Figure 4.67b Code for the composite structure - part of the Controller class

Key to the whole operation here is to ensure that the outport object *AScontrollerOutPort* is connected to the correct inport object *FAinPort*. How this is done is shown in figure 4.67c, everything hinging around the use of the pointer to the SsigInPort object (*pConnectingInPort*).

```
// ============= Part class CsigOutPort =============//
     class CsigOutPort
     {
     public:
          SsigInPort* pConnectingInPort1;
          SsigInPort ConnectingInPort1;
          void RunCsigOutPort();
     }; //end class CsigOutPort
// ============= End class  -  CsigOutPort =============//




void Controller::CsigOutPort::RunCsigOutPort()
{
    // Written for simplicity of explanation
    ConnectingInPort1 = *pConnectingInPort1;
    //THIS IS THE CALL OF A FUNCTION IN THE SsigInPort OBJECT.
    ConnectingInPort1.UpdateSsigInPort(int ElData, int AzData);
} // end RunCsigOutPort




void Bind (Controller &Cont, FlightActuator &FA)
{
    Cont.AScontrollerOutPort1.pConnectingInPort1 = &FA.FAinPort;
} // end Bind
```

Figure 4.67c Code for the composite structure - binding the ports together

Loading this with the correct inport address is done by the Bind function, which is called in main (figure 4.67d).

```
void main()
{
Controller AutostabiliserController;
FlightActuator FlightActuators;

        Bind (AutostabiliserController, FlightActuators);
        while(1)
        {
                AutostabiliserController.RunController();
                FlightActuators.RunFlightActuator();
        } // end while
} // end main
```

Figure 4.67d Code for the composite structure - running the system

4.7 Building larger modular structures - components.

4.7.1 Some background.

The component construct has been developed as a means of implementing larger systems, in particular the development of model-driven architectures (MDAs). One of its primary aims is to promote the building of software using sets of plug-compatible units, a 'software-lego' approach. Another key point is the ability to use existing components as part of new designs (software reuse on a large scale). So, having said that, exactly what is a component, what (if anything) does it contain and how is it instantiated? To answer these, consider the following extracts from the UML Superstructure document:

1. A component represents a modular part of a system that encapsulates its contents and whose manifestation is replaceable within its environment. It is a subtype of Class.
2. A component defines its behaviour in terms of provided and required interfaces.
3. A component may optionally have an internal structure and own a set of Ports that formalise its interaction points.
4. A component is modeled throughout the development life cycle and successively refined into deployment and run-time.
5. A directly instantiated component is defined at design time and 'is instantiated as an addressable **object**'.
6. An indirectly instantiated component is defined at design time 'but at run-time an object specified by the component does not exist'. The component is instantiated (indirectly) 'through the instantiation of its realising classifiers or parts'.

It's easy enough to understand the general principles of components. However, trying to pin down specifics (in particular code implementations) feels like wrestling with jelly; the multitude of times that you meet the words 'option', 'optionally', 'alternatively', 'can also be' and 'may also be' in the UML document is legion. Therefore we'll use a subset of the available constructs, sufficient to let us to build embedded systems in a sensible way.

4.7.2 Components - constructs and notation.

The component icon is nothing more than a simple rectangle denoted by:

<< component >>

See figure 4.68.

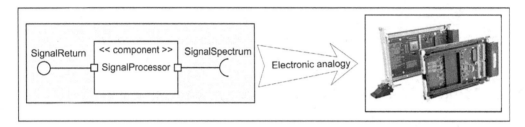

Figure 4.68 The component - external view

Strictly speaking this represents the specification of the component, but that's a somewhat pedantic point.

We have decided to use ports as the conduits for messages going to and from the component, and also specified its interfaces using ball and socket notation (note that, unlike composite structures, interfaces are *not* optional).

A good analogy for the component is, in electronic systems, a modular part of a complete system (e.g. a PCI circuit board). Ports are equivalent to the plugs/sockets of the board, the interfaces corresponding to connector pins. The protocol of the PCI bus dictates what the various pins should be used for. The board's intended function is defined by the circuit design, the equivalent of the software specification.

Now that we have our desired set of components we can proceed to wire them together to produce the overall system functionality, figure 4.69. An electronic analogy to this is the interconnection of a set of modules via a backplane bus (either a standard one such as PCI or else a home-grown one). Similarly our software components are 'plugged' into a software bus such as CORBA, .NET, EJB, etc. (for explanation see list of acronyms).

Suppose we had specified a VME modular structure instead of a PCI one. How would the model change? Well, the concepts are exactly the same but interface details would change to comply with the VME specifications. Likewise, a component-based design could be implemented in one case using CORBA technology, in another EJB - without any need to change the high-level design.

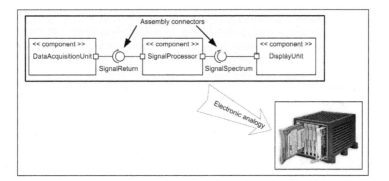

Figure 4.69 Wiring components together using assembly connectors

Components can also have internal structures containing, for example, components (figure 4.70) and classes (figure 4.71).

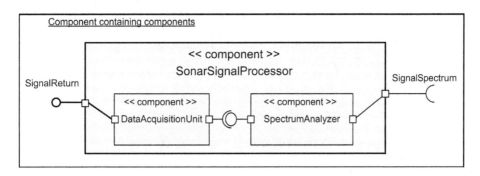

Figure 4.70 Component containing components

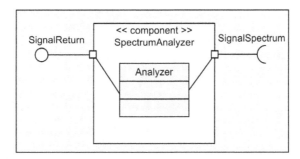

Figure 4.71 Component containing a class

All this seems to be clear and understandable; now we have to consider the instantiation of components. Unfortunately no guidance is given by UML 2.x as to how to show such instantiations (the objects) in diagrams. The component diagram, as defined in the UML documents, is a classifier, whose implementation is considered typically to be some type of file. These include source code, binary code and executable code files, collectively called *artifacts*. Normally artifacts are seen to be part of the deployment model, so we'll leave further discussion to that topic.

But that still leaves the issue of component instances hanging in the air. At least UML 1.4 was helpful here; it states '*A component diagram has only a type form, not an instance form. To show component instances, use a deployment diagram (possibly a degenerate one without nodes).*' Moreover, in our view, if software designs are based on instantiated components, then we need diagrams to show such structures. This need was also recognized by the IBM Rational Software Architect Real Time CASE tool developers. Their response was to provide an icon so that designers could model component instances on deployment diagrams, figure 4.72.

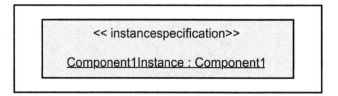

Figure 4.72 Component instance - IBM symbol

Observe that it extends a standard object symbol, the stereotype being labelled 'instancespecification'. Taking this as our cue we decided to use the following notation for an instantiated component (loosely a 'component object'), figure 4.73.

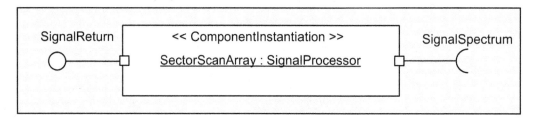

Fig. 4.73 Component instantiation (stereotype) - external view

Where components have internal structures we can extend our stereotyping to take this into account as, for example, figure 4.74. This depicts the internal structure of a component object, one that is formed as a set of intercommunicating composite objects.

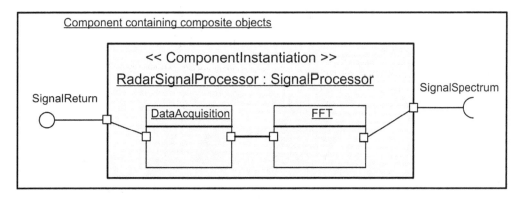

Fig. 4.74 Component instantiation - internal object structure example

4.7.3 Practical aspects of using components.

UML implicitly assumes that, to design and implement component models, we use defined component technology mechanisms. It also assumes that we intend to build large systems. Unfortunately for us it seems that component technology has rarely been applied to practical embedded developments; few real products are available. However, there is one technology worth taking a look at: real-time CORBA. This, it is claimed, has been used in real-time applications. Some aspects of the technology are described below, just to give an idea of the rationale behind such an approach. It also highlights the amount of development support provided by these development environments.

The starting point is to define object interfaces using CORBA's Interface Definition Language, IDL. This can be considered to be a 'programming' language, not too unlike C++.   A very important point: it doesn't define object implementations, only object interfaces, figure 4.75.   Figure 4.75a shows a UML component having two interfaces, a provided and a required one. Let's have a look at how we turn these into compilable Java source code, specifically the provided interface *LoopError*. First we specify and name the interface using IDL code, as given in figure 4.75b. The interface details are added to this, shown within the conceptual boundary of figure 4.75c. These are grouped within an IDL module, this providing a boundary of encapsulation for the interface code, figure 4.75d (if we extended the example to include the interface *ControlSignal*, its code would be added to the module). At this point we submit the IDL code to the target language compiler (in this case Java), the result being that of figure 4.75e.   Here the module has been translated to a Java package, the interface definitions generating a set of Java interfaces and classes (stubs/skeletons). It is now up to us to fill in all the details needed to fully implement the component object.

Well, that's quite a lot of work, and you could reasonably ask why we shouldn't go straight to the Java code.   But then *we* would have to take on the burden of interconnecting the various objects, making sure that they are correctly wired together and that all inter-object messaging is handled properly.   Instead we leave this to the provided facilities of CORBA, this acting as a 'middleware' technology (sometimes defined

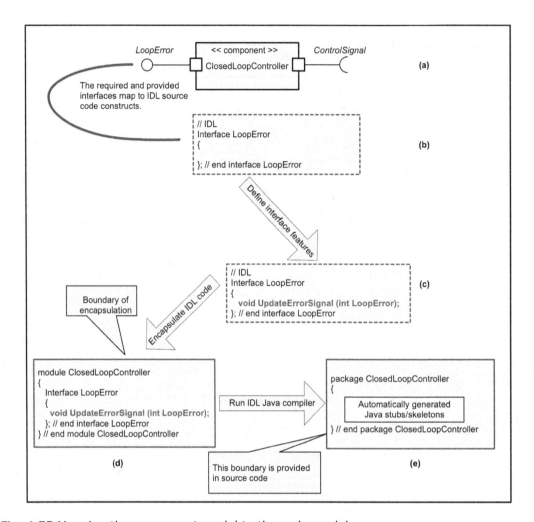

Fig. 4.75 Mapping the component model to the code model

as 'interconnecting software'). These facilities also allow us to interface to operating system software, to define concurrent units (e.g. threads) and to specify the timing attributes of these units.

There's little point in taking this topic further, for a very practical reason; at the detailed level all component architectures are different. But I hope this makes you think carefully about developing UML component models, especially if you haven't got a suitable implementation mechanism.

A closing point; at present, for the embedded field, the nearest equivalent technique to CORBA et al is the Architecture Analysis & Design Language (AADL). This is an architecture description language which is used to model the software and hardware architecture of embedded, real-time systems. A number of research projects have successfully used AADL, see http://www.aadl.info/aadl/currentsite/ for more details. However, it seems that a more popular approach to developing model-based designs is to use the Systems Modeling Language, SysML (http://www.omgsysml.org/). This, though, is beyond the scope of our work here.

4.8 Packages, artifacts and deployments.

4.8.1 Why things need to be organized.

Scenario: suppose during development we need to make changes to the class (logical) model. Assume for simplicity that only one class is affected. Finding and modifying the class in the design model is unlikely to be a problem. However, we now need to consider a most important question; will the design change impact on clients of the class? Can we evaluate the change effects? Answering these is not necessarily easy but isn't usually a major problem. But what about clients of the clients? And their clients? Now it's beginning to look a much more formidable issue.

The message here is that when systems have a large number of classes (or any other software elements), design maintenance isn't trivial.   Relying on tools to help you out is a little like putting up scaffolding on an unsound building. What we need to do is to build it correctly in the first place; use an organized, structured approach in the development of the design model. And this is where the package diagram can be very helpful.

4.8.2 Packages and package diagrams.

One of the simplest features of UML – yet an extremely useful one – is the package. In simple terms this is nothing more than a holder or container for other items.   You use it to group things together in a sensible manner for sensible reasons. These 'things' can be classes, components, packages, subsystems, what you will. Thus we can have packages of packages, packages of classes, packages of components, etc.

The basics of the package diagram are shown in figure 4.76, which is pretty-well self-explanatory.

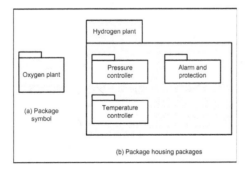

Figure 4.76 Basic package diagrams

Figure 4.76a shows the symbol for the package, a 'tabbed' rectangle or folder. The name of the package is written within the main area. In figure 4.76b the package 'Oxygen plant' itself contains three packages. Observe that the name has been written within the tab, the recommended notation when packages have contained elements.

As stated earlier, we can group many items together using packages. In practice its greatest use has been the handling of classes, so we'll concentrate on that aspect.

Suppose you are brought in as a trouble-shooter to an on-going failing project, described as 'drowning in classes'. Massively complex class diagrams exist, but hardly anybody can make sense of the overall design (this is based on personal experience; it is how a senior project manager once described to me the state of a large Radar project). How should we attack this problem? Well, it's time to go back to basics; reduce the problem complexity. We can do this by bringing in the package to provide a simpler (and hence more easily understood) structure.

Consider the packaging of classes as being similar to forming modular structures. That's a good start; it's the first step in producing an organised structured model. However, it's not enough merely to package classes; a badly thought-out scheme will only make things worse. A golden rule is 'package together classes that logically belong together'. If your choices are good you should find that:

- Most of the class interactions occur within the package (intra-package associations).
- Few class interactions take place between packages (inter-package associations).

A simple example is shown in figure 4.77.

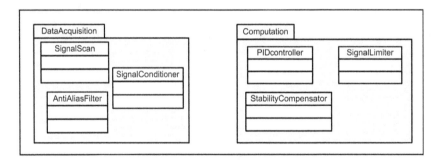

Figure 4.77 Packaging classes

Package diagrams form part of the design or 'logical' model of software. These, though, have to be translated to a code form (the 'physical' model), ready to be compiled, linked and located, figure 4.78 Observe that the package icon maps to a source code unit, its purpose being to contain the relevant source code. The example here is based on the Java package; the Ada package is similar. For C++ though, there is a problem as we don't have Java and Ada equivalents; the best we can do is to use a combination of .h and .cpp files.

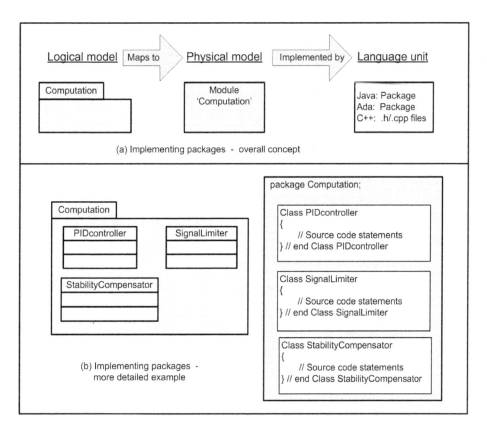

Figure 4.78 Logical and physical models of software - example

In figure 4.78 the classes have, for simplicity, been shown as individual, separate elements; in reality they usually are interdependent.   Dependencies *within* a package are easy to see; just look at the associations.   But what about dependencies *between* packages?   Where this occurs we can identify it using the notation shown in figure 4.79.   The dotted-arrowed lines show that packages *Welding controller* and *Cutting sequencer* somehow depend on the package *System operating parameters* (note the direction of the arrows).   It may be, for instance, that the values of the system operating parameters are used by the dependent packages; thus changes to these will almost certainly affect the behaviour of the welding and cutting units.

Showing such dependencies explicitly is an important part of the configuration control of software (it shouldn't need saying that as software becomes more complex it becomes increasingly difficult to manage).   But package diagrams can make our job a lot easier by showing clearly the structure of the software, figure 4.80.

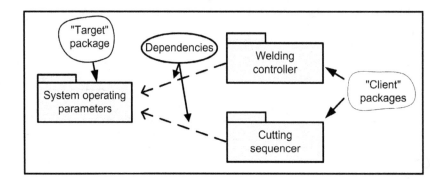

Figure 4.79 Package dependencies

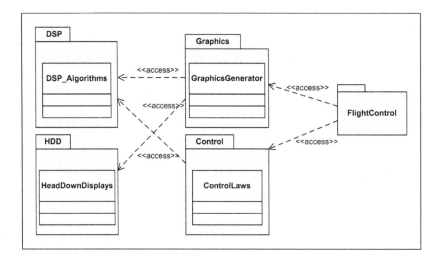

Fig. 4.80 Showing compilation dependencies - example

We can read this to mean that:

- Package *Graphics* can access the contents of packages *HDD* and *DSP* (an 'access' dependency) .
- Package *Control* can access the contents of package *DSP*.
- In turn package *FlightControl* can access the contents of *Graphics* and *Control.*

UML defines a second form of dependency, 'import'. We won't discuss this further as the way that dependencies are implemented is highly language-dependent.

4.8.3 Artifacts.

The final steps in developing software for embedded applications involves :

- Constructing language-specific source code files.
- Compiling these to linkable files.
- Linking separately compiled files to form executable files.
- Defining the memory areas to be used for read-write volatile data (RAM), read-only non-volatile information (the program code and software constants (ROM)) and read-write non-volatile information (EEPROM or Flash).

All files produced during this process are examples of UML artifacts, figure 4.81.

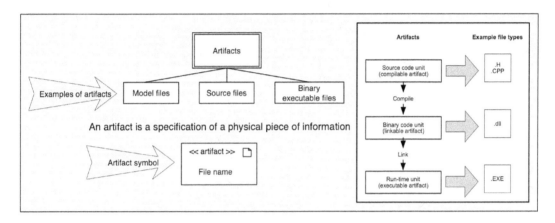

Figure 4.81 Examples of artifacts

A package for example, can be specified using an artifact, figure 4.82.

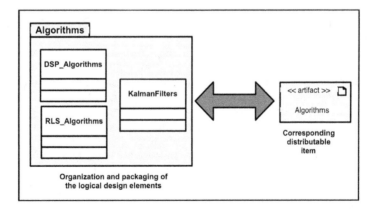

Figure 4.82 A package and its corresponding artifact

UML-speak:

An artifact is the specification of a physical piece of information that is used or produced by a software development process, or by deployment and operation of a system. Examples of artifacts include model files, source files, scripts, and binary executable files, a table in a database system, a development deliverable, or a word-processing document, a mail message.

A minor point: it is optional to underline the name of the artifact.

In a project as a whole we can use both package and artifact diagrams to show structures and, most importantly, dependencies, figure 4.83.

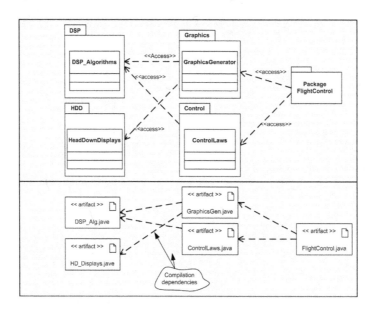

Fig. 4.83 Relating packages, artifacts and dependencies

You might by now begin to appreciate how useful the artifact construct can be for software configuration and version control.

Now for a few practical points. First, when we come to test and debug code we deal with artifacts, not design models. And anything that makes our life easy at this stage is welcome. Hard gained experience has shown that we should produce code units having a very clear purpose (high cohesion) and few interconnections (low coupling). However, to deliver these you have to start from the right beginning. Central to this is how you partition your class design in the first place (in other words, how you package it up).

A second aspect relates to your code development environment. Many, many embedded developers are producing code for flash-based microcontrollers using IDEs such as the IAR Embedded Workbench and the Keil (ARM) µVision. In such circumstances there really isn't such a thing as a distributable item; everything is integrated. So the artifact, in itself, is relatively unimportant. However, a word of caution; just because the environment is integrated doesn't mean that it's easy to see all the relationships and dependencies. You, as a designer, need to put mechanisms in place to deal with this.

4.8.4 Deployment diagrams and nodes.

Deployment diagrams are used to model the physical aspects of systems. They consist primarily of nodes, node relationships and components. In UML-speak a node is *a physical piece of equipment on which the system is deployed, such as a workgroup server or workstation. A Node usually hosts components and other executable pieces of code, which again can be connected to particular processes or execution spaces. Typical Nodes are client workstations, application servers, mainframes, routers and terminal servers.*
The symbol for a node is a three-dimensional box, figure 4.84.

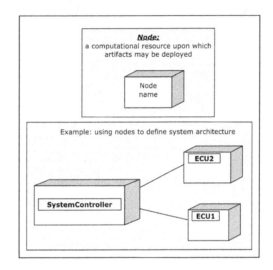

Fig. 4.84 Nodes and system architectures

Nodes are used in Deployment diagrams show the overall physical architecture of systems, i.e. the various pieces of kit together with their interconnections. There are three types of node: 'plain' (or general-purpose item such as workstations), 'device' and 'execution environment', figure 4.85. An example of their use is demonstrated in figure 4.86. Here we have two device nodes, *PortEngineController* and *StbdEngineController*, each containing an execution environment node. Both are labelled *VxWorks*, indicating that the software in these nodes is executed under the control of the VxWorks real-time operating system. Each node houses an artifact, this denoting the run-time code.

4.9 Review.

You should now:

- Know what classes and objects are, how they relate to each other, how they are shown in diagrams and what information is provided in such diagrams.

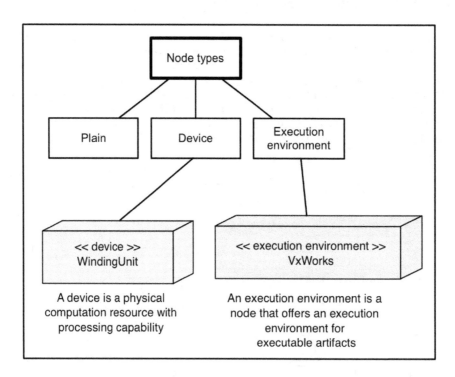

Fig. 4.85 Example node types

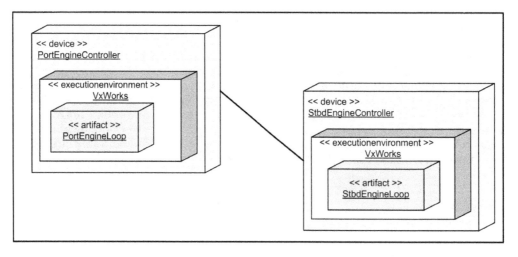

Figure 4.86 Example deployment diagram

- Appreciate how items in the class diagram map to source code.
- Understand that an object has two major sections: a public interface and a hidden, private part.
- Appreciate how items in the class diagram map to source code.
- Appreciates why objects are formed in this way and what, typically, the two parts contain.
- Understand that when code is to be generated automatically from class diagrams, all public and private features must be explicitly denoted in the diagrams.
- Know what the following are: provided and required interfaces, links, messages, operations and methods.
- Understand the fundamental aspects of client-server and peer-to-peer object relationships.
- Know what is meant by associations (uni and bi-directional) and how these are represented in class diagrams.
- Appreciate that the mapping from object diagram to class diagram is unique but that the reverse is not true.
- Appreciate the advantages of building software in modular fashion.
- Know what is meant by composite aggregation and how it is denoted in the class diagram.
- Know how to show modular structures on class and object diagrams.
- Understand what inheritance is and why we use it.
- Know how to show inheritance structures in class diagrams.
- Appreciate the essential difference between implementation inheritance and interface inheritance.
- Be confident to classify the objects of object diagrams and, using this information, produce the corresponding class diagrams.
- Understand the distinction between inheritance and adaption and know the pro's and con's of the two methods.
- Know what is meant by superclass, subclass, abstract class, static polymorphism and dynamic polymorphism.
- Appreciate why polymorphism is used.
- Appreciate that to build robust software structures it isn't sufficient to have good modularity and good interfaces; it's also essential to be able to wire components together simply and easily.
- Understand how the UML composite object having ports provides means to build such robust structures.
- Know the content and structure of composite object diagrams.
- Know what is meant by an object role and how to show it on a composite object diagram.
- Know what a composite structure diagram is and what connectors are used on such diagrams.
- Know how to denote ports having provided and required interfaces using ball and socket notation.
- Understand what software components are and why they are used as the building blocks of model-driven architectures.
- Know the notation used for components and be able to show how they can be wired together using assembly connectors.

- Know that components can have internal structures such as components, classes and objects, for example.
- Understand that component-based designs are translated to source code using some defined component technology mechanism.
- See how CORBA's interface definition language may be used to map a component model into a source code one.
- Know what packages are, why they are used and how they are shown on diagrams.
- Understand what is meant by the logical and physical models of software.
- Know how to show package and compilation dependencies.
- Know what artifacts are and how they relate to various types of file.
- Know how to relate packages, artifacts and dependencies.
- Understand what deployment diagrams are, what they contain and why they are used.

END OF CHAPTER

Chapter 5

The behavioural interactions model

The objectives of this chapter are to:

- Introduce active and passive objects.
- Explain why we need the two object types, and describe their behaviour.
- Show what sequence diagrams are, why we use them and what information they contain.
- Describe the basics of the UML sequence diagram and the notation used.
- Show how CASE tools influence diagramming techniques and notation.
- Describe methods that help us handle sequence diagrams efficiently and effectively.
- Show how timing information can be added to sequence diagrams and illustrate the various presentation options.
- Introduce the communication diagram and show how it describes object interactions (collaborations).
- Show how sequence and communication diagrams relate to each other.

5.1 Object types and their interactions.

The structural model should give us a good picture of the make-up of systems and how their individual pieces are connected together. Well, that's fine as far as it goes; it tells us, in great detail, *what* needs to be built. But that is only part of the story; we also need to know:

- What a system does - its functional behaviour.
- When things happen, and for how long - its temporal behaviour.
- When and why the component parts interact.

As pointed out earlier, what a system actually does depends on the collaborations and interactions of these component parts. We *can*, from the structural model, deduce some information relating to the three points mentioned above; but that's as much as we can do. Consider, for example, the robotic system shown earlier in figure 1.10. Experienced engineers would be able to make some pretty good guesses about its operation and behaviour. But that's all they'd be: guesses. To answer the questions raised above we need to model the behavioural interactions of the system (first introduced in chapter 1). And *that* is the subject of this chapter.

Before we get into it in detail there are a few important preliminaries to consider (otherwise some later material just won't make sense). In chapter 4 the object models were, in the main, implemented using sequential code constructs. And with sequential code, one and only one object can run at any one time: object executions are non-concurrent. Yet real embedded software consists of both non-concurrent *and* concurrent code units (true concurrency with multiprocessors, quasi-concurrency in single processor units). UML recognises this by providing two object types, the active and passive ones (figure 5.1).

Figure 5.1 Active and passive objects

For reasons that we ourselves don't understand, many newcomers to UML have problems grasping the concepts involved here. In fact it is quite easy to appreciate the differences between the two types by looking at how target code actually executes. So, let's start

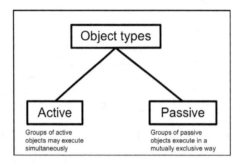

with describing active object behaviour.

An active object is said to have its 'own thread of control'. From an abstract point of view it begins to run as soon as it is created. After that it behaves as an independent, collaborating software unit, figure 5.2.

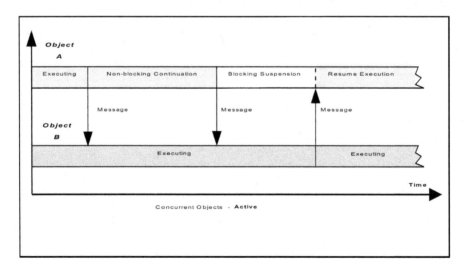

Figure 5.2 Active object behaviour

This demonstrates some examples of typical interactions between active objects (in this case two only, objects A and B). Assume that object A is executed by one real processor, object B running on a second one in a multiprocessor unit. Thus what happens in each processor depends entirely on the code of its object *and* its interactions with the other processor (i.e. other object).   For the scenario shown, object B executes without interruption over the whole time period. Object A runs until it sends its second message to object B, at which time it *voluntarily* enters a suspended state (that decision is made in its own code, which you, the programmer, are responsible for).   It resumes execution when signalled to do so by object B.

Next, consider the execution of these objects on a single processor device, using multitasking/multithreading   methods.   Does this change things?   Yes, but *not* to the conceptual object model; the behaviour of figure 5.2 is maintained.   It's in the run-time model that any differences show. And that's because task/thread execution is not actually concurrent but is, in fact, quasi-concurrent ('pretend' concurrency).   With this, one (and only one) code unit can run at any one time.   The implications and effects of this are beyond the scope of this book; see http://www.amazon.com/dp/B00GO6VSGE.

Passive objects behave quite differently, as can be seen from figure 5.3. Once again, for simplicity, we'll look at the interactions between two objects, A and B.   The single most important point here is that when object A executes, object B is inactive. Likewise, when B is active A is inactive.   Execution is thus mutually-exclusive (in fact, if you implement your design in a sequential code unit, you will always get this type of behaviour).   Moreover, this particular case represents a client/server relationship, A being the client and B the server.   For *our* work we will always consider this to be a specification (or description) of objects executing on a single processor unit.

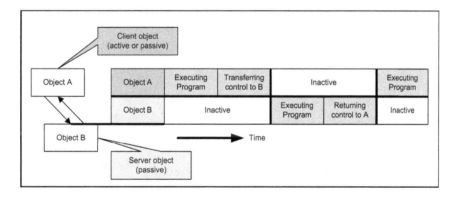

Figure 5.3 Passive object behaviour

The UML symbol for an active class can be seen in figure 5.4a.

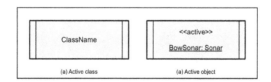

Figure 5.4 Active class and object - notation

There isn't any symbol for an active object in UML 2.x, so we'll use stereotyping to do this, figure 5.4b. And, for consistency, we'll *always* underline names to make it clear that these are instantiations.

5.2 Modelling interactions - the basics of sequence diagrams.

5.2.1 Introduction.

The fundamental purpose of sequence diagrams is to show interactions between items (usually objects) as time elapses. The basic concept for a two-object system is shown in figure 5.5. In essence it shows;

- What messages are sent.
- When messages are sent.
- Who the sender and receivers are.
- How much time elapses during the various message transactions.

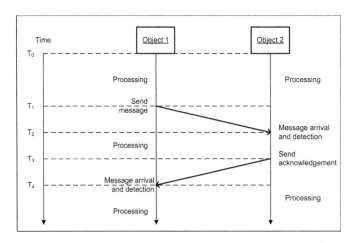

Fig. 5.5 Basic sequence diagram showing object interactions

However, UML extends this generalised notation in a number of ways. It:

- Distinguishes between concurrent and sequential program operations and
- Uses a number of different arrows to denote different forms of messaging.

5.2.2 Basics of UML sequence diagrams.

   Before giving examples of sequence diagrams it is necessary to understand a little more of the basic semantics and syntax used. First, a variety of messages are defined by UML, figure 5.6.

116

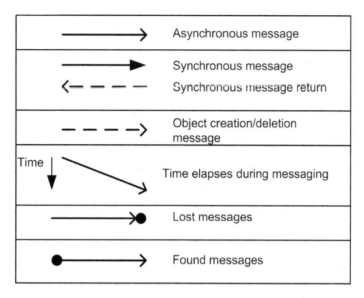

Figure 5.6 UML message notations

(i) Asynchronous message or flat flow of control: a request where the sending object does not have to wait for results generated by the receiver, denoted using an open arrowhead.
(ii) Synchronous message or nested flow of control: a request where the sending object waits for results generated by the receiver, denoted using a solid-arrowhead.
(iii) Synchronous message return (optional): shown as a dashed arrow shaft having an open arrowhead.
(iv) Object creation/deletion: a message sent to create (delete) an object during program execution.
(v) Message transfer time: defined by using slanted arrows bounded by the sending and receiving times.
(vi) Lost message: a message sent to a destination that is outside the scope of the current description.
(vii) Found message: a message received from a source that is outside the scope of the current description.

A sequence diagram consists of a set of object lifelines, figure 5.7. A lifeline is defined to be the combination of the object symbol (the rectangle) together with the dotted vertical line. To show when an object is actually doing something (either directly or indirectly, see later) we add a narrow rectangle to its lifeline, see object 2 of figure 5.7. This is called an 'execution specification', often abbreviated to 'execution'.   Just for information; UML has a number of irritating features, one being that names and/or definitions are sometimes changed as new versions are released. An 'execution specification' was previously called an 'activation', also a 'focus of control'. As these words are quite descriptive, well known and widely used, we'll continue to use them as synonyms for 'execution specification'.

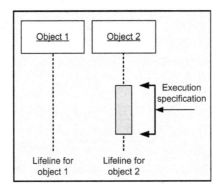

Figure 5.7 UML sequence diagram, object lifelines and execution specification

So, in summary; figure 5.7 shows a sequence diagram that is intended to model the interactions between two objects. Object 1 is present but, as shown, doesn't actually do anything. Object 2 is also present but *does* carry out work for the time of its activation. Now let's extend this to show some sample scenarios.

The first applies to concurrent operations (figure 5.8), both objects being active ones. This shows a set of interactions between two objects in a particular time period. The objects are assumed to be alive continuously as long as the processor is powered up. It can be seen that the first message in the sequence is *StartMeasurements*. This is generated by object 1, being sent to object 2. Some time later 2 sends the message *StoreData* to 1.

The next message, *PrepareForRun*, is also sent as a flat flow of control from 1 to 2. Following this is the message *OpenHatch*, sent from 1 to 2. In this case object 1 chooses to suspend until it is later awoken by a reply from object 2. When this – the message *ElevateMissile* – is received, object 1 is reactivated and resumes execution.

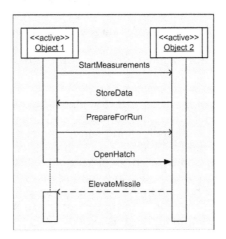

Figure 5.8 UML sequence diagram - concurrent operations 1

A second interaction scenario is shown in figure 5.9, this done to illustrate the 'busy-wait' behaviour of object 1.

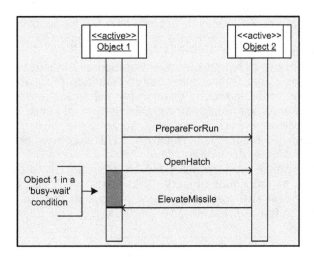

Figure 5.9 UML sequence diagram - concurrent operations 2

With this object 1 is always active; it does not suspend.

Now let us deal with sequential operations, (more specifically, operations that are implemented in sequential code). But first, two points for your consideration.

Point 1: In an object-based sequential program, one, and only one, object can be active at any one time. This may seem too obvious to be worth mentioning; yet many designers appear to be oblivious to this truism.

Point 2: The more complete definition of focus of control is that it shows the period during which an object is performing an action _either directly or through a subordinate procedure_. This is highly relevant to sequential operations, as shown in figure 5.10.

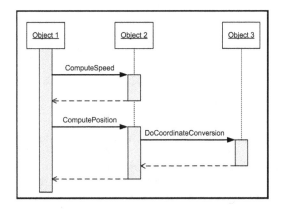

Figure 5.10 UML sequence diagram - procedural (sequential) operations

Assume that object 1 is a form of control object, responsible for the running of the system. Initially it is the one that is active. Now, as this is a procedural program, objects 2 and 3 must therefore be inactive.

At some later time object 1 sends the message *ComputeSpeed* to object 2, so activating it. The message is, of course, really a procedure or function call; hence it must be a synchronous (blocking) one. Program control is thus transferred from object 1 to object 2, which, on completion of its work, returns control to object 1.

During this latter period, although object 1 was actually inactive, it was still shown as having a focus of control. This, in line with the full definition of focus of control, is correct; its action was being performed indirectly through the subordinate, object 2.

The next set of interactions demonstrate this feature in more detail. The message *ComputePosition* activates object 2, which, some time later, sends the message *DoCoordinateConversion* to object 3. Whilst object 3 is computing, object 2 still has a focus of control (as, of course, does object 1).

In this simple example you aren't likely to misread the diagram concerning the execution occurrences of individual objects. However, what actually happens is much clearer to see if you adapt the diagram so that a focus of control denotes only that an object is executing, as in figure 5.11.

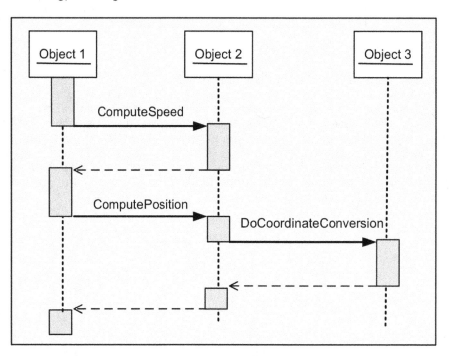

Fig. 5.11 Modified sequence diagram showing the flow of execution

The would be especially helpful when working with complex procedural sequence diagrams. Unfortunately, it isn't legal UML. However, beating your breast over such issues is pretty pointless once you start using a CASE tool; that's going to determine what your diagrams look like, legal or not.

5.2.3 CASE tool issues.

The following examples demonstrate some issues relating to CASE tool usage, the material being produced using the EA tool (once again, this is done merely to show how CASE tools may dictate what you end up with; it is *not* an EA tutorial!).

First, consider figure 5.12 which shows a set of passive object interactions. Observe that the diagram is framed and has been denoted as type 'sd', its name being *UpdatingADvectors*.

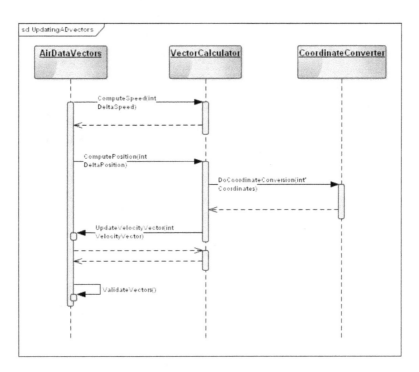

Fig. 5.12 Sequence diagram CASE tool example 1

By now you should be familiar with most of the diagram features, but two aspects need further explanation. First, at one point the object *VectorCalculator* sends the message *UpdateVelocityVector* to the object *AirDataVectors*. Observe the execution that ensues when this message arrives. Also, it would be logical to show the call return as flowing out of this occurrence, but the tool doesn't (seem) to permit it.

Second, the final message generated by the object *AirDataVectors* is actually sent to itself. What this means is that it's internal code calls on one of the object's public methods. And to keep the diagram clear the call return has been suppressed.

A second CASE tool generated sequence diagram is given in figure 5.13, this describing an interaction scenario involving three active objects. Observe that we have chosen to show the sequence numbers of the messages.

This is yet another example that points out that once you use an automated tool you have to live with its features. A major issue here is how it denotes the various execution occurrences (which, for active objects, may not represent what *actually* happens). This raises questions concerning the usefulness of the construct (opinions are quite split on this issue!). Consider figure 5.14, for example. Here the diagrams (a) and (b) are almost the same but with just one presentation difference: the use of the focus of control construct. The 'standard' style is used in figure 5.14a, whereas in 5.14b the foci of control have (almost) been suppressed, resulting in a cleaner diagram. This 'cleaner' style appeals to designers who just want to model the object interactions (and generally consider focus of control aspects to be a distracting side-issue).

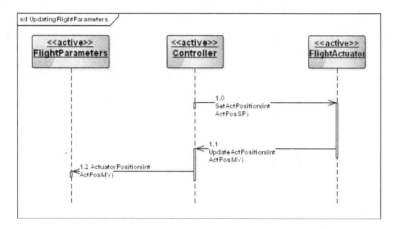

Fig. 5.13 Sequence diagram CASE tool example 2

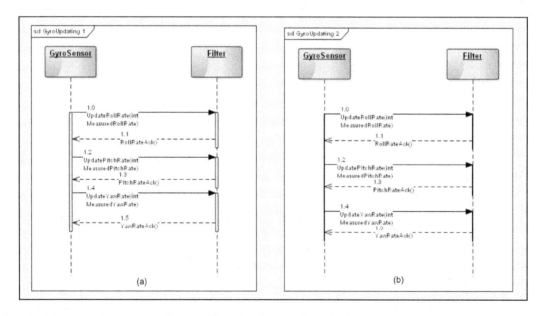

Fig. 5.14 Example presentation options for focus of control

5.2.4 Some lesser-used constructs.

Finally, let's review a few sequence diagram constructs that, in our experience, aren't widely used in real-time embedded systems (figure 5.15).

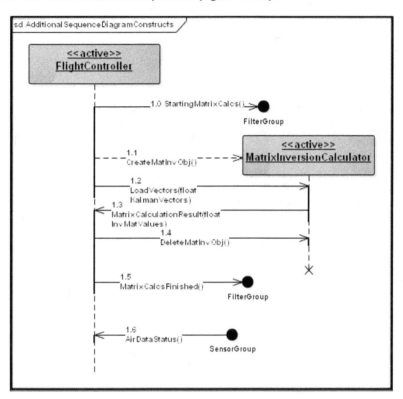

Fig. 5.15 AdditionalSequenceDiagramConstructs

First point to review is the lost message *StartingMatrixCalcs*, shown as an asynchronous message to *FilterGroup*. Now, the destination object is regarded as being outside the scope of the current model; it is described on a separate sequence diagram. What actually happens when the message arrives at it's destination isn't of interest to us *within this scenario*. However, the notation gives us a useful way of showing that, as part of the scenario, this message must be generated. Yet we don't need to worry *precisely* where it goes to and what effects it produces.

Likewise, we can adopt the same viewpoint in the handling of the incoming found message *AirDataStatus*. We know it has to be handled but don't need to concern ourselves with its origins.

Next to look at is the dynamic creation of an object during program execution. This is denoted by the message *CreateMatInvObj*. Observe that the lifeline of the created object *MatrixInversionCalculator* starts with the arrival of the creation message. It ends, in this case, when the message *DeleteMatrixInvObj* arrives (the X symbol at the end of the line denotes that the object's life has finished).

Dynamic objects are conceptually simple and, in practice, easy to implement. They have their uses in the softer, less critical, dynamically-changing systems (e.g. PDAs, mobile phones, etc.). But their use should be minimized where systems:

- Are required to be robust.
- Have limited RAM storage.
- Need fairly predictable behaviour.

For highly-critical systems (e.g. aircraft fly-by-wire) they are forbidden.

5.3 Modelling interactions - efficiently handling sequence diagrams.

5.3.1 Brief introduction.

Sequence diagrams are an immensely powerful way to describe when and why interactions take place between entities (be they people, vehicles, components, software units, etc.). Also, the examples we've looked at so far have been easy to read and understand. This simplicity, unfortunately, may fool you into thinking that working with sequence diagrams is child's play. Believe me, this illusion will quickly disappear when you meet your first complex real-world problem.

There are, it seems, three distinct areas that cause problems for designers:

- Updating and modifying diagrams (loosely 'maintenance'),
- Navigating through the diagram(s) quickly and efficiently ('navigation').
- Correctly and rapidly understanding complex interactions ('comprehension').

5.3.2 Diagram maintenance.

Most designers produce sequence diagrams using either drawing packages or CASE tool diagram editors. When you come to generate a diagram in the very first place there seems to be little to choose between them; a good drawing package is as effective as a CASE tool (and a bonus feature of drawing packages: there are free open-source versions available). However you may well find difficulties when you later come to make changes to the diagram (such as adding objects, deleting objects, modifying messages, etc). CASE tools tend to excel at this. Moreover, with a tool-based approach you will (or should) be working in an integrated environment, handling *all* the project software diagrams. Thus it is much easier to maintain consistency of the diagram set *and* to carry out effective version control.

5.3.3 Diagram navigation.

The sequence diagrams that we've looked at so far could be described as 'single layer' types; all information is at the one level. Now, much earlier in the book we discussed the difficulties that people have in handling complexity. No matter how good we are, there comes a point when everybody makes mistakes. And the only solution to this is to reduce the problem complexity; just simplify things.   What we have also seen is that, when dealing with diagrams, a layering (essentially top-down) approach is a very effective technique.   And that's what we now need to do with the sequence diagram.

The technique used is to break the single large sequence diagram into a set of simpler ones.   Key to this is the use of 'interaction fragments', figure 5.16.

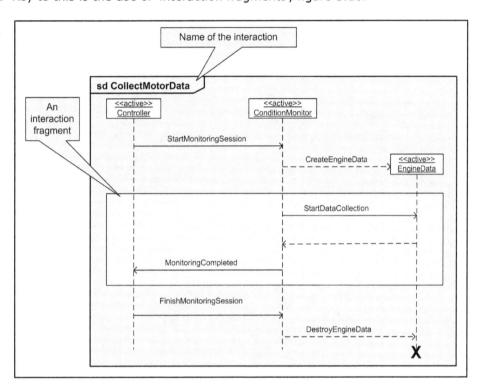

Fig. 5.16 Sequence diagram interaction fragment

Here the overall diagram represents the interactions that take place for the scenario *CollectMotorData*.   An interaction fragment merely depicts some of the interactions of the overall scenario.   We, as designers, can decide exactly how many fragments to use, as for example in figure 5.17   What we've done is to first 'mop up' the set of interactions shown in figure 5.17a into two interaction fragments; then draw a simpler higher-level diagram based on these fragments, figure 5.17b (note: there is no defined UML notation for a 'simple' interaction fragment).

This gives us a clear overview of the overall structure of the scenario interactions and, note, suppresses all interaction details.   This informal approach is formalized in UML as an interaction overview diagram, figure 5.18.   Each collected set of interactions is called an 'interaction use' or 'interaction occurrence' (an older and widely-used term).   An interaction use is denoted by a diagram frame having the identifier 'ref'.   No messaging details are given within the frame, so treat the construct as being a *reference* to another sequence diagram (one that contains all the interaction information).

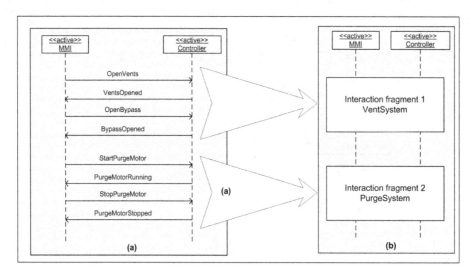

Fig. 5.17 Interaction overview concept

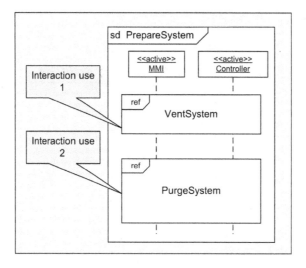

Fig. 5.18 Interaction overview diagram

UML actually defines the interaction overview diagram to be a specialization of the activity diagram (see later). So for the moment we'll limit its use to specifying the ordering of a set of interaction uses. We will, though, return to this when covering activity diagrams for a fuller discussion of the topic.

Interaction occurrences are also a helpful simplifying feature when we wish to show interactions between sequence diagrams, figure 5.19 (CASE-tool generated).

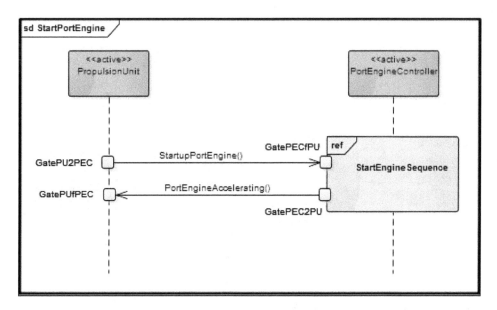

Fig. 5.19 Passing messages between sequence diagrams

The overall sequence diagram is *StartPortEngine*, this containing an interaction occurrence *StartEngineSequence* (shown on the lifeline of the *PortEngineController* object). This, as previously stated, is a reference to another diagram, so nothing new here. But what *is* new is the construct of messages being sent to an interaction occurrence (in this case *StartEngineSequence*) from other objects (and vice versa). We read this to mean that such messages (e.g. *StartPortEngine* and *PortEngineAccelerating)* are handled somewhere *within* the fragment. Four points have been identified as being 'gates'. Gates are nothing more than connection points, marking the source and target of messages. Note that the gate identifiers, the squares and associated names, are informal notations.

What we have here is a classic aspect of information hiding; compartmentalize the problem and show only what is necessary (minimize brain-loading). Tackle the problem a piece at a time.

Once we've fully understood what happens at the higher level we can then drill down into the detail, figure 5.20. This example message sequence is very simple; no new features have been used. However, two important points to note are that:

(a) Using gates makes it easy to navigate between the outside and the inside of an interaction occurrence.
(b) Objects can exist purely within the occurrence (i.e. *PortEngine*); they play no part in the interactions of the overall sequence diagram.

These features are really very useful for modelling the interactions in systems built using composite object structures.

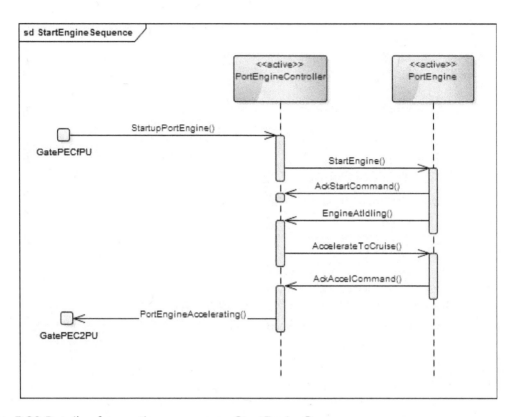

Fig. 5.20 Details of execution occurrence *StartEngineSequence*

5.3.4 Diagram comprehension.

It's been easy to understand the examples given so far for one good reason; all messages shown formed part of a simple sequence of transactions. But we know (especially from structured programming) that other very important transaction types have to be handled. Two of the most widely-used ones are selection (alternative courses of action) and iteration (looping operations). Let's deal first with selection.

The sequence diagram of figure 5.21 consists of two interaction fragments, whose executions are mutually exclusive. As shown here the notation is informal, describing what is a classic if-then-else execution.

This informal notation has, in the past, worked well, but only up to a point. To improve things and make it easier to comprehend the diagrams, UML2 introduced a construct called the 'combined fragment'. What this does is group interactions together, specifically those that are executed only when specified conditions are met. Figure 5.22, for example, shows a combined fragment which handles the alternative courses of action first defined in figure 5.21.

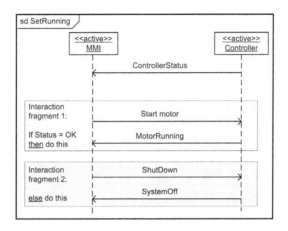

Fig. 5.21 Informal notation specifying alternative courses of action

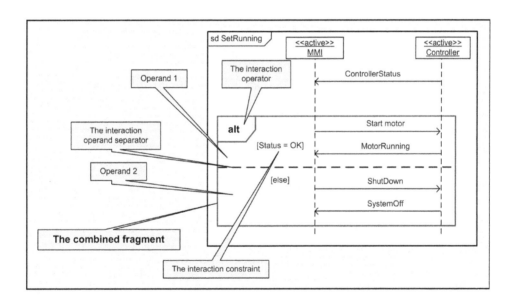

Fig. 5.22 Combined fragment specifying alternative courses of action

The combined fragment notation is that of a diagram frame with an interaction operator, this defining the purpose of the fragment. Here the operator is 'alt' (self-explanatory). Each possible sequence execution is called an 'operand'. Note that these operands are separated by a dotted line, the 'interaction operand separator'. Whether Operand 1 or Operand 2 gets selected is determined by its 'interaction constraint' (sometimes called a 'guard'). More precisely, we evaluate the constraint, and if it's 'true', then its operand is actioned. Clearly, only one constraint can ever be true at any one time. A further point is that we can show as many alternative courses of action as we wish; we're not limited just to two (this is equivalent to the 'if-then-elseif-elseif-elseif-else' or similar programming construct).

Please note that figure 5.22 is *not* an overview diagram; there is no hiding of information.

A variant on the selection action is the 'if-then' construct, where we either do something or just skip over it. This, defined to be an optional action, is illustrated in the combined fragment of figure 5.23.

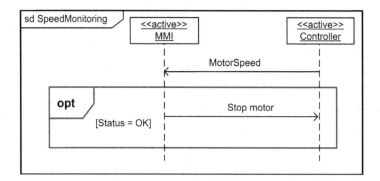

Fig. 5.23 Combined fragment specifying optional actions

Here the interaction operator is 'opt'.   Note; there can be only one operand in this construct.

To show iterations we use the loop combined fragment, figure 5.24.

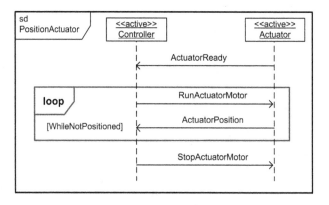

Fig. 5.24 Combined fragment specifying a loop

It's important to clearly understand that the operand is executed while the guard is true. In other words it represents a controlled loop construct, and can also be designated to have a range of values (i.e. having low and high limits).

Combined fragments are especially useful when dealing with complex interactions. For example, we may have a loop that contains selections where the selections in turn may contain further selections, etc.

Sequence, selection and iteration can be considered to be the 'bread and butter' constructs of sequence diagrams. However, there are also a number of other interaction operators which, in our experience, are less widely used. Possibly the more important ones are:

critical: denotes a region (the 'critical region') where the sequence *must* be completed without a break. In embedded terms this would be used to model a non-interruptible section of code.

ignore: Denotes interactions that should be ignored during the defined scenario. For example, when a plant is running it might be forbidden to amend its alarm limits, figure 5.25.

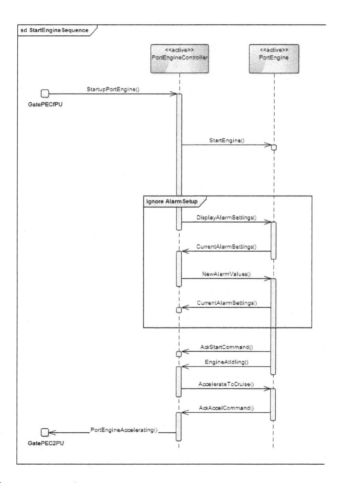

Fig. 5.25 Use of ignore operator

Break: denotes interactions that *must* be carried out instead of the whole of the interactions within a scenario. A practical use of this is to define where/when exceptions should be raised during normal operations, as in figure 5.26.

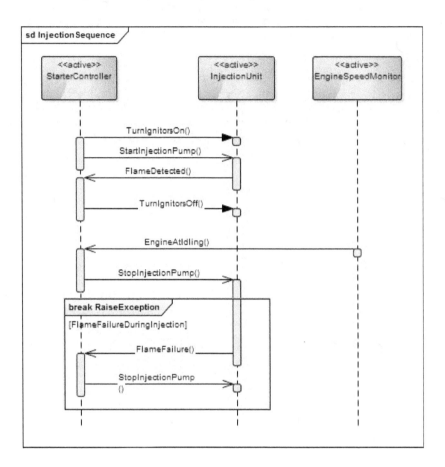

Fig. 5.26 Use of break operator

This scenario illustrates the messaging that takes place during a start-up sequence of an engine. If all goes well then the interactions within the combined break fragment aren't executed. However, if at any time during startup a flame failure is detected, then the normal scenario is abandoned. Instead the break combined fragment is executed (and note; there can be *only one* operand in this fragment).

   In the real-time embedded world the following operators seem to have limited use:
par: denotes fragments that are executed in parallel (i.e. concurrently), figure 5.27. Here there are two operands, each controlled by a guard. Provided both guards are true then the messaging specified in each operand (for simplicity omitted here) execute concurrently.

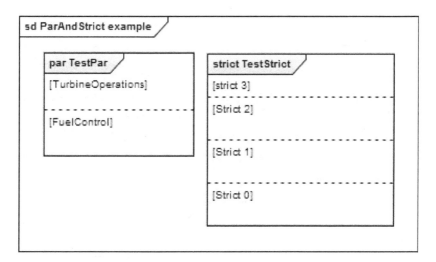

Fig. 5.27 **par** and **strict** example

strict: denotes a sequence of messages that must (and the operative word is *must*) be executed in the specified order. The structure of the combined fragment is shown in figure 5.27, which denotes that the interactions specified in the first operand (guard is 'strict 3') execute before those of the second one and so on. You can, if you wish, use this construct to specify the sequential structure of an interaction scenario (where the guards are assumed to be implicit and set to 'true'). Please note that all the remaining combined fragments described below have similar diagram structures with one proviso; neg and assert must have exactly one operand.

seq: defines a 'weak sequencing' fragment, one that relaxes the requirements of strict sequencing. Refer to the UML superstructure document for a fuller description of this operator.

consider: specifies interactions that should be considered within this combined fragment, meaning that any other message will be ignored. I haven't yet seen a believable use of this construct.

neg: specifies messages that could occur during the scenario but shouldn't be there (e.g. as a result of a fault). Thus they are considered to be invalid and should not be actioned.

assert: denotes that the messages shown in this combined fragment are the only valid ones that can occur in the scenario being modelled. Any others should be considered as being invalid.

5.4 Modelling the timing of interactions.

So far we haven't considered whether object interactions have to meet specific timing requirements. In fact that's probably true for the majority of interaction scenarios, such as the simple example of figure 5.28.

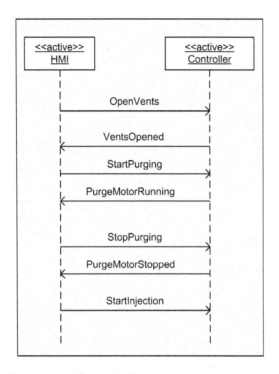

Figure 5.28 Sequence diagrams without timing issues

But now let us add timing requirements to this scenario, as follows:

1. The signal *OpenVents* is produced by push-button operation, a momentary action. To protect against spurious warnings (e.g. noise or input signal stuck) it is to be evaluated between lower and upper time limits (in this case 0.1 to 0.5 seconds).
2. The signal *VentsOpened,* an acknowledgement reply, must arrive between 1 and 2 seconds after *OpenVents* is sent.
3. The signal *PurgeMotorRunning,* an acknowledgement reply, must arrive between 0 and 1 seconds after *StartPurging* is sent.
4. The signal *StartInjection* must be received within 0.5 seconds of its sending.

The original sequence diagram can now be amended to show these specifications, figure 5.29. Notes have been added to clarify the meaning of the notation on this CASE-tool generated diagram (using UML-based terms), as follows:

- Duration Constraint: defines the duration between two time instants.
- Duration Constraint (between messages): this, non-standard UML, defines duration between two time instants on a lifeline.
- Time Observation: specifies the time instant when a message is sent.

- Time Constraint: specifies the time limits between the sending of a message and its reception.

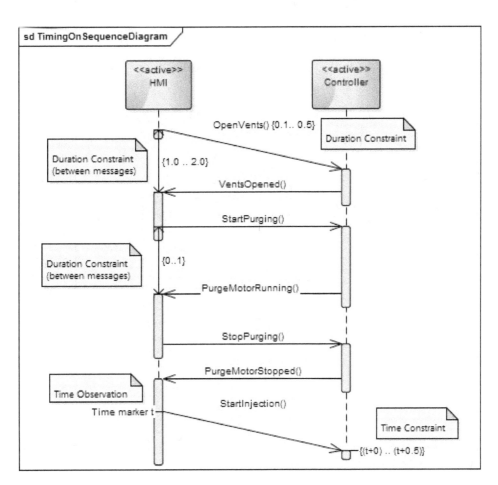

Fig. 5.29 Sequence diagram - example timing information

One other time-related item that may also be specified (not shown in figure 5.29) is:

- Duration Observation: normally used to denote that a message should be observed and also specifies the duration of this observation.

We've now got a good overall picture of the interactions that take place during a particular scenario, together with their important timing features. But later (when we get into state modelling) you'll find that it's important to describe the behaviour of the objects involved in these interactions. Now, using sequence diagram information, we can relate this overall behaviour to that of the individual objects, figure 5.30.

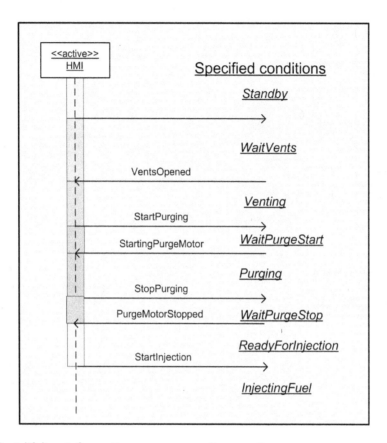

Fig. 5.30 Object lifeline information - sequence diagram form

Here we'll concentrate on one object only, the HMI of figure 5.29. As we walk down the lifeline we, the designers, define the various conditions (states) of the HMI object. Having done so we can now model the behaviour of the object as time elapses, figure 5.31. In this, the 'state lifeline' diagram, the horizontal axis is the timeline, having a range of 0 to 13 seconds. States are shown as discrete levels on the vertical axis, these being derived from figure 5.30. The 'graph' shows how the object progresses from state to state as time passes. Specifically it denotes *when* transitions occur together with the events (the *why*) that specify these transitions.

The same information can be shown in a more compact form, the 'value lifeline' diagram, figure 5.32. This should be self-explanatory.

If we wish we can produce a diagram that combines the lifeline information of all objects involved in a scenario. The example of figure 5.33 contains the lifelines of two objects, *Hydraulics* and *Controller*. Here we've shown the state lifeline of *Hydraulics* and the value lifeline of *Controller*, together with important signalling between them.

Please note that we could have used any other valid combination of lifeline diagrams (i.e. state/state, value/value, value/state).

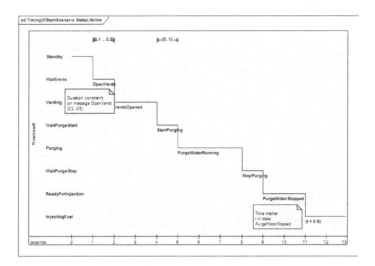

Fig. 5.31 Timing details of object behaviour - the state lifeline diagram

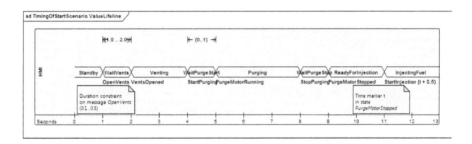

Fig. 5.32 Timing details of object behaviour - the value lifeline diagram

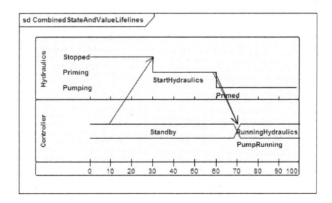

Fig. 5.33 Combined state and value lifelines

Figure 5.34 wraps up this section by giving an overview of UML sequence diagram timing notation.

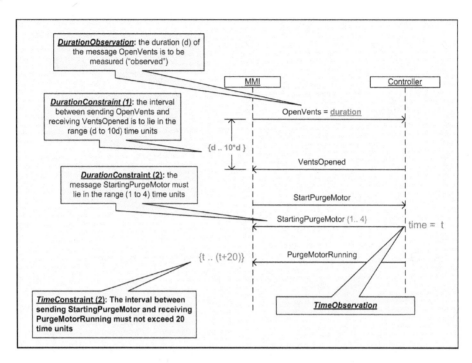

Fig. 5.34 Overview of timing information

5.5 The communication diagram.

Recap: the purpose of an object diagram is to show the objects of a system and their relationships. In this section we now extend the object diagram to produce the object *communication* diagram. It, in fact, is simply an object diagram that also shows the interaction(s) between the objects. This is demonstrated in the following example, the design diagramming of a simple conveyor belt system, figure 5.35, (for completeness the class structure is also provided, figure 5.35a). The object diagram, figure 5.35b, shows that the system as designed consists of a hall controller and two conveyor belts. Each conveyor belt object has two operations which can be invoked (called on) by other objects: Start and Stop. These operations are activated by passing messages to the objects, as shown in figure 5.35c, the object communication diagram. Here the messages have, for clarity, been given the same name as the operations. We can, if we wish, define the time ordering of messages by attaching numbers to them. Thus in this example the first message is Start, sent to the output conveyor belt. The next one starts the input conveyor belt, the third one stops the output belt, etc.

Communication diagrams are easy to produce and easy to understand, even as they become more complex, figure 5.36.

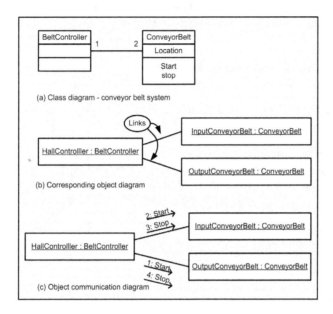

Figure 5.35 Objects and their collaborations

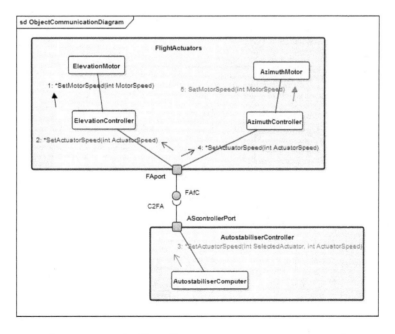

Fig. 5.36 More complex communication diagram

It's worth pointing out at this stage that communication diagrams aren't limited to describing just object interactions; they can, in fact, be used much more generally.
Now for two very important questions concerning communication diagrams:

- How do they relate to sequence diagrams?
- Why bother to use them?

To answer these we'll look at a very simple example of interactions between objects, as follows:

A communication system consists of two objects, a primary station (PS) and a secondary station (SS). There are two modes of transmission: PS to SS and SS to PS. Transmission is always initiated by the primary. Produce the sequence diagrams and the corresponding communication diagrams for the following scenarios:

(a) Scenario 1: PS obtaining SS data.
  PS sends a POLL message to SS.
  (i) If no data is available SS replies with a NACK message. This is the end of the transaction. PS terminates the session.
  (ii) If SS data is available, then SS sends the full data stream. When all data has been received PS sends ACK to SS to finish the session.

(b) Scenario 2: PS sending data to SS.
  PS sends a SEL message to SS. SS responds with ACK. PS sends data. When all data has been received by SS it sends ACK. PS terminates the session.
Scenario 1 is modelled in figure 5.37, while figure 5.38 describes scenario 2.

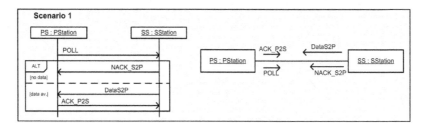

Fig. 5.37 Relating sequence and communication diagrams - scenario 1

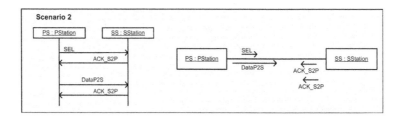

Fig. 5.38 Relating sequence and communication diagrams - scenario 2

Please study these in detail to confirm that they are complete and correct.

From this you can see that the sequence and communication fundamentally show the same information but in different form. In a way they can be treated as 'two sides of the same coin' in that they emphasise different aspects of the interactions. For the sequence diagram the emphasis is the time-ordering of messages and the various interaction occurrences (as we've already seen in many earlier examples). For the communication diagram it's the messages themselves. Observe that in scenario 2 the message ACK_S2P has been shown twice on the communication diagram. This corresponds to the occurrence of the same two messages on the sequence diagram (if the messages were time-stamped on the communication diagram they would be numbers 2 and 4). So what is the key relationship between the two diagrams? It is that all objects and messages on the sequence diagram must also appear on the corresponding communication diagram (and vice-versa). Given a sequence diagram we can *automatically* produce its equivalent communication diagram (in fact some CASE tools can do this). However this is not generally true for the reverse case unless the scenarios are very simple (e.g scenario 2) *and* messages are time-stamped.

So this leads us to the second question, 'why bother to use communication diagrams?'. Frankly, based on what we've done so far (producing a communication diagram for each scenario), it's hard to see what we've achieved. It seems to be a case of diagramming for the sake of diagramming. And yet this is the 'default' UML approach. Well, ignore that; let's do something sensible and useful instead, figure 5.39.

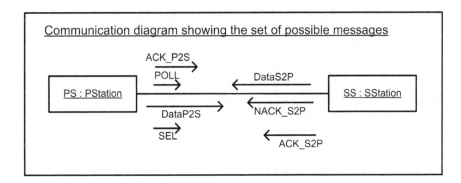

Fig. 5.39 Combined communication diagram

Here we've taken the information from the individual scenarios and used it to build up a single communication diagram. Also, there is no duplication of messages, nor time-stamping. The end result is a very useful, practical diagram that shows:

- All the objects of the system under design.
- The messages that flow between these objects.

This is a very powerful diagram for describing how systems work. Moreover, if you take an object-first design approach, this will be a key part of your work. A second major factor from a design point of view concerns the presentation of the messages. You can see at a glance all the distinct messages within the system *and* where they flow to/from.

Using this information you can define precisely the requirements of the required and provided interfaces of the various objects.

A final point: the time-stamping of messages. This hasn't been done for two reasons. First, there is no intent of the diagram to show message ordering. Second, I have found that it's worse than useless when used in practical designs; confusion rather than enlightenment is the result

5.6 Review.

You should now:

- Know what active and passive objects are, how they behave and how they are depicted in UML diagrams.
- Realize that the reason for having the two types is to allow us to model concurrent and non-concurrent object execution.
- Know how to describe active classes and objects in UML diagrams.
- Understand what a sequence diagram is, what it shows and why we use it.
- Know the notation used in UML sequence diagrams, the various message types used and how they are represented in the diagrams.
- Understand what an object lifeline and an execution specification (focus of control) are.
- Be able to model interactions involving concurrent (active) objects only, passive objects only and a mix of active and passive objects.
- Appreciate why, in passive object-based designs, one object can only ever execute at any one time (i.e. object executions are mutually exclusive).
- Realize that passive object-based designs map naturally to sequential (procedural) code.
- Recognize why you might choose to omit the foci of control from sequence diagrams.
- Know how to model the creation and deletion of objects during model execution.
- Appreciate how CASE tools can help in the maintenance of diagrams.
- Understand that CASE tool-generated diagrams may diverge from standard UML notation.
- Know what interaction fragments and interaction occurrences are, why we use them and how they simplify the handling of sequence diagrams.
- Understand the concepts and use of interaction overview diagrams.
- Know what combined fragments are and why we use them.
- For combined fragments, know what the following items are: operators, operands, interaction constraints and operand separators.
- Know, when using combined fragments, how to show alternative, optional, iterative and parallel actions.
- Know how and why to use the break and ignore operators.
- Know what type of timing information can be shown on sequence diagrams and how it is presented.
- Understand the structure and content of state and value lifeline diagrams and what they're used for.
- Appreciate that combined lifeline diagrams can be produced
- Understand what an object communication diagram is and how it relates to class and object diagrams.

- Understand the relationship between sequence and communication diagrams and be able to explain why they are 'two sides of the same coin'.
- See how communication diagrams can be generated automatically from sequence diagrams but the reverse isn't usually true.
- Understand that there is little value in producing communication diagrams on a scenario by scenario basis.
- Understand the reasons for and benefits of producing a single system-wide object communication.
- Appreciate that communication diagrams can be applied to model interactions between various software entities, not just objects.

END OF CHAPTER

Chapter 6

The behavioural dynamics model

The objectives of this chapter are to:

- Give various examples of dynamic functions.
- Introduce the general state transition diagram and the UML state machine diagram.
- Show how state machine diagrams may be used to define the dynamical behaviour of systems and units.
- Cover, in detail, the basic UML state model, including both transition-related and state-related behaviours.
- Describe hierarchical state machines, composite states, superstates and substates.
- Show the role and use of concurrent state modelling.
- Describe ways to clarify and declutter diagrams.
- Show how a state machine can be implemented in sequential code.

6.1 Introduction to dynamical modelling.

6.1.1 The basics of state modelling.

All the following statements have been extracted from **system** specification documents for real-time applications:

- 'The autopilot will have three ride modes - soft, medium and hard.'
- 'The shaft brake is to be released when the engine is running and the throttle moved past the idle position.'
- 'At (T+2.5) seconds IPN is injected into the starter and the ignition is switched on. If flame is not detected by (T+2.75) seconds initiate an emergency shut-down of the starter system.'
- 'The Sonar range gate is to be opened 300 microseconds after pulse transmission'.

From these it can be seen that the behaviour of such systems varies over time – the behaviour is dynamic.   At any instant in time each system has a specific mode of behaviour, its 'state'.

   In the examples above the specifications are quite simple and clear. For cases like these text is perfectly good enough to 'model' such behaviours. But many real systems behave in much more complex ways, resulting in complex text descriptions. In these situations it's no surprise that we turn to diagrams and diagramming to help us out; enter the state transition diagram (STD). In UML this is called the 'state machine diagram', so to avoid confusion we'll stick with that term (or for brevity, just 'state diagram'). First, though, a number of points need to be made before we get into detail:

- The behavioural dynamics model can be used to describe many entities, including systems, components, devices, electronics and software.
- The core aspects of this chapter are the hows and whys of modelling software systems and individual units.
- All items being modelled are considered to have a finite number of definite, discrete states.
- Dynamical behaviour is described using a graphical finite state machine (FSM) model.

6.1.2 State machine fundamentals.

The core constructs of the state machine are shown in figure 6.1.

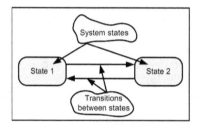

Figure 6.1 Basic state machine diagram

This represents a system that has two states only, as denoted by the rounded rectangles. It can be seen that the system can move (make a transition) from State 1 to State 2 and vice-versa (hence the origin of the name state transition diagram). Please, when it comes to building practical models, use meaningful names, ones taken from the problem domain, figure 6.2.

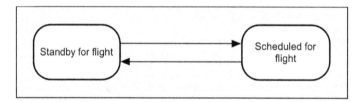

Figure 6.2 Simple state description

This model represents the state of a passenger waiting in an airport check-in area (a very simplified situation, of course). We'll assume that the scenario being modelled starts after he has arrived at check-in, in possession of a standby ticket. Hence he's placed into the standby queue, his state being *Standby for flight*. At some stage it is decided to include him in the flight schedule - a transition to *Scheduled for flight* state. But then the unfortunate passenger loses his place on the flight and is put back on standby.

This is a very simple scenario, but with one problem; what's caused the transitions? We really don't know - the information on hand is incomplete. What needs to be done is to define the causes of, or the events leading to, such changes. This we do as shown in figure 6.3.

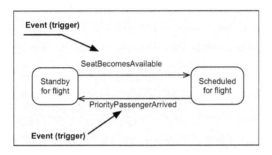

Figure 6.3 Events causing state changes

It can be seen that each transition has an associated event (strictly speaking, UML 2 states that a transition is provoked by a 'trigger'. See note at the end of this section). Thus the transition from *Standby for flight* to *Scheduled for flight* is caused by the event *Seat becomes available*. The next stage change occurs if a priority passenger arrives, leading to a return to the standby state.

To model this using UML notation, the constructs given in figure 6.4 may be used.

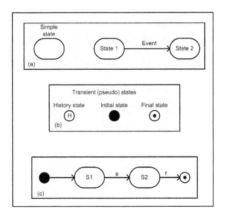

Figure 6.4 Basic UML notation

We've already met the notation used here for states, transitions and events. New, though, are the transient states; initial, final and history. There are others but these are some of the more important ones in UML. Let's deal first with the initial and final states and look at the use of the history state later.

Transition states, often called pseudo-states, can be likened to route markers for the transitions. Systems merely pass through such states, doing nothing on the journey. But, they are key to describing and understanding state models.   First, every state model execution *must* have a defined starting point (this is a key aspect of finite state automata theory, which underpins FSM modelling).   That is denoted by the transient state *Initial*. The point at which the model ceases executing is defined by the *Final* state.   Hence figure 6.4c is read as follows: when the model comes into being, it automatically enters the S1 state.   It remains there until event e occurs, at which point it makes a transition to state S2. When event f occurs state S2 is exited, a transition to the final state is made, and the model ceases execution.

The rules concerning final states are *not* the same as those that apply to the initial state. First, there doesn't even have to be a final state. This arises when a system, once activated, executes continuously (that, in fact, is typical of many embedded applications). Second, there may be more than one final state, as we'll see in a moment.

Frequently people have difficulty in understanding exactly how model execution starts and ends. In reality it depends on what is being modelled. One very simple example is, for instance, the use of a state model to describe the dynamics of a C++ program function. The model itself is, of course, a permanent feature, but it only begins executing when the function is called.   This corresponds to a transition from the start state. Likewise, the final state represents the completion of the function, when it returns control to the calling unit.

The key point to note is that the model specifies what happens when software actually runs.   If the software cannot run then the model has no meaning, the most extreme example being when the processor is powered down.

So let's now build a simple state model using the features shown in figure 6.4. Suppose that we work for a company that receives orders via email and need to describe how these are handled. We can do this using state modelling as per figure 6.5. By now you should be able to work your way through this diagram and fully understand what happens. Although this is simple, do not dismiss it as trivial.   I have seen such approaches used very effectively to describe the life cycles of both credit cards and legal documents.

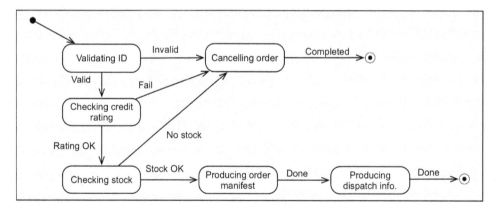

Figure 6.5 State modelling - simple example describing the processing of an order

If a state model is used mainly to describe the various stages of a process (as with the ordering process of figure 6.5), no more need be said. However if you wanted to know *exactly* what is done as the order is handled, then more information is needed. Key to this is that any processing carried out is a result of responses to the events. For completeness such information needs to be shown in our model. In practice there are three ways to do this, in each case by associating *actions* (responses) either with:

- Transitions: transition-related behaviour (the Mealy machine) or
- States: state-related behaviour (the Moore machine) or
- Both transitions and states (the UML state machine).

The Mealy and Moore machines (named after their developers) form the bedrock of graphical FSM modelling, figure 6.6.

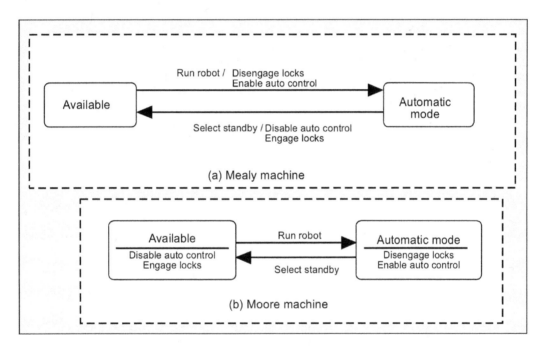

Figure 6.6 The Mealy and Moore machines

Both machines describe the same dynamic operation of a very simple two-state robot. State 1 is *Available* and state 2 is *Automatic mode*. Transition from *Available* to *Automatic mode* takes place in response to the event *Run robot*. Similarly, the event *Select standby* causes a transition from *Automatic mode* to *Available*. Thus, in terms of state and event information, both diagrams are much the same. The essential difference is to do with the actions. In the Mealy machine actions are associated with events. For the Moore machine actions are linked to states. Take, for instance, figure 6.6a. Assume the robot is currently in the *Available* state. When the event *Run robot* arrives it causes a state change to take place. It also generates two action, *Disengage locks* and *Enable auto control*. Now consider figure 6.6b.   When the same state transition takes place the same actions are generated. However, these are connected with the state, not the transition. Hence when the system is in *Available* mode (figure 6.6b), the actions *Disable auto control* and *Engage locks* are performed.

Thus both diagrams show the same information (they are, after all, describing the dynamics of the same system).   However, the presentation of information - and its interpretation - differ; and both machines have their advantages and disadvantages. UML sets out to get to get the best of both worlds by combining them (and also adding in some constructs developed in Statecharts by David Harel).   So we'll start by seeing how to model transition-related behaviour with UML, leading onto state-related models, finally combining it all.

To round off this section two small points need a mention. First, the topic discussed here is, strictly speaking, that defined in UML as the 'behavioural state machine'. There is also a second UML type, called a 'protocol state machine'.   This is defined to be 'a specialization of behavioral state machine and is used to express usage protocol or lifecycle of a classifier'. See the UML 2 superstructure if you wish to follow this up.

A second point for discussion concerns the meaning and use of the term 'trigger' (this section is dedicated to UML pedants). The use of 'event' as a triggering mechanism is well established in state machine terminology (starting with its original use in the design of digital electronic circuits). Moreover, UML 1.4 actually states that 'In the context of state diagrams, an event is an occurrence that can trigger a transition'.   Unfortunately (and confusingly for practitioners) some redefining of terms was done in UML 2. However, for our work we can (in my view) generally interchange *event* and *trigger* without causing confusion.   And there's a lot to be said for keeping the more generally-used and well-established term *event*.

In conclusion, here's a couple of examples of other authors take on the subject.

- *The Unified Modeling Language Reference Manual,* by Rumbaugh, Jocobson and Booch (known as the 'three amigos' UML gurus): In this 'Trigger' is called a 'trigger event'. It also states that 'the trigger is an event'.
- *UML Distilled*, by Martin Fowler: He (correctly) uses 'trigger-signature' in place of 'trigger', and states 'this is usually a single event'.

6.2 Transition-related behaviour.

This section looks at typical events and responses found in state machines where such responses are associated with the transitions. So, let's extend the scenario of figure 6.3 to show responses to the events on the state diagram, figure 6.7.   Assume that the passenger is in the *StandbyForFlight* state and a seat becomes available.   The event (trigger) *SeatBecomesAvailable* causes two things to happen:

- A response by the system (in this case the passenger is checked in) and
- A transition to the next state (here *ScheduledForFlight*).

It should be clear from the diagram what happens next when the event *PriorityPassengerArrived* occurs.

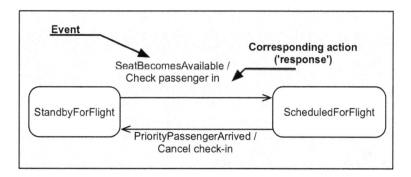

Figure 6.7 Responses to events

Important point: all changes in the theoretical model are assumed to take place instantly (and not over a period of time). Thus the response and the transition occur together; there isn't any idea of ordering or dependency. However this really isn't the case in practical implementations, something that will be discussed later.

Note that the term 'response' is an informal one; more generally these are called 'actions' or 'effects'.

There are times when events occur but we wish to react to these only under specified conditions. For example, it might be specified that :

'Provided that the start command has been received and the system has reached stage 3 of the start-up sequence, the clutch is energised and the system changes state'.

What this means is that we first evaluate the status of the start command event. If this is true we then proceed to check the start-up sequence to see if it's in stage 3. Provided this is also *true* (it is treated as a boolean variable) then the transition takes place ('fires'). If it isn't then the transition doesn't fire; the system stays in the same state. Thus what we have here is an event, an action and a *guard* on the transition, figure 6.8a.

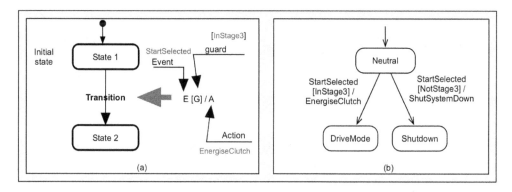

Figure 6.8 State diagrams and guards

On the surface the use of the guard construct appears to be straightforward. This certainly is the case when it evaluates to *true*. Unfortunately, when the guard is *false,* things become a bit murky. Many articles and books on UML merely state that 'it remains in the same state'. Others say, for example, 'it stays in the same state and the event occurrence is consumed'. We all agree that it remains in its original state, but what then? Most importantly, for real systems, when/why do we re-evaluate the event (and how do we go about doing this)? It seems to be open to individual interpretation, an unacceptable situation. What we *need* to do (to eliminate any ambiguities or ambivalences) is to make the specification more robust. To do this, rewrite the original specification as follows:

> *'Provided that the start command has been received and the system has reached stage 3 of the start-up sequence, the clutch is energised and the system changes state to the DriveMode state. If it isn't in stage 3 when the start command arrives then the system shuts down and changes state to Shutdown'.*

This is modelled in figure 6.8b, where clearly one of the guards *must* be true.

There are situations, of course, where it is intended that the guard does bar a transition to the next state. It is highly recommended to show it explicitly on the diagram using, for example, a self-transition (see later).

In embedded systems we frequently need to deal with compound events, those best described as combinational logic problems. For example: *'when the start button is pressed **and** the interlocks are clear then energise the starter relay'*. UML doesn't specifically address these aspects, but they are easily handled, as shown in figure 6.9. Here the combination of the two events are treated as if they're a single boolean value. This is equivalent to a logic AND gate, where the output only goes true when *all* its inputs are true. Moreover, there's no sense of order; it doesn't matter which one occurs first. In practice this means that the events are evaluated until both become true, then the transition is made.

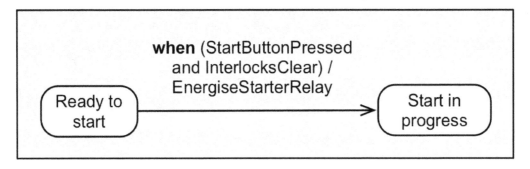

Figure 6.9 Multiple events

You should appreciate that we can handle many combinational logic variations such as NAND, OR, NOR, AND-OR, etc. You should also be able to work out why the guard construct is not a suitable way to implement such constructs. And just a point of syntax; the keyword 'when' was defined in UML 1.x, but appears to have disappeared in UML 2. As it's a very expressive term we choose to continue using it.

Frequently we need to produce multiple responses to a single event, e.g. 'when lock is selected, both the doors and the hatch are to be locked'. UML doesn't appear to consider such situations, but they're easily dealt with, as in figure 6.10.

Figure 6.10 Multiple responses

This is very straightforward, and you shouldn't have any difficulty in handling multiple responses. Implicit here is that there is no time ordering of the responses (in an ideal model both occur simultaneously; this is unlikely to be the case in real systems). If time ordering *is* important you could denote it on the diagram. However, if you are concerned with the robustness of implementations it is best to change things: introduce extra states. Also, if you want to control the evaluation order of multiple events, use the same approach.

To round this section off we'll look at two lesser-used constructs. First, how would you model the following specification: 'A sonar pulse is transmitted, and after 300 microseconds the range gate is opened in order to process echoes'. We *could* resort to the use of a guard, but a neater solution is shown in figure 6.11.

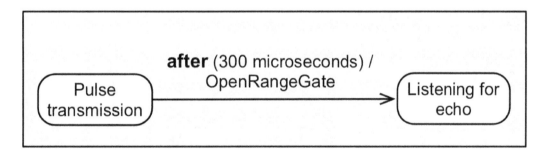

Figure 6.11 Transition caused by time elapse

Here the keyword 'after' is used to denote that the transition is triggered after the required time delay. Like the keyword 'when', 'after' was defined in UML 1.x but not in UML 2. As before we choose to continue using it.

The second construct is that shown in figure 6.12, the addition of an attribute to the event.

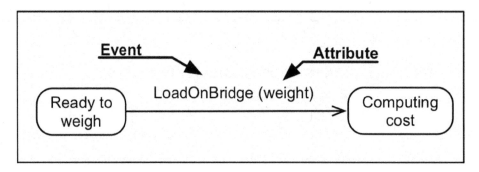

Figure 6.12 Event-attribute notation

This specifies that when the event *LoadOnbridge* occurs a transition is made and the weight value is passed to the next state.

6.3 State-related behaviour.

We now move on to the Moore machine aspects of state modelling: associating actions with states. The state models we've developed so far do very little while they're in an individual state. In fact all they do is wait for events that cause the state to be exited. However, with state-related behaviour, operations are performed *within* the states (and not on the transitions). Three important cases to consider are code executions that run:

- To completion.
- For a limited time.
- Continuously until the state is exited (typical of control loops).

These are all defined to be 'do-activities', figure 6.13.

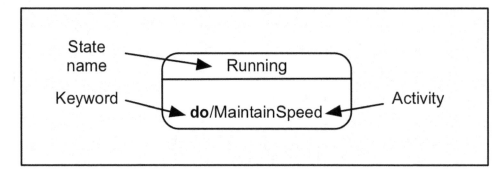

Figure 6.13 Activity within a state - a 'do-activity'.

This defines that when the state *Running* is entered the activity *MaintainSpeed*, identified by the keyword 'do', is started. We can infer from the wording that the activity runs continuously but there is no formal way to confirm this. Also, we're not restricted to one activity only; there can be multiple entries if so needed.

In practice state diagrams can become complex, and this may cause problems when states are entered via different routes. You may find that when you have different entry transitions the actual state conditions may vary; a state inconsistency problem. It isn't, of course, something we've planned for in the design; it's just a mistake that hasn't been picked up. This is a difficult problem to deal with; you need to be very precise and rigorous with your design (more on this when composite states are covered). However, one aid to good design is the **entry** action, figure 6.14. What this specifies is that when a state is entered, any activity denoted as an entry one is carried out. Moreover, entry actions are the first ones to be performed. This guarantees that such actions are *always* carried out irrespective of our route into the state.

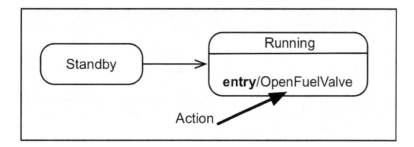

Figure 6.14 Entry action

There is an equivalent construct to deal with leaving a state, the exit action, figure 6.15.

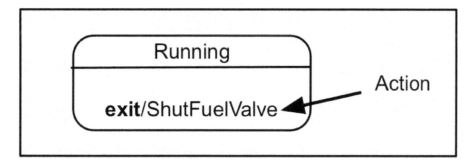

Figure 6.15 Exit action

The diagram is self-explanatory.

A further requirement we sometimes meet is, once we're in a state, to deal with specified events but *without* leaving that state. To handle this the UML state machine has a construct called an 'activity within a state', figure 6.16.

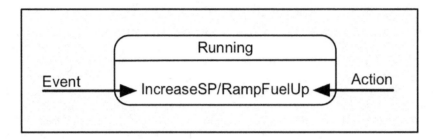

Figure 6.16 Activities within a state

This specifies that while we're in the *Running* state and the event *IncreaseSP* occurs then we perform the action *RampFuelUp* (which, in this case, is a run-to-completion action). No changes of state take place.

6.4 Combining state-related and transition-related behaviours.

It's a very simple step from the two individual models to one that combines all the features mentioned earlier. And the first example introduces yet another construct, the self-transition (figure 6.17).

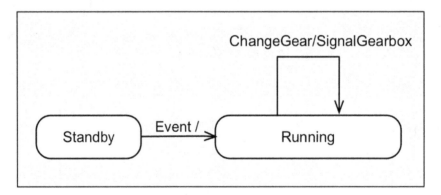

Figure 6.17 State machine - self-transitions

The meaning of this is quite simple. When the system is in the *Running* state and the event *ChangeGear* occurs we leave *Running*, perform *SignalGearbox*, and then return to where we came from (*Running*). Now, in terms of the response itself, this appears to be almost identical to an activity within a state. However, the significant difference is that as the state has been left and then re-entered, any specified exit and entry actions *must* be carried out.

All the features covered so far are illustrated in figure 6.18.

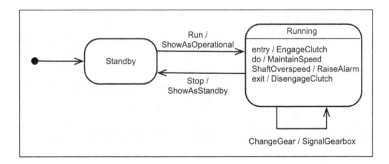

Figure 6.18 Example of combined transition and state related behaviour

You should, by now, recognise all the constructs shown and be able to navigate through the diagram.

6.5 States and substates - composite states.

6.5.1 Composite states and sequential state machines.

In the example state models given so far, all states have been at the same level. This, as previously noted, results in a one-level or 'flat' state diagram. Now, for illustration and explanation purposes, this is fine. However, when dealing with real applications such diagrams may end up being cluttered, complex, difficult to understand and hence difficult to use. Yet this is something we should avoid like the plague; diagrams are supposed to be a help, not a hinderance. Fortunately help is at hand: the UML composite state machine. What this does is allow us to 'decompose' a single state into a more detailed sub-state model, figure 6.19.

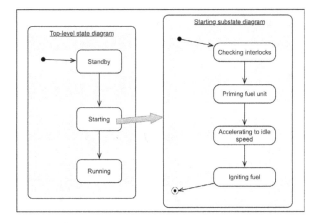

Figure 6.19 Refinement and substates

As shown here there is a top-level flat state diagram, consisting of three states only. However, the state *Starting* is really a high-level view of the behaviour given in the substate diagram.   So when the model runs it initially enters the *Standby* state, then progresses to *CheckingInterlocks*, on to *PrimingFuelUnit*, etc.   The transition in the substate model from *IgnitingFuel* to its final state is actually a transition to *Running*. Hence what we have here is a classic example of an information hiding, top-down, stepwise refinement technique.   Note also; it is permissible (and often quite useful) to further decompose the states within the substate machine.

A small point: you can, if you wish, show the substate diagram details on the top-level diagram.   This, to me, seems to defeat the aim trying to simplify things.   Hence the recommended approach is to have a separate diagram for the substate model.   To show that state details are described in a separate substate diagram, the top-level state includes a decomposition indicator, figure 6.20.   This is a helpful navigation guide, especially when a substate is itself a composite state (it's perfectly ok to decompose down as many levels as needed by the design).   CASE tools normally automate navigation between the various levels.

Two further constructs that can be usefully applied to composite state diagrams are the entry point and exit point pseudo-states, figure 6.21.   This diagram is directly equivalent to that of figure 6.19, but now the entry and exit points are explicitly denoted.   Observe that using consistent naming on both diagram simplifies the job of dealing with separate diagrams (especially as, in practice, we may not be able to view both simultaneously). Note that the event *RunningSelected* on the top-level diagram is also shown in the substate model; it's the one that causes a transition from the state *IgnitingFuel* to the exit point *ToRunning*.   Observe also the we specify the name of the substate machine (the 'referenced state machine') as part of the 'parent' state name: *Starting:StartingSubstates*.

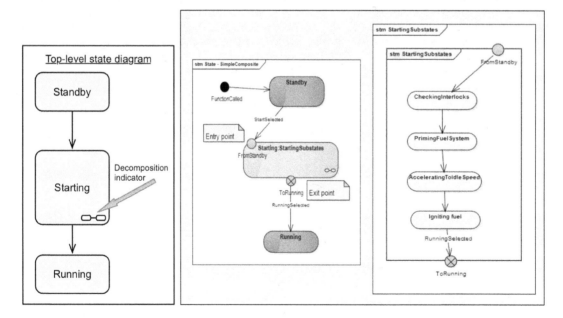

Figure 6.20 Decomposition   Figure 6.21 Entry and exit points
            indication

This diagram is simple, easy to follow and easy to use. However, for this particular example, the use of entry and exit points is overkill; we don't need them. But consider their role in a more complex case, figure 6.22 (this is just a fragment of a larger state diagram).

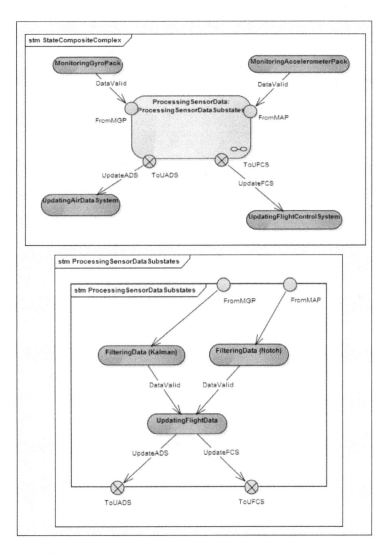

Figure 6.22 Entry and exit points more

To begin with you'll enter either one of two states: *MonitoringGyroPack* or *MonitoringAccelerometerPack*. As you can see the successor state for both of them is *ProcessingSensorData*. However, they enter it via two different entry points, thus entering different substates. Hence the model execution proceeds either as:

1. *MonitoringGyroPack => FilteringData(Kalman) => UpdatingFlightData* **or**
2. *MonitoringAccelerometerPack => FilteringData(Notch) => UpdatingFlightData*

There are two possible transitions from *UpdatingFlightData*, one to exit point *ToUADA*, the other to *ToUFCS*. The associated events are *UpdateADS* and *UpdateFCS*.

It is permissible to omit events on transitions that emanate from exit points; thus the events *UpdateADS* and *UpdateFCS* could be left off figure 6.22. The decision to include or to omit such events is really a matter of personal choice. However, omitting events has a down-side when using the top-level diagram; we can deduce only that a transition has been triggered by *some* event within the substate machine. Without checking the substate diagram we can only guess at the reason.

6.5.2 Concurrent state machines.

In all the examples given so far, model execution proceeded as a set of sequential steps: from initial state to the next state, then the next one and so on. This works well when the behaviour of individual, complete items (e.g. machinery, systems, software units, etc.) needs to be modelled. But there are times, though, when it is necessary to model concurrent behaviour. Consider, for example, the pump unit of figure 6.23.

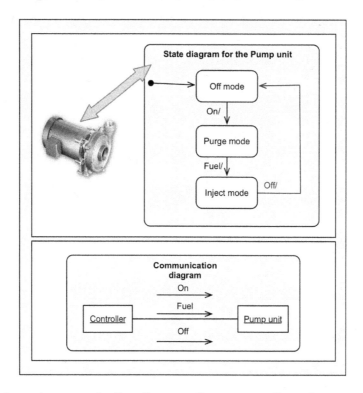

Figure 6.23 State and communication diagrams for a composite unit - overall behaviour

From the outside this is seen to be a single unit, having the behaviour defined in the state diagrams of figure 6.23. Observe that here there is no final state, thus the machine runs indefinitely (more practically, while power is on).

The communication diagram has been added to figure 6.23 to bring home the point that events are often real-world signals (especially important in embedded systems). And that raises the interesting question of just how the state machine gets to know about these signals. We'll have a look at this (very important issue) later, in the concluding part of the chapter.

It turns out that in our example the pump unit is actually made up of two sub-units, a valve and a motor. Now, suppose that we had to delve into the innards of the pump unit, perhaps for maintenance. It's then necessary to treat it as a composite unit that is made up of the two separate sub-units. These operate concurrently as individual items, having their own modes of operation as defined in the state diagram of figure 6.24.

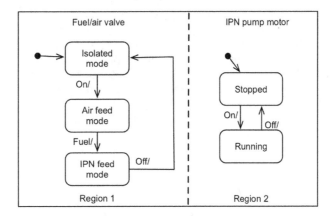

Figure 6.24 Concurrent state modelling in UML

Although they run concurrently their behaviour is determined only by the events arriving into the unit (and, in this case, not on interactions between the sub-units). If you work your way around the model you can verify the relationship between the individual state machines and the overall one, figure 6.25.

Event	Pump unit state	Valve state	Pump motor state
Power on	Off mode	Isolated mode	Stopped
On	Pump mode	Air feed mode	Running
Fuel	Inject mode	IPN feed mode	NO EFFECT Running
Off	Off mode	Isolated mode	Stopped

Figure 6.25 State relationship for the pump unit

161

Please verify that it's correct.

In this example it's quite easy to cross-check the relationship of the individual state models with that of the overall one.

Now, if we'd started with the individual models then, to produce the overall model, they have to be combined. The way to do this (in general) is to first define all potential combinations, then delete those that can't happen. It can be see that there are six potential combinations:

1. Isolated mode AND Stopped;   2. Isolated mode AND Running.
3. Air feed mode AND Stopped;   4. Air feed mode AND Running ;
5. IPN feed mode AND Stopped;   6. IPN feed mode AND Running ;

In practice three combinations cannot occur and, when these are deleted, we're left with the valid combinations. We can now populate the overall state diagram with the valid states (adding in events and transitions as appropriate).

This example was easy to deal with. Even so we needed a good knowledge of the overall unit behaviour to arrive at the correct result. This, I hope, will make it clear that the job of combining complex state models is not simple; it may turn out to be really quite difficult. Our advice? Wherever possible try to develop designs that *don't* require you to combine state models. Moreover, the reverse of this, splitting a high-level state model into separate sub-models, can be equally difficult.

At this point we can introduce two more pseudo-states, the fork and the join, figure 6.26.

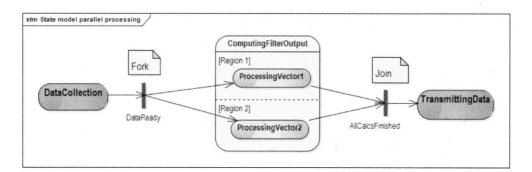

Figure 6.26 State model of parallel processing

Here, just for simplicity, events have been omitted from the diagram. Assume that the diagram models the behaviour of the software in a multicore processor. The processing of the incoming data is split across two cores, these executing in parallel (concurrently). The state *ProcessingVector1* applies to software on core 1 say and *ProcessingVector2* to core 2.

To explain what happens, first assume that the model is in the *DataCollection* state. An event now arrives that causes a transition to the fork pseudo-state (*DataReady*), where the transition splits. Two transitions emerge from *DataReady*, one to *ProcessingVector1*, the other to *ProcessingVector2*. These are simultaneous. When processing is complete in each state a transition is made to the join pseudo-state *AllCalcsFinished.* The cores may, of course, have different calculation times, thus the incoming transitions arrive at different times. However, a transition isn't made out of *AllCalcsFinished* until <u>both</u> incoming transitions are present. At that point the model enters the *TransmittingData* state. Hence *AllCalcsFinished* (the join) acts as a synchronizing mechanism.

Modelling using concurrent regions is fine for simple diagrams and, in some cases, can be very helpful. The previous example, for instance, has very neatly shown where concurrent units <u>must</u> synchronize their activities. However in many practical cases the state models of the individual units are quite complex; putting this information on one diagram can result in confusion, not clarity. This is especially true where concurrent activities interact, something that usually happens in task-based designs. If such tasks are dynamically complex then they need their own state models (usually shown in separate state machine diagrams). If there is any task-to-task signalling, this can be shown on the individual state diagrams using the constructs of figure 6.27. As shown here the transition from state 1 to state 2 takes place when eventA occurs. The event, in our example, is actually a signal received from a different concurrent unit. If we wish to show this *explicitly* on a state diagram a 'signal receive' icon can be used. Likewise, a 'signal send' icon can be used to denote that an event provokes a sending of a signal to another state machine (the action).

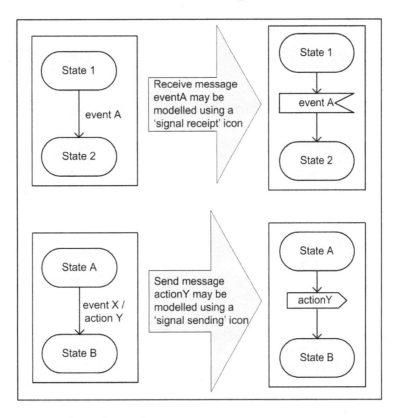

Figure 6.27 Receive and send signals

A simple example showing signalling between tasks is given in figure 6.28.

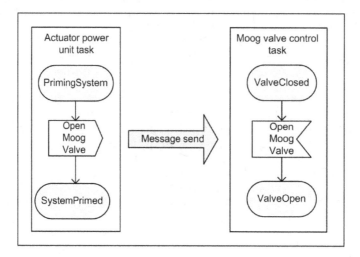

Figure 6.28 Signalling between concurrent units

It also makes sense (from a design/implementation point of view) to augment the diagram with notes explicitly defining the sources and destinations of messages.

6.6 Minor topics - diagram simplification and decluttering.

6.6.1 History pseudostate.

Consider how we'd model the following behaviour:

'The vehicle infotainment unit has three modes of operation: Tuner, DVD and Aux. When electrical power is applied to the unit it first enters a standby state, transitioning to an operational state only when the unit On/Off button is pressed and released ('depressed', a soft-key action). When this button is next depressed the system returns to the standby state.

When the unit enters the operational mode the first time after power is applied tuner is selected.

A mode button is used to change the operational mode, but the order is pre-defined: Tuner to DVD to Aux to Tuner and so on. The mode button action is also a soft-key one. Each depress moves the system into the next pre-defined mode.

As stated above, when the unit is in an operational mode and the On/Off button is depressed, the system returns to the standby state (irrespective of its specific operational mode). When On/Off is once again depressed the system returns to the operational mode it had last been in.'

The corresponding state diagram is that of figure 6.29.

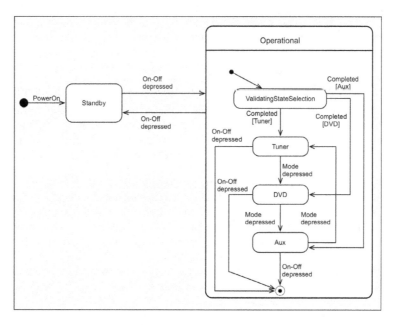

Figure 6.29 State model - simple infotainment unit

Here, for completeness, the event *On-Off depressed* has been shown on both the high-level and the substate level state machine diagrams.

To cater for situations like this UML has a pseudostate called 'history'. The icon for this (an H within a circle) is used in the substate diagram of figure 6.30, replacing the original initial pseudostate of figure 6.29.

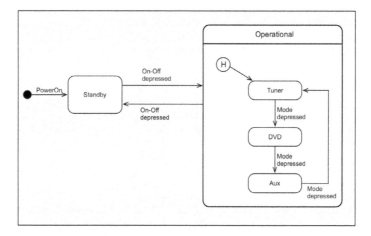

Figure 6.30 State model with history

This defines that when the substate model is entered for the first time, the history state acts as the initial state. Subsequently when the substate model is running and the *On-Off depressed* event occurs, then a transition is made from *Operational* to *Standby*. More precisely, the transition could have come from the *Tuner*, *DVD* or *Aux* substate.

Following this, the next time the event *On-Off depressed* arises, a transition is made from *Standby* back into the substate that it had previously been in.

It can be seen how this construct leads to a much simpler and clearer state machine diagram. And, provided you're au fait with the rules, very easy to understand.

Well, that's fine for producing and reading diagrams. But don't be fooled by this simplicity if your intention is to translate this state diagram to code. The reality is that any code implementation will be driven by the state model of figure 6.29 (or something similar).

So, the semantics of the the history state as described so far are simple. They specify that, on a return to a composite state, one of the substates *visible at that level* will be entered. This, strictly speaking, is called 'shallow' history in UML. Now, though, consider where substates may themselves be decomposed into substates, also having a memory feature. As an example, suppose that the Tuner substate was decomposed into substates which define the tuning presets. Assume that we're in 'FM104' say and *On-Off depressed* occurs. This means that we exit the sub-substate 'FM104', going to *Standby*. Now when *On-Off depressed* next arrives we need to make sure that the systems transitions back into to 'FM104'. To specify such a requirement we *could* add a history state to the decomposed substate. However, UML gives us a second history form, 'deep' history, for use with examples like this. This is used in place of the shallow history indicator, and denotes that *all* sub-substates have a memory feature.

A personal comment; I prefer to take a consistent approach and use the shallow memory state icon only (and note that some CASE tools may not supply the deep history icon).

6.6.2 Junction and choice pseudostates.

Here we once again use pseudostates to simplify diagrams and so reap the benefits of such simplification. Take, for example, the fragment of a state machine shown in figure 6.31. To properly understand even this quite small scenario takes much care and

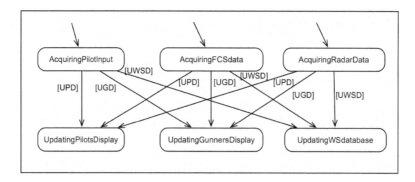

Figure 6.31 A complex state diagram fragment

patience. Now visualize the situation where this is just one part of a much larger state diagram. How much effort, do you think, would be needed to fully understand and work with such information? A somewhat rhetorical question, methinks. Simplification is badly needed. And here we can employ yet another pseudostate, the junction.

Junction states come in two flavours, merge and split, figure 6.32.

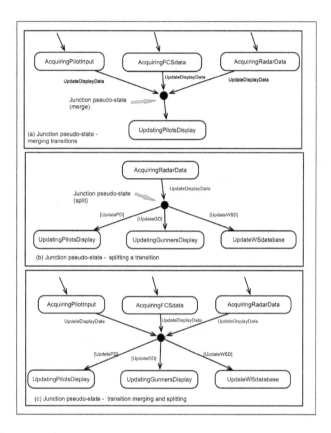

Figure 6.32 Junction pseudostates

The merging action is shown in 6.32a, where all transitions are all routed through the junction to the destination state *UpdatingPilotsDisplay*. And, in accordance with the rules of sequential state diagrams, our system can be in one state only. So only one actual route can be taken, this depending on the originating state.

Figure 6.32b shows the splitting of a transition, where there are three possible successor states. Remember, these are mutually exclusive, so it is essential to define which transition is taken out of the junction. This we do, as you can see, by the use of guards.

Now for a final point concerning junctions; they can be used to specify both merging and splitting, as per figure 6.32c. This, a combination of figures 6.32a and 6.32b, is in fact the redone state model of figure 6.31, but using the merge/split junction. The resulting clarity speaks for itself.

Repeating something said earlier; don't think this simplifies the code implementation of the model. It is merely a diagramming technique.

We'll finish this section by reviewing the meaning and use of the choice pseudostate, figure 6.33.

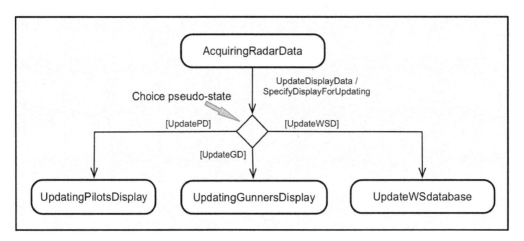

Figure 6.33 Choice pseudostate

It looks as if this performs exactly the same function as the split junction, which is true up to a point. For some reason (which I find rather esoteric) UML distinguishes between the two, as follows (UML-speak):

> Junction pseudostate realizes a **static** conditional branch. Here the guard constraints are evaluated before any transition containing the pseudo state is executed.
> Choice pseudostate realizes a **dynamic** conditional branch. The guards are evaluated when the transition reaches this pseudostate.

So, in figure 6.33, the guard conditions could be updated as a result of executing the action *SpecifyDisplayForUpdating*; only then are they used to select the valid outgoing transition from the choice pseudostate.

Personally I'm totally underwhelmed by this distinction. However, there may be situations where it's important for you to know the difference between the two (e.g. if you are reviewing the work of others).

6.7 Code-related aspects.

This section deals with the translation of the state machine model into source code. Here, though, it is limited to implementation in a sequential code unit (the area where it is most likely to be used). Key factors central to the approach taken here are the:

- Provision of code to manipulate the state machine itself (the 'state controller').

- Minimization of coupling between the controller and the state code units.
- Localization of all *processing* code to the individual states.
- Localization of *decision-making* to the code of the individual states.

There are many ways to implement state machines but this method is simple, clear, proven and robust (a much deeper coverage of this issue is given in 'Practical Statecharts in C/C++' by Miro Samek).   An important point to understand is that, when using sequential code, events don't 'magically' arrive; they have to be obtained. Generally this means reading the value of a program variable or obtaining an input from a real-world device. Once a event is deemed to be 'true' then the appropriate response is generated. Moreover, from the state diagram information, the state 'knows' which transition to take; i.e. which state is the next one.   In the program design technique used here each individual state *must* specify the destination of the transitions.

Consider an example of a generalized state machine, figure 6.34.

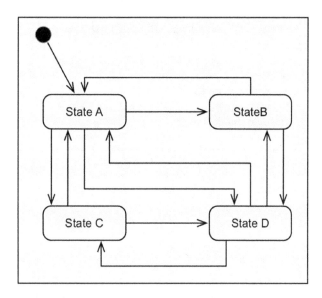

Figure 6.34 Generalized state machine

The controller code that implements this is relatively simple, as shown in figure 6.35. Here the processing code of each state is wrapped up in a single function 'RunStateX. Thus a call on this starts the execution of the the state code, which then runs to completion.   On its return to the calling unit, (*RunStateController*) it brings with it the name of the next state to be run.   The state so identified is subsequently called into execution by the action of the code switch selection mechanism (which is itself running in an endless loop). Observe that on first call of *RunStateController* the variable *NextState* is initialised to *StateA*.

We'll defer discussion of the processing carried out within the states until activity diagrams have been covered.

```
typedef enum {StateA,StateB, StateC, StateD} SystemStates;
void RunStateController (void)
{
static SystemStates  NextState = StateA;

   while(1)
   {
     switch (NextState)
      {
      case   StateA:     RunStateA(&NextState);
             break;
      case   StateB:     RunStateB(&NextState);
             break;
      case   StateC:     RunStateC(&NextState);
             break;
      case   StateD:     RunStateD(&NextState);
             break;
      default: RunErrorWarning();
      } /* end switch */   } /* end while */
}/* end RunStateController */
/*--------------------------------------------------------*/
```

Figure 6.35 Code for generalized state machine - the state controller

6.8 Review.

You should now:

- Appreciate why many real-time systems have a changing pattern of behaviour.
- See how the state machine diagram allows you to model such operations.
- Understand the concepts of states, transitions, events (conditions) and actions (responses).
- Understand the rules and notation of the Mealy and Moore finite state machines.
- Appreciate that an event is required to cause a state change.
- Understand that, in some circumstances, the completion of processing can be considered to be an event.
- Realise that an action is not necessarily produced. Also realise that, when an action is generated, it is a response to an event.
- Understand the syntax of the UML state machine model.
- Understand what entry and exit actions are and how they relate to both self-transitions and activities within a state.
- Know what composite states are and why we use them.
- Appreciate the use of entry and exit points in substate diagrams.

- Know the syntax and semantics of the following pseudostates: initial, final, history, join and choice.
- Appreciate the use of the history (memory) feature.
- Be able to model concurrent states (using fork and join pseudostates if needed).
- Appreciate what receive and send signals are and why we'd use them.
- Understand how to map a state machine to sequential code to form a state controller.

END OF CHAPTER

Chapter 7

The processing model

The objectives of this chapter are to:

- Introduce process modelling and models.
- Illustrate the usefulness and widespread application of such models.
- Explain how processing models can be developed using the UML activity diagram.
- Describe a limited but useful set of activity diagram constructs and how they can be used.
- Show how activity diagrams can model both sequential and parallel processing.
- Describe the use of activity diagrams for specifying program structures (the program structure diagram).
- Explain how structured, top-down designs can be developed using activity diagrams.
- Show how to map program structure charts to source code.

7.1 Introduction to process modelling.

Process modelling (loosely 'the hows and ways of doing things') has been an integral part of business, engineering and science activities for aeons. In general the diagram formats and the symbols used are many and varied, having been developed mainly in ad-hoc ways, figure 7.1a. Yet they are usually quite easy to understand, even for the non-specialist. As a result they are an excellent communication vehicle for team work, especially cross-disciplinary ones. What is also interesting is that such models have been used for a variety of purposes.

- The Telecomms example, figure 7.1b, is an aid for fault-finding and general diagnostic testing.

- The Medical example, figure 7.1c, is used to specify how a new system is intended to work.

- The Local government example, figure 7.1d, is an evaluation guide for the use of employees.

- The Purchase Order Process example, figure 7.1e, defines how a specific business process (handling purchase orders) should be done.

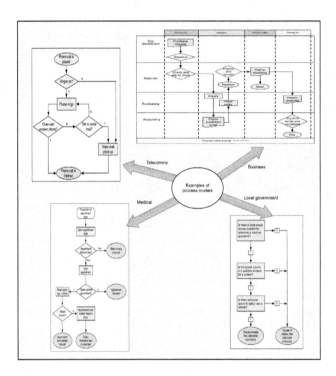

Figure 7.1a Examples of process models

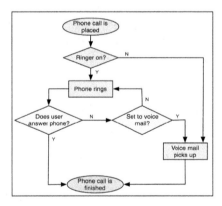

Figure 7.1b Telecomms example

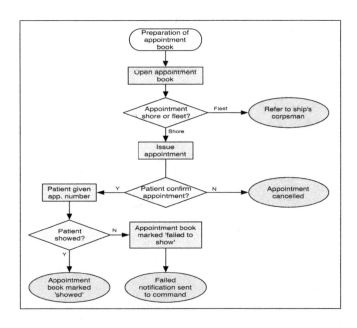

Figure 7.1c Medical example

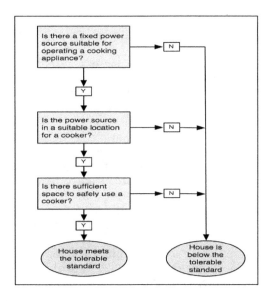

Figure 7.1d Local Government example

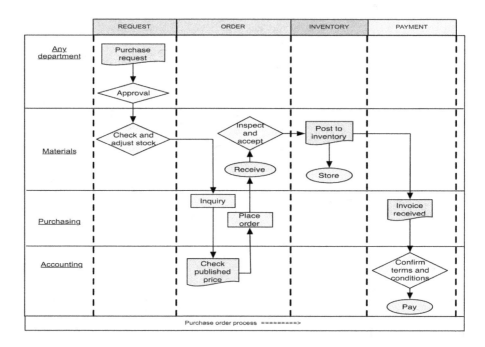

Figure 7.1e Order processing example

The final example, the processing of a purchase order, is especially relevant to our work; so please read through it and assimilate its details. Observe that while, like the others, it performs a set of sequential actions (involving decision making at times) it also:

- Specifies all participants taking part in the process (Accounting, Purchasing, Materials Management and Any department).
- Shows that some actions are carried out in parallel (during the 'ORDER' processing phase).

Note, though, it does not define that these parallel actions are necessarily carried out *simultaneously*.

Note also the style of wording used to specify the actions to be taken (e.g. Check and adjust stock, Place Order, Post to inventory, etc). These tell us what to do (contrast this with state naming, which tells us where we are). On a pedantic note, it's the contrast between the transitive and the present participle verb forms (now I'm sure you feel better for knowing that!). But forget the grammar; just stick to using the active form of the verb.

At this point I can understand that you might consider such advice to be somewhat trivial. Not so; it is actually quite important. Because, in my experience, the use of passive expressions can easily result in wooly and sloppy implementations. Active terms such as 'measure sensor data' are much more focussed than casual passive expressions such as 'data collection'.

Well, now that the general aspects of process modelling have been covered, we can move onto the UML version.

7.2 Basics of UML process modelling - activity diagrams.

7.2.1 Introduction to activity diagrams.

In UML, process modelling is done using activity diagrams. Unfortunately, what was a relatively simple topic in UML1.x became something really quite complex in UML2.x (Martin Fowler gives you a taste of what to expect when he talks about 'the demonic depths of the UML specification'). Yet, in practice, it seems that few of the newer features are widely used. So here we'll restrict activity diagram modelling to things that, in my opinion, are really very useful:

- To describe general processing operations.
- To act as a program specification model - the program structure chart.

The set of symbols used in our diagrams are shown in figure 7.2, where many (if not most) will be readily recognized.

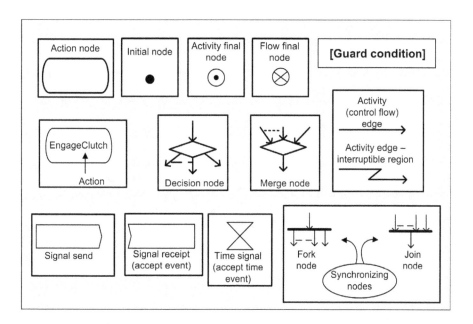

Figure 7.2 Activity diagram symbols (basic)

In simple terms an Activity is a "job" to be done. An Action is a specific piece of processing (or "work") carried out as part of the overall activity. The most basic activity diagram uses a combination of action and control nodes (initial, decision, merge and final), as in the example of figure 7.3.

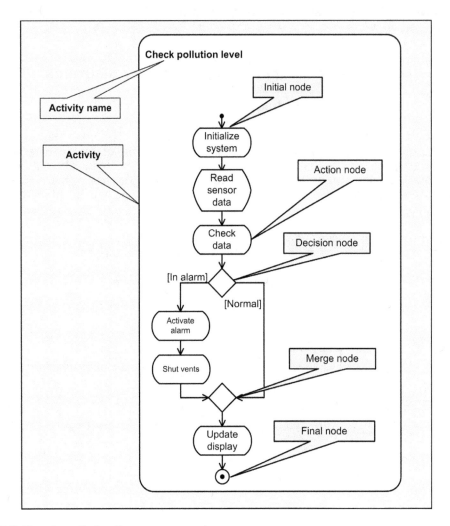

Figure 7.3 Simple activity diagram example

This could, for example, be used to specify the processing to be carried out by a software function (in this case named 'Check pollution level'). The model becomes active when the function is called, finishing when control is returned to the calling unit (after the action *Update display* is performed).

You should find this to be very straightforward to use because of its similarity to a flow chart. Note how the guard conditions define which route is to be taken out of the decision node (clearly when the guards are evaluated only one can be true). Also, you can have as many output control flows as you like, it's not limited to three. Likewise, a merge node can have multiple inputs, as dictated by the design.

Activity diagrams can also show combinations of sequential and parallel actions, figure 7.4.

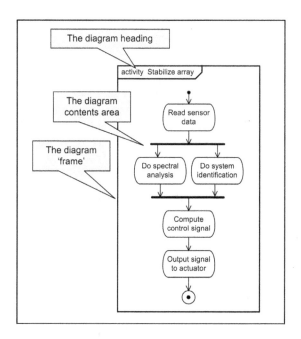

Figure 7.4 Activity diagram describing sequential and parallel processing

The diagram here is framed in the standard way, with its type ('activity') and name ('Stabilize array') shown at the top left. Included here are the control nodes fork and join, used to synchronize the two actions *Do spectral analysis* and *Do system identification*. We read the diagram as follows:

When the model starts the action Read sensor data is carried out. The control flow from this goes to the fork node, where it splits into two outgoing paths (implicit here is that the data output from Read sensor data forms the input to the parallel actions). Both outputs are fed to the synchronizing node (implicit is that the results are combined); only when both are present is progress made to the next action node where Compute control signal is performed.

This example used the activity diagram to emphasise the overall process, not to act as a program structure chart (although it could eventually be used for such a purpose). In particular it defines where parallel actions take place and what they are, something essential for parallel processing.

In many cases it is necessary to explicitly specify where the parallel activities take place. This is where activity partitions (also called 'swimlanes') come into use, figure 7.5. As you can see the total set of activities has been partitioned across three processors: *Data acquisition*, *Spectral analysis* and *System identification*. This type of presentation is very good at showing the overall processing activities carried out by systems. And, a bonus point, they are readily understood by non-specialists.

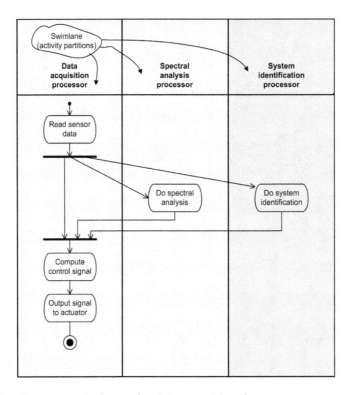

Figure 7.5 Activity diagram swimlanes (activity partitions)

7.2.2 Using signals.

The basic activity diagram can be a very useful way to describe the processing carried out by an individual software object. However, practical designs consist of sets of collaborating objects. In such cases it can be helpful (sometimes necessary) to show inter-object messaging on the activity diagrams. To do this we use send and receive signals to handle the messaging actions. An example of this is given in figure 7.6, showing interactions with an object *Profiler1*. Read through the diagram to make sure that you can follow the program flow. By now this shouldn't present any difficulty (and if you're new to activity diagrams then it can act as a useful consolidation exercise). There is, however, one important point to note relating to signal input (accept) nodes. When the execution flow reaches a signal input, UML specifies that it waits until the signal is accepted. In many (most?) embedded applications this just wouldn't be acceptable, so some sort of time-out protection is necessary. Such protection can be provided by using a time signal (more formally called a 'wait time action'), as shown in figure 7.7a. From this you can see that once the action *Switch water heater on* is completed flow continues to the time signal *Wait 30 minutes*. The arrival of the flow starts the timer action and then waits. Only when the timer expires does flow continue onwards to the action *Open*

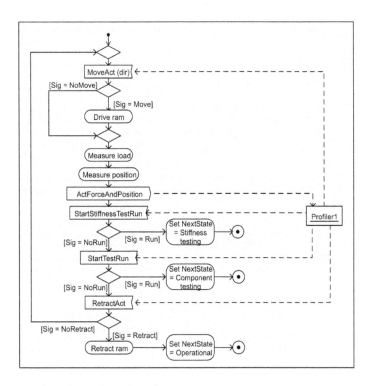

Figure 7.6 Using send and receive signals

discharge valve. Note also that if a time signal hasn't got an input it is assumed to be permanently enabled (we could use this, for example, to trigger a periodic task), figure 7.7b.

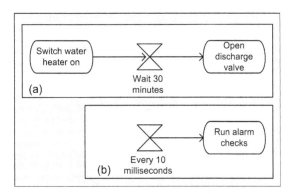

Figure 7.7 Use of time signal

7.2.3 Important but lesser-used constructs.

Two constructs that you're not likely to use very often (but are still important) are:

- The final flow node and
- Exception handling and interrupt invocations

An example that uses the final flow node is given in figure 7.8. This represents processing carried out within a multitasking system, here involving two tasks only. Processing begins with performing the action *Start all tasks*, which starts two parallel (in this case concurrent) processing operations, *Run purging task* and *Initialize plant*. When *Run purging task* completes, this activity stream finishes (behaviour typical of a run-to-completion task). However, this has no effect on the rest of the processing, which continues until the system pressure is OK. At that point the activity terminates.

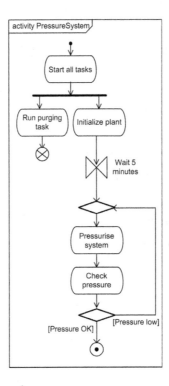

Figure 7.8 Use of the flow final node

The second construct, exception handler, would normally be implemented in code using a 'raise exception' call. Its purpose is to invoke some action to protect a system if software problems are detected (e.g. data out of range, number overflow, etc.). This concept is shown in figure 7.9a.

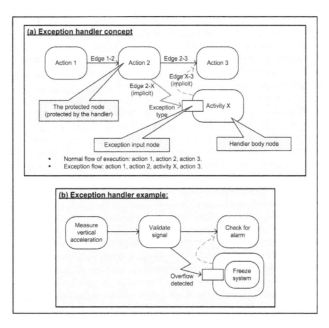

Figure 7.9 Exception handling and interrupt invocation

Strictly speaking there are two parts to the protection action, fault detection and exception raising. Here the processing to be protected is that of 'Action 2', defined to be a protected node. If the code here detects a program violation it unconditionally transfers program control to the exception handler activity 'Activity X'. A concrete example is given in figure 7.9b, where the the protected node action validates the incoming signal data. If overflow is detected then an exception is raised and control transferred to the exception handler *Freeze system*. According to the UML specification the next action to be performed is *Check for alarm*. Unfortunately, in reality this is something that we'd rarely (if ever) do in real-time embedded systems. So, if you use this construct but intend to deviate from the specified behaviour, please provide a note on your diagram.

If your programming language doesn't include an exception raising mechanism you can mimic it by invoking an interrupt (either hardware or software, as you wish).

7.3 Why program structure diagrams?

Program structure diagrams, when used for design purposes, *specify* the code structure of programs. But, in reality, how useful are such diagrams? This section sets out to answer that question; it also aims to convince you that it really is a good idea to employ these diagrams.

Let's start by considering the situation depicted in figure 7.10. Here the requirement is to implement a complex algorithmic specification in source code.

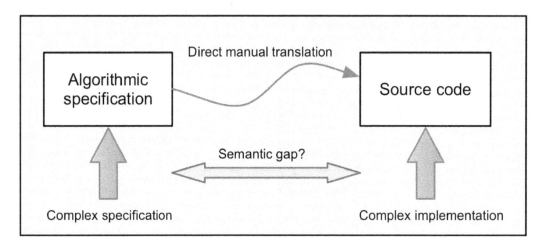

Figure 7.10 Specification to code - a semantic gap

Clearly, if the specification is complex then the resulting implementation will also be complex. And that is a very undesirable situation as it may very well cause problems, in two ways:

- First, we may not properly understand the specifications and thus incorrectly specify the code requirements. So, while the code implementation may be faultless, it doesn't solve the right problem.
- Second, we may make mistakes in implementing the (correct) specification, thus failing to solve the problem correctly.

With very complex issues there can be a huge semantic gap between the problem and the solution domains. In such cases it's always possible that we may also incorrectly solve an incorrectly specified problem. Once again we look to diagramming to help us to tame this complexity. Specifically we'll use the activity diagram both to describe the software requirement *and* to specify the resulting program structure (see next section).

Some of you may well feel that it's sufficient to work with class diagrams; anything beyond that isn't for real coders! So let's look at taking on the requirement to produce a code solution to the following algorithmic requirement:

===

Activity: Run System Supervisor
(Part of an algorithmic specification for an experimental avionic adaptive autopilot controller)

Compute the average of the absolute value of the control error. Perform a stability check and decide whether the process is fully stable, unstable or marginally stable. If fully stable, no further action is to be taken. If unstable, reset the controller to a sub-optimal but stable condition. If the process is marginally stable, carry out a trend analysis of the data to determine further action.

If unstable: To determine the next best controller action, first detune the self-tuning regulator adaptive mechanism. Then load the controller with a known (predetermined) safe set of control parameters and reset it. Call on the expert system to determine if the problem is due to an incorrect model assumption, an inappropriate identification assumption, too great a demand on the capabilities of the controller and/or unaccounted or extraneous environmental disturbances.

If marginally stable: Call the trend analyser to perform linear curve fitting on the data and so predict future changes to stability margins. If the trend is towards full stability, no action need be taken. If the margin is predicted to deteriorate, call the expert system as detailed above.

==

This, by the way, has been taken verbatim from the technical manual of a real avionic project; it isn't a made-up problem.

A class-based approach to this could well result in the solution shown in figure 7.11, involving one class only.

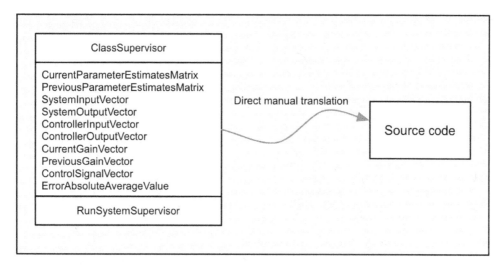

Figure 7.11 Specification to code - how helpful is the class diagram?

As you can see, the class has many attributes but needs only one public method. It hasn't taken much effort to arrive at this result, but now for the really important question. Has it helped in any way to close the semantic gap between the real requirements and their code solution? I think that you can very easily work out the answer to that. But, will we fare any better by using activity diagrams?

Earlier it was pointed out that there are two distinct aspects to this work. The first one is to make sure that the correct problem is being solved; that's what we'll take on now. Applying activity diagrams to formalize written requirements brings great rigour to the analysis process. And, as previously mentioned, these diagrams can be used as a communication medium: in particular to provide feedback to our 'customer'. Figure 7.12 shows the result of re-defining the text specifications as an activity diagram; please check that it correctly represents the original specification.

And now for a small digression into design practices. Many of you may be surprised at some of the details, in particular the duplication of actions 'Run the expert system' and 'Record info for post-flight analysis'. This has come about because the diagram has been developed using the rules of structured programming, discussed in the next section. Both actions are likely to be implemented as functions, and so the duplication will result in extra function calls in the code (requiring more ROM space). Some programmers would regard this as an unnecessary waste of resources, but is it really a problem? No; in reality it's a trivial overhead (and if you're worried about this overhead you really do need to have a good look at your design). What we gain, however, is a robust, easily testable and easily maintainable code structure, something to be prized

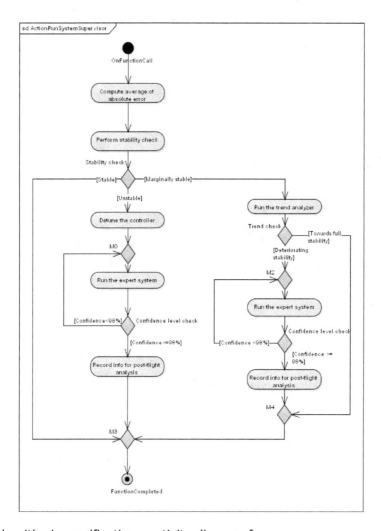

Figure 7.12 Algorithmic specification - activity diagram form

7.4 Structuring and decomposing activity diagrams.

The original flow charts were quite good at dealing with small problems. However, when they were used to tackle larger ones (i.e. full programs) they really didn't scale up very well. Such designs usually ended up scattered across many pages, making it extremely difficult to:

- See the overall picture.
- Debug existing programs.
- Evaluate the effects of changes.
- Maintain the design.

These deficiencies led to the development in the 1960's and 70's of structured, multi-layered structure charts such as those of Yourdon, Jackson, Rothon and Nassi-Schneiderman. And then the activity diagrams of UML 1 brought us full circle back to the 1950's!

Fortunately UML 2 has remedied things to some extent by allowing activities to be decomposed. With this we can produce designs that minimize the problems listed above, by building them in a structured, top-down stepwise manner. Let us now do this with the autopilot algorithm discussed earlier, starting with a top-level design (figure 7.13).

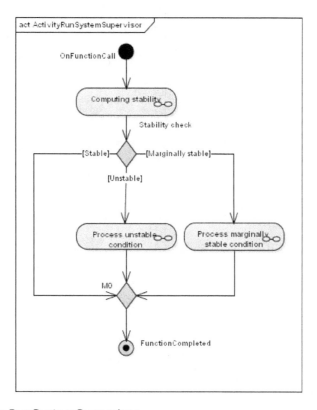

Figure 7.13 Activity RunSystemSupervisor

The overall activity consists of three sub-activities, each of these showing a decomposition symbol (the standard decomposition symbol of an activity looks like a small rake; the one here is CASE-tool specific).   What this tells us is that each sub-activity is actually the topmost part of some hierarchy of activities or actions.   For simplicity we'll call these 'structured' activities. When we invoke a structured activity we actually start a lower-level activity, as shown in figures 7.14 and 7.15.

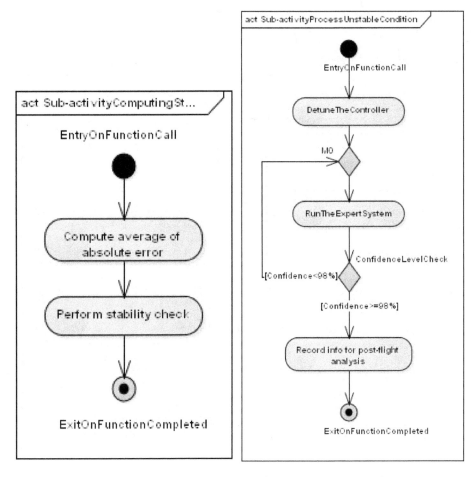

Figure 7.14 Sub-activity1
ComputingStability

Figure 7.15 Sub-activity 2
ProcessUnstableCondition

The advantages of using this technique in the design of software have been well and truly discussed; further words are unnecessary.

7.5 Applying activity diagram symbols to interaction overview diagrams.

Interaction overview diagrams were introduced in chapter 5 as part of the behavioural interactions model. The examples given were fairly straightforward, involving sequential sets of interaction fragments. However, by incorporating activity diagram symbols into the overview diagrams, we can describe much more complex situations, as in figure 7.16.

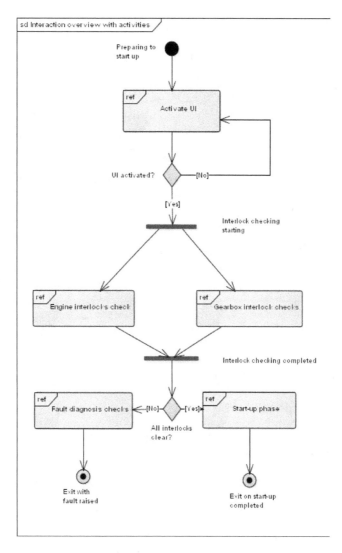

Figure 7.16 Interaction overview with activities

This is a very straightforward topic and the diagram should (at this stage) be self-explanatory.

7.6 Code-related aspects of program design.

For us a keystone in program design is the use of structured programming (SP) techniques. There are sound theoretical and practical reasons that support this approach; in fact I can't think why you wouldn't go down this route. However, a detailed discussion is beyond the scope of this book, so for the moment just take it on trust.

SP has three basic control constructs: sequence, selection and iteration, figure 7.17.

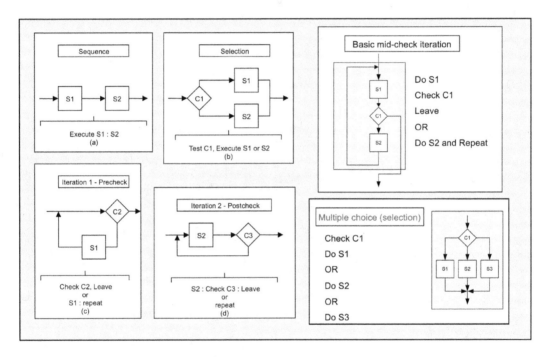

Fig. 7.17 Basic control structures of SP

Iterations actually come in three forms: pre-check, post-check and mid-check. Also, the simple selection example is really a special case of the more general multiple choice one. And that's all you need for the building of sound programs!

Central to these structures is the rule that unconditional transfers of control are forbidden (aka the great 'GO TO' debate). In practice we do have to use such operations in embedded software, but only for abnormal conditions (such as exception handling). And you've already seen how to portray this in activity diagrams.

Now, as an exercise, let us develop ways to show the standard constructs using pseudo-code. Having done that we can then map these into our actual programming language using defined mapping methods. Referring to figure 7.17:

==

Simple selection:

```
If CheckTestConditionTrue
   then
      DoActionS1
   else
      DoActionS2
end If
```
==

Pre-check iteration:

```
WhileTestConditionTrue
   DoActionS1
end While
```
==

Post-Check iteration:

```
Repeat
   DoActionS2
UntilTestConditionTrue
end Repeat
```
==

Mid-check iteration:

```
Loop
   DoActionS1
   ExitIf CheckTestConditionTrue
   DoActionS2
end Loop
```
==

Multiple choice (selection):

```
Check TestConditionValue
      TestCondition = Route1; DoActionS1; exit
      TestCondition = Route2; DoActionS2; exit
      TestCondition = Route3; DoActionS3; exit
      else exit
end Check
```
==

The result of applying these to figure 7.13 is as follows:

```
==================================================

ProgramStart
  DoComputingStability
  Check StabilityStatus
    StabilityStatus = Stable; Exit
    StabilityStatus = Unstable; DoProcessUnstableCondition(); exit
    StabilityStatus=MarginallyStable;DoProcessMarginallyStableCondition(); exit
    else exit
  end Check
ProgramFinish
==================================================
```

Mapping this into C or C++ gives the following program fragment:

```
==================================================

switch (StabilityStatus)
{
    case Stable: break;
    case Unstable: ProcessUnstableCondition;
    break;
    case MarginallyStable: ProcessMarginallyStableCondition;
    break;
    default: break;
}
==================================================
```

It is very strongly recommended that you define precisely how the diagram should be mapped to source code. If you do this then, when you look at an activity diagram, you know exactly what to expect in the source code. This is makes code reviewing a much simpler process and it also helps in debugging. For instance, suppose the code doesn't execute properly but you know that the design is correct. Also, you verify that the mapping to code has been done correctly. So, what does this tell you? It is that the problem must lie in the detailed code implementation. Over to the programmers!

7.7 Review.

You should now:
- Understand what process modelling is and how it helps in the specification and analysis of designs.
- Understand how UML activity diagrams relate to process modelling.
- Know what the following items are, how they are used and how they are shown diagrammatically:
    - Action nodes and actions.

- Flow final, decision, merge, fork and join nodes.
- Guards.
- Send, receive and time signals.
- Activity partitions (swimlanes)
- Exception handlers.

- Be able to model sequential and parallel flows using activity diagrams.
- Appreciate why errors may occur in both analyzing and implementing complex requirements.
- Understand how activity diagrams can be used both to formalize requirements and to specify program structures.
- Be able to employ activity diagram constructs on interaction overview diagrams.
- Appreciate why activity diagrams help to reduce errors in the source code.
- Perceive that structured, top-down step-wise refinement techniques make it easier to design and implement software.
- Know what a decomposition symbol is and what it signifies.
- Know how to implement structured design methods by decomposing activities.
- Know the basic control structures of structured programming and be able to implement these in your chosen programming language.
- Understand how to use activity diagrams as program structure charts.
- Appreciate why we should use defined rules for the mapping of activity diagrams to source code.

END OF CHAPTER

Chapter 8

The usage model

The objectives of this chapter are to:

- Introduce the topic of use case analysis.
- Demonstrate the content and application of the use case model and the use case diagram.
- Describe what scenarios are and how they relate to use cases.
- Show how use cases may be described and structured.
- Illustrate why use case documentation needs structuring.

8.1 Introduction to usage modelling - use case analysis.

Without a doubt, the analysis methodology of use cases has made an immense impact on the software scene. It is probably **the** dominant requirements analysis and specification method in the software world of business systems. Although less widely used in the embedded world, it is still a very important topic. What the methodology sets out to do is help us to:

- Analyze clients requirements.
- Organize and present requirements in a way that is useful, meaningful and complete.
- Minimize confusion and misunderstanding between clients and suppliers.
- Validate system-level designs.
- Develop specifications for the software system itself.
- Define the outlines of system acceptance tests (for function, performance and usage).

Unfortunately the UML specification gives only a very limited coverage of this topic. Essentially what you get is a sparse description of how to apply various diagrams without any real reasoning about their use. Yet to employ use case methods effectively, you *do* need a deeper understanding of the subject. Hence the purpose of this whole section is to provide a good appreciation of use case basics.

The underlying ideas are really quite simple, being based on the fact that people are users of systems, figure 8.1   And, in general, system requirements are related to the whats, whens and hows of people/system interactions. *That* is what we set out to define as part of the requirements analysis process.

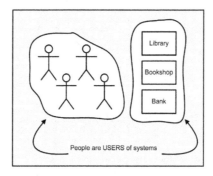

Figure 8.1 Use cases - setting the scene

Of course, the real world contains many people and many systems.   First we must establish exactly what is of interest to us, which could be shown as in figure 8.2.

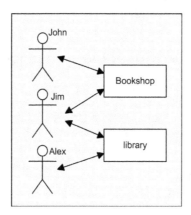

Figure 8.2 Systems and their users

Although this is a step in the right direction, the diagram has one great shortcoming. We have no idea *why* the people are using these systems. This leads on to the basics of the use case diagram, figure 8.3. It shows (figure 8.3a):

- The system of concern is a bookshop.
- There are two users (specifically two individuals).
- The individuals are using the system to order a book (or books). Any illustration of the usage of a system is defined to be a 'use case'; hence this example is the use case 'order book'.

From the system's point of view the two users are essentially the same; both are customers.   Therefore, rather than focussing on individuals, we try to identify the 'roles' they play in the interaction. In this example both people are 'customers', figure 8.3b.

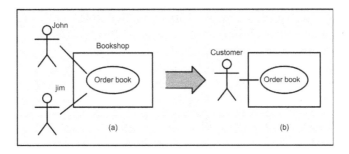

Figure 8.3 The basics of the use case diagram

At this stage most of the ideas of the use case model has been established. However, it still isn't complete; we have no idea what actually goes on when a customer tries to order a book. Thus the diagram symbol needs to be backed up by a text description, figure 8.4. Here we have the essential components of a use case: a diagram symbol and a text description of the user/system interaction.

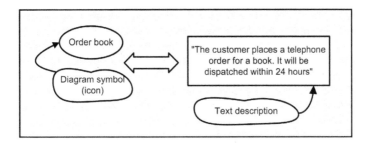

Figure 8.4 The two components of a use case

And, please note: there is no need to limit yourself to text; anything which imparts information can be used. But more of that later.

From this it is but a small step to establish the components of the use case *model*, figure 8.5.

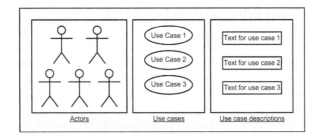

Figure 8.5 The components of the use case **model**

This consists of actors, use cases and use case descriptions. Each system will have its own model, with actors depicting users (more correctly, roles performed by users). The reasons why these actors are using the system are shown as a set of use cases within the system boundary. Supporting these are the use case descriptions. Two simple examples are given in figure 8.6.

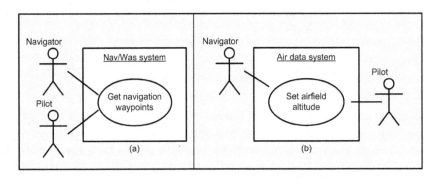

Figure 8.6 Example use case diagrams

Each system is drawn as a rectangular box, with the relevant use cases shown as ellipses inside them. Outside the system boundary are the actors, connected via lines to the use cases. In 8.6a both the navigator actor and the pilot actor interact with the navigation/ weapon aiming (Nav/Was) system in the same way; they use it to find out what the navigation waypoints are. Information flow is a two-way process. In 8.6b, the navigator uses the air data system to set airfield altitude: again a two-way process. However, in this case, the pilot merely receives information from the system; the role played by the actor is thus a 'passive' one.

Summarizing things to date: the use case diagram shows all users of the system and their reasons for using the system. It should go without saying that all items on the diagram must have useful, relevant and meaningful names. Moreover, we have to be clear exactly where our system boundary lies. In the example given, both systems are *within* the overall aircraft system (figure 8.7).

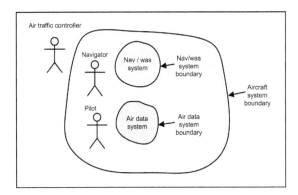

Figure 8.7 System boundaries

However, from the perspective of an air traffic controller the pilot and navigator themselves form part of the *aircraft* system.

A small aside at this point. There have been many definitions of the term use case. Here we'll define it as 'a way that an actor uses a system to achieve some desired result'. This result or 'goal' should determine the wording used on the use case diagram. If you can't express your goals simply then you don't understand what you're trying to do.

8.2 Describing, structuring and packaging use cases.

Now let us look into the use case text descriptions in more detail. It is *strongly* recommended that the initial one should be short, clear and use ordinary language, figure 8.8a. A structured, formalized version can be used to expand on this at a later stage, figure 8.8b. Trying to do this in the beginning is often a hindrance to clear thinking.

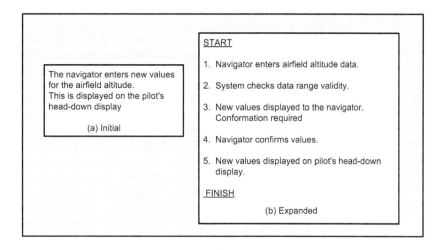

Figure 8.8 Text description - initial and expanded versions

Observe that, in the example, the text is enclosed between a START and a FINISH marker. The starting point is pretty self-evident; when the actor begins to use the system. Thus a use case always has a single starting point. This however, is not necessarily true for the finish condition, a point of much confusion. Alistair Cockburn's definition (see note at the end of this chapter) is clear and practical: 'a use case is finished when the goal is achieved or abandoned'. That's good enough for me. And this nicely leads into the topic of *scenarios*, figure 8.9.

Figure 8.9a is a description of what happens assuming that everything is ok. This is one *scenario* (a particular sequence of actions and interactions) for the use case 'Set airfield altitude'. The scenario, identified as 'Data within valid range', has a single finish point. But what of the situation where the data entered is *not* within the pre-defined range? The interactions which take place in these circumstances are shown in figure 8.9b. Here, if the data is invalid it is rejected and a request made for new data. This is a second, valid sequence of interactions for the use case, a second scenario.

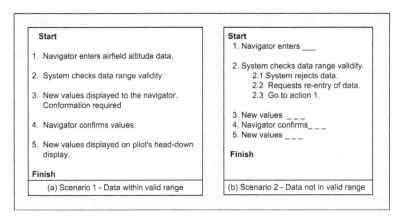

Figure 8.9 Scenarios - text description

We can simplify our paperwork by combining scenarios as shown in figure 8.10a. Moreover, if it helps, we can use diagrams to show the logic of the scenarios, figure 8.10b. This also brings out that there are two distinct routes through the use case text: therefore two scenarios.

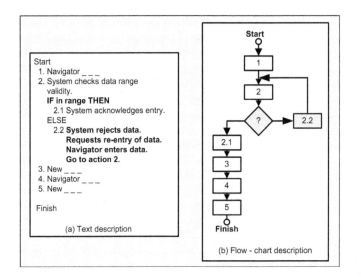

Figure 8.10 Combining scenarios

Showing the logic of the scenarios using flow charts (or activity diagrams) is an informal way of doing things. The UML specification gives an example showing the behaviour of a use case using a state machine (as, for example, figure 8.11). Unfortunately it doesn't make it clear whether this is *the* preferred method or merely a demonstration.

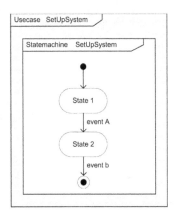

Figure 8.11 Use case behaviour - state machine description

Now, returning to scenarios. In reality here are three kinds of scenarios, as follows:

- Normal (error-free) use of the system.
- Uses where errors occur but which can be dealt with as part of the interaction process (e.g. entering invalid data).
- Uses where errors occur but which cannot be dealt with as part of the normal processing (exceptions).

   As we combine more and more scenarios, text documents soon become complex, difficult to read, difficult to understand. Hardly a step forward for mankind, as the whole point of use cases is to make things understandable. One way of simplifying documents is to take a leaf out of programming techniques; use the equivalent of subprograms and subprogram calls (figure 8.12).

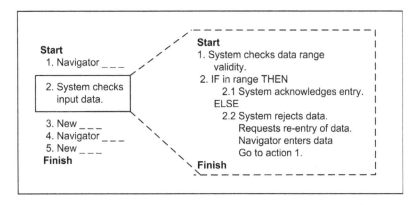

Figure 8.12 Simplifying use case descriptions

Here we aim to write the 'top-level' text as a set of sequential operations; where necessary these can be expanded in a separate text document. In fact, the separate text can be treated as a use case in its own right, figure 8.13.

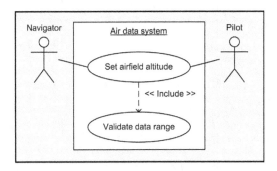

Figure 8.13 Use case diagram for figure 8.12 – the include relationship

The use case 'Set airfield altitude' – the *base* use case - is considered to include that of 'Validate data range'; this is defined to be an *includes* relationship. We can read the diagram to mean that the base use case *will* use the behaviour of the included use; moreover it will do so at explicit points. One last aspect of the includes relationship; the included use case should always form some part of a base use case. It is not meant to be a use case in its own right. Moreover, the included use case is an integral part of the base one; without this the base use case is incomplete. Observe the notation used and the direction of the arrow.

Now there are situations where a base use case is complete, as per the 'Check alarm status' of figure 8.14.

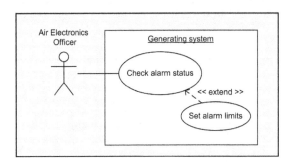

Figure 8.14 The extend relationship

Here the Air Electronics Officer starts the base use case 'Check alarm status' to check out the generating system alarms. Most of the time this is the only action which is carried out. However, on certain occasions it may be necessary to (re)set alarm limits. In these circumstances extra functions are performed, defined in the use case 'Set alarm limits'. Thus the functionality of the base use case is *extended* by the second one. This is denoted by drawing an arrowed line from the extended class to the base class.

The distinction between includes and extends causes much confusion. One way to resolve this is to ask the question 'if I remove the (included/extended) use case, is the base use case complete?' Another view is that:

- Include use cases collect in one place behaviour common to a number of base use cases, figure 8.15a.
- Extend use cases show variations on a theme, figure 8.15b.

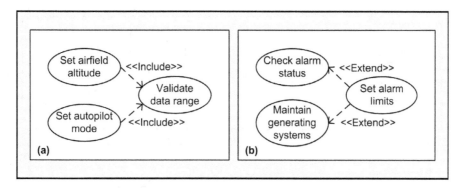

Figure 8.15 Comparing the includes and extends relationships

Up to this point we have used actors to represent the roles of people. But frequently systems interact, not only with people, but with other systems, figure 8.16a.

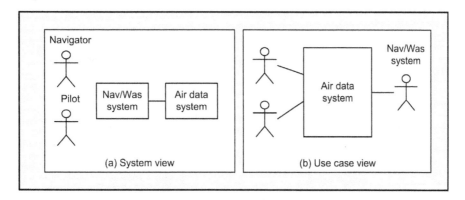

Figure 8.16 External systems as actors

Here the Nav/Was system uses information provided by the air data system. Thus, from the point of view of the air data system, the Nav/Was system is merely another actor, figure 8.16b. Where devices are treated as actors the notation of figure 8.17 can be used to identify them (note that these notations can also be used in place of the stick figure wherever appropriate).

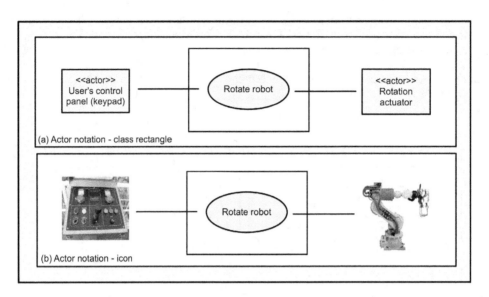

Figure 8.17 Representing devices as actors - UML notation

A major weakness with use case diagrams are that they are essentially one-level types; there really aren't constructs to support top-down modelling with decomposition via step-wise refinement. So if you intend to actually employ use case methods, read Cockburns work. He gives some excellent advice on this topic. The best we can do with standard UML is to carve up large use case diagrams into smaller, more manageable chunks, figure 8.18. Here the overall use case diagram has been packaged into smaller units, based on areas of concern.

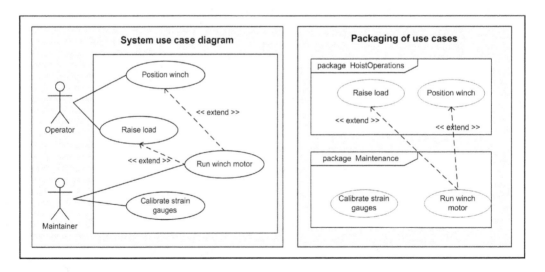

Figure 8.18 Use cases and packages

8.3 Review.

You should now:

- Understand the basics of use cases, use case models and use case diagrams.
- Feel confident to start developing use case models for real systems.
- Know what actors are, and distinguish between users and roles.
- Understand that actors can be used to model both people and systems.
- Be able to define the detailed actions within use cases using activity and state diagrams.
- Understand what scenarios are and how they relate to use cases.
- Appreciate that when scenarios are combined, the resulting documentation may be complex.
- Understand the need for structuring use case documents in larger systems.
- Know how to use include and extend use cases.
- Appreciate how large use cases diagrams can be partitioned using package diagrams and why we'd want to do this.
- Understand the basics of a goal-driven approach to use case structuring.

END OF CHAPTER

Chapter 9

Practical diagramming issues

The objectives of this chapter are to:

- Explain why it's important from a diagramming perspective to have well-structured software.
- Describe in outline terms how large programs should be structured and explain how to design and build such software.
- Introduce the concept and practicalities of application-level and service-level software.
- Give a broad-brush view of Object-Oriented Design and Object-Oriented Programming techniques.
- Show how UML diagrams relate to the four major design models: usage, structure, behaviour and processing.
- Give guidance to help you choose the diagrams most suited to particular levels of software design.

9.1 Setting the scene.

When you first come to UML it's easy to be overwhelmed by the sheer amount of information. With all these diagrams to choose from, just where do you start? Which ones are going to be useful? How will they fit into *your* project? Are they *really* going to help you to produce better designs? These are difficult questions to answer if you have little experience in using diagrams for design. So what this section sets out to do is to give advice and guidance to help you choose what's right for you. It's also important that you understand that such advice and guidance is basically descriptive and *not* prescriptive. In real life there's never a single right way to do things. Moreover, different problems after require different solutions.

   A major assumption is that you will produce the diagrams using either CASE tools or drawing packages. CASE tools are significantly more powerful than drawing tools, so that's our recommended approach. However, if you *do* decide to use a drawing package, at least get one that includes UML diagram templates. Once you have chosen your tool it's now essential to understand what it can and can't do vis-a-vis standard UML. Find its restrictions, limitations and extensions, then adopt the tool features as *your* working standard. There's no reason to adopt *all* the tool features, a subset may be perfectly good enough for specific projects. A golden rule is to avoid complexity like the plague; simplicity and clarity are the keywords. And if you are working on a team project, consider producing a 'style' guide for diagram production.

9.2 Building well-structured embedded software.

If you structure your software in a clear, logical manner, then you'll be able to use diagrams in a more effective and efficient way. By that I mean it becomes much easier to decide *which* diagrams to use, *where* to use them and *how* to use them. The modern way of constructing well-structured software is based on the concept of independent design and build, as depicted in figure 9.1.

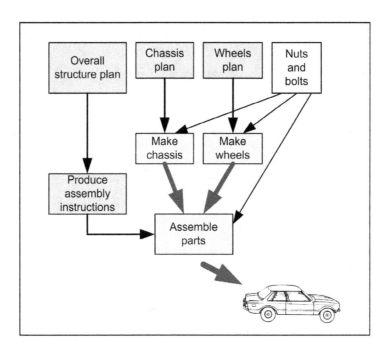

Figure 9.1 Independent design and build concept

This is a simplified view of automobile manufacture, sufficient to explain the basic principles. The key point is that building the vehicle is primarily an assembly of pre-built components. These components have previously been made in accordance with their design specifications; now they are integrated to form the whole vehicle. What is also extremely important here is the choice of the pre-built components; cohesive functionality and simple interfaces are central factors.

The software equivalent of this is shown in figure 9.2. This is very general in concept, and applies to different structures. For example, if it represented a sequential program build then the sub-systems are likely to be individual software modules. These, in turn, could be based on composite object structures, especially where the subsystems are complex. Similarly, in a multitasking design each subsystem could represent an individual task. In all cases, however, a crucial point is the separation of the software into two major groups, application and service levels.

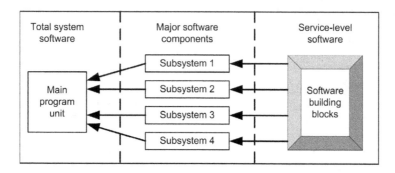

Figure 9.2 Fundamental structure of large programs

Application-level software is exactly what it says; it's the software that's needed for the system to operate correctly, both functionally and temporally. Service-level software is concerned with all the low-level building blocks, so named because these provide a service to the application layer, figure 9.3 (the term 'driver' doesn't really reflect the extent of such software).

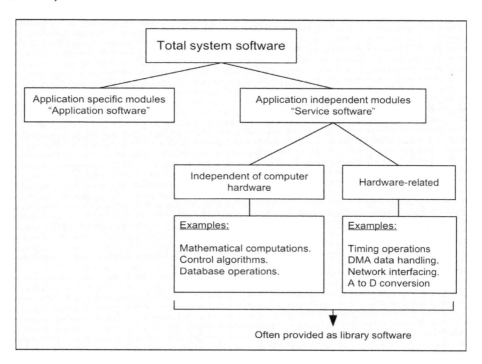

Figure 9.3 Application and service modules

Moreover, their functions are essentially independent of the applications (although we may well develop a piece of such software for a specific application). Broadly speaking, service software splits into two groupings, hardware-related and hardware-independent. Much of this will have to be developed in-house, though we may also be able to use vendor-supplied Commercial Off The Shelf (COTS) software.

9.3 Using the right diagrams - 1.

9.3.1 General comment.

Sometimes it seems that designers produce diagrams just for the sake of producing diagrams. But, as pointed out right at the beginning of this book, diagrams are a means to an end. Therefore it's essential that you first identify your particular ends (your objectives) for each stage of the design process. Having done that you then need to decide precisely which diagrams are *needed* to meet these objectives. As shown earlier there are four major design models:

- Usage
- Structure
- Behaviour
- Processing

In the following sections some general guidance is given to help you choose the diagrams that *should* be produced when building these models.

9.3.2 Usage.

Remember, the purpose of the usage model is to analyse system requirements and, from these, generate the software specifications. The requirements of many small embedded systems are relatively straightforward, especially if there aren't user interactions (hence no need for HMIs). In such cases text descriptions are all that are needed; diagrams are a bit of an overkill. However, once systems need to interface to external 'users' (either people or other systems) then use case techniques should be employed. At the very minimum this should include use case diagrams and associated scenario descriptions. As interactions become more complex these should be augmented using flow charts (or activity diagrams) and/or state diagrams. All important timing requirements should also be included with the use case descriptions.

9.3.3 Structure.

Structure diagrams should always be produced for application-level designs. Class and object diagrams are the core aspects of such design, but we don't necessarily need both. A design that excludes classes is here called an object-oriented design (OOD) method; when classes are included we define it to be an object-oriented programming (OOP) method. Let us deal first with OOD techniques, specifically the use of the object diagram.

   Put simply, the aim of the object diagram is to specify how a system should 'work' (or, for an existing system, how it actually works). However this diagram, in itself, doesn't contain sufficient information; what we also need to show is all system messaging, both between objects and to/from the outside world. Adding messages to the object diagram results in, of course, the object communication diagram. The information given there enables us to specify two things (figure 9.4):

- The structures of the software machines that implement the objects and
- The structure and behaviour of the executable code.

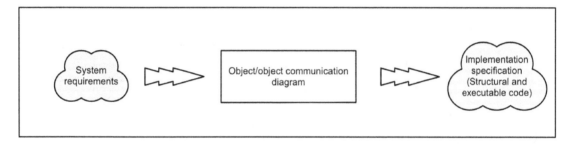

Figure 9.4 Object-first OOD design approach

   As the design doesn't include classes it can (if desired) be implemented using procedural languages such as C. In this case it is entirely up to the designer to decide how the objects should be built and how messaging is supported. One simple method is to implement the objects using functions (sub-programs), having parameter passing as the communication mechanism.

   A frequently asked question is 'what's the upper limit to the number of objects in any one design?'. There isn't a simple answer to this; much depends on individual designs and the degree of coupling between objects. Based on personal experience, I believe that if you have more than 10 objects showing at any one level, the design should be carefully re-assessed. Above this number it becomes increasingly difficult to quickly and easily understand the design structure and its operation. Review your design, look at how you arrived at the object model in the first place, and consider using modular objects to simplify the design.

   The basis for the OOP technique is shown in figure 9.5. Here, as before, the object and object communication diagrams are the first to be produced. From these we can generate the specifications for the executable code structure and behaviour. Next, the class model can be derived from the object model via a classification process (as described earlier).

This is used to specify the structure of the software machines needed to implement the objects.

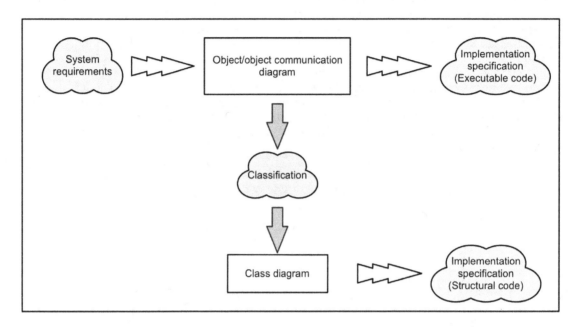

Figure 9.5 Object-first OOP design approach

Now for a very personal point of view. I consider that the client-server software model is a poor choice for the development of embedded software systems. Instead, right from the word go, base your design on a materials flow model using composite connectable structures. This, of course, doesn't preclude client-server techniques (or publish-subscribe methods), but these should be used sparingly.

Don't even consider using model-based designs unless you:

- Are developing quite large systems and
- Have the appropriate technology at hand.

Finally, what of package, artifact and deployment diagrams? Although they have interesting and useful features, many developers instead prefer to use commercial products such as:

- Integrated development environments.
- CASE tools.
- Analysis, visualization and maintenance tools such as Understand (scitools.com) or Polyspace (mathworks.com)

9.3.4 Behaviour and interactions.

If your design includes concurrently executing software units it is *essential* to describe the details of their interactions. And the best way of modelling such interactions is to show them using sequence diagrams. Being more dogmatic; all intercommunication between concurrent units should *always* be modelled using sequence diagrams. Moreover, important timing information should also be included on such diagrams. The purpose of this is to explicitly specify (to implementers) exactly what the software performance requirements are.

Sequence diagrams can also be very helpful during the development of sequentially-executing software units. A particularly useful feature is to show the message flows through the system (on a scenario by scenario basis) and so test the object model design. This same technique should, of course, be applied to concurrent software designs.

9.3.5 Behaviour and dynamics.

Where systems and/or software are dynamically simple, then text is sufficient to describe their behaviour. However, as things become more complex, so too does the complexity of text descriptions. It is much much better to now replace such text with diagrams. And the most appropriate one is the state diagram.

State modelling is a very powerful technique, one that should *always* be applied to complex dynamical systems. It is at its best when used to describe the behavioural aspects of *individual* entities including, for example:

- Real devices such as robots, digital watches, smart televisions, etc.
- Software units such as components, tasks, threads and modules.

A personal view: state machines are *not* well suited to describing the collective behaviour of concurrent units. If you go down this route then you'll find yourself regularly having to split and/or combine individual state models: not a trivial task.

9.3.6 Processing.

First, it is worth clarifying the distinction between the dynamical and the processing models (in diagram terms, state diagrams vs activity diagrams). A simple view is that state diagrams essentially define *when* things should be done; activity diagrams describe exactly *what* is to be done. Recognize that these are complementary, not alternatives.

As you will have seen from the processing model chapter, activity diagrams have a number of uses. They are, for example, a neat way to describe the processing carried out by concurrent units, especially where activities have to be synchronized. In cases like this they are mainly used to explain how systems work or to specify how they *should* work. We don't necessarily intend to translate such diagrams directly into code (their role being more of a communication rather than implementation mechanism). Also, when parallel activities interact, such interactions should *always* be described using activity diagrams (unless the interactions are trivial).

In practice the greatest use of activity diagrams is to describe the processing carried out by software units (these acting as program structure diagrams).   Any processing beyond the very simplest should *always* be defined in this way.   Therefore we'd expect to find activity diagrams being used in virtually all software projects, irrespective of size.

9.4 Using the right diagrams - 2.

If you've understood the advice given so far you should have a good idea which diagrams best suit your needs. In effect you've selected the range of diagrams most useful to you. But there is still one question left unanswered; which ones are you going to use in specific situations?   So to help you on your way this section sets out to provide some useful, practical guidance.   And please, treat it only as guidance; in the end you have to make your own decisions.
   Nine levels of software complexity are shown in figure 9.6, level 1 being the simplest, level 9 the most complex.   So, which diagrams should we use in these various situations? And note well: it's implicit here that the software requirements for these cases have already been established.

Software level	Software complexity	Example system	
Application level	9. Multicomputer designs - distributed systems	Advanced landing gear system	Concurrent software
	8. Multitasking designs - true concurrency (multiprocessor or multicore units)	Flight control system	
	7. Multitasking designs - quasi-concurrency (single processor)	Control, monitoring and alarm protection for a small plant	
	6. Complex dynamic functionality	Small plant sequence controller	Sequential software
	5. Simple dynamical-type application	Robot single axis control	
	4. Algorithm-type application	3-term digital controller	
Service level	3. Complex interfacing s/w	Serial comms interfacing	
	2. More complex board-specific s/w	Board self-test routines	
	1. Simple functionality	Configuration of port	

Figure 9.6 Software project complexity levels

(a) Level 1 - Simple functionality.
An example of simple functionality is the work need to configure a programmable I/O port on a processor or peripheral chip.   This, while usually quite detailed, normally requires only a few lines of sequential code for its implementation. There really is no need to use

diagrams in situations like this; well-commented source code is perfectly good enough. Typically we use software functions to encapsulate the code.

(b) Level 2 - More complex board-specific software.
Now consider a somewhat more complex example: the code needed to implement board level full self-test routines. Although much of this is sequential in nature it usually employs many conditional and repetitive operations. In such cases it may be difficult to quickly and correctly understand the software function and operation from text descriptions. A far better approach is to describe such aspects using activity diagrams.

If programming is to be done using an OO language, it may be useful to develop a board test class.

(c) Level 3 - Complex interfacing software.
Higher levels of complexity are often a feature of driver software. Take, for example, the software needed to provide full interfacing to a 4-colour inkjet cartridge unit via a serial link. Here the required code is usually extensive, having a variety of operational modes. Any text description is going to be complex, possibly tortuous and likely to be difficult to understand.
Diagrams should definitely be used, the most appropriate ones being the activity and the state diagram.

For an OO implementation a class may be used to encapsulate the code.

(d) Level 4 - Algorithm-type application.
Typical of this is the software needed to implement a digital three term controller. The code is basically algorithmic in nature (with little or no dynamics), best described using activity diagrams.

For an OO implementation a class may be used to encapsulate the code.

(e) Level 5 - Simple dynamical-type application.
Requirements of this nature are frequently met in applications such as single-axis robotic control. Such systems usually have a number of distinct operational states, each one involving specific (and sometimes extensive) processing. This calls for the use of both state and activity diagrams.

As before, for an OO implementation, a class may be used to encapsulate the code.

(f) Level 6 - Complex state functionality.
Applications such as sequence controllers for small plants (e.g industrial air treatment units, pick and place units, etc.) usually involve complex state functionality. To model this we need, at the very least, to employ state and activity diagrams. For somewhat larger systems we may well develop a full object model, bringing into use sequence, object communication and (possibly) class diagrams.

(g) Level 7 - Multitasking designs (quasi-concurrency).
This level of complexity is often met in single-processor designs used for control, monitoring and alarming functions in small plants. Here the required concurrency is usually provided either by interrupts or a real-time operating system (RTOS). Thus a full-blown design must be carried out, involving object communication, sequence, state, activity and (possibly) class diagrams.

(h) Level 8 - Multitasking designs (true concurrency, multiprocessor/multicore units)
Multiprocessor or multicore structures are normally used where system performance requirements can't be satisfied by single-processor designs. The overall software design approach is very similar to that used in the previous level; hence the same set of diagrams should be produced. However, extra information is needed if the *designer* is responsible for allocating code to the various processors. It is necessary to show how the design is partitioned and where the resulting executable code is housed. If you don't really care about being totally semantically correct, then you could press the package diagram into use (but risk the ire of UML pedants). The deployment diagram doesn't really suit, especially for multicore designs. An alternative path is to use non-UML diagrams, such as the block diagram of SysML.

(i) Level 9 - Multicomputer designs, distributed systems.
This is the most complex level, and so you'd expect to be using just about the full range of UML diagrams. But it's really impossible to generalize beyond this as there are many and varied multicomputer architectures. Take, for instance, federated structures, where individual units may be designed and produced by different manufacturers. Here the role of the system designer is to get all the units working together correctly; software design doesn't enter the equation. Conversely, with avionic Integrated Modular Electronics, system designers may well carry out very high-level software design. Some form of deployment diagram is needed to show the location and interconnection of the individual units (in my experience these are usually company-specific; the UML deployment diagram is a somewhat bland piece of work).

A concise view of the use of diagrams at the different design levels is given in figure 9.7.

9.5 Review.

You should now:

- Understand the concepts of the independent design and build of software.
- Appreciate the distinction between application-level and service-level software and recognize that this split makes for good structuring.
- Know that service software contains modules that are essentially independent of their application.
- Be able to give examples of hardware-independent and hardware-related service modules.
- Be able to specify precisely what the following are used for and when they *should* be used:
  - Use case diagrams and associated scenario descriptions.
  - Object and object communication diagrams.
  - Class diagrams.
  - Sequence diagrams.
  - State diagrams.
  - Activity diagrams.
- Understand what OOD is and see how such designs can be implemented using procedural languages.

- Understand what OOP is and see that that such designs are best implemented using OO languages.
- Feel confident to categorize the complexity level of your own projects.
- Be able to select the set of UML diagrams best suited to your own work.

Software Complexity	Example system	Recommended diagrams	
9. Multicomputer designs - distributed systems	Advanced landing gear system	Sequence, object communication, state, activity and (possibly) class diagrams. Some form of deployment diagram.	Concurrent software
8. Multitasking designs - true concurrency (multiprocessor or multicore units)	Flight control system	Sequence, object communication, state, activity and (possibly) class and package diagrams.	
7. Multitasking designs - quasi-concurrency (single processor)	Control, monitoring and alarm protection for a small plant	Sequence, object communication, state, activity and (possibly) class diagrams	
6. Complex dynamic functionality	Small plant sequence controller	State and activity diagrams. Possibly also sequence, object communication and class diagrams (depending on complexity)	
5. Simple dynamical-type application	Robot single axis control	State and activity diagrams. Possibly class diagram	
4. Algorithm-type application	3-term digital controller	Activity diagram. Possibly class diagram.	Sequential software
3. Complex interfacing s/w	Serial comms interfacing	State and activity diagrams	
2. More complex board-specific s/w	Board self-test routines	Activity diagram	
1. Simple functionality	Configuration of port	Diagrams not needed	

Figure 9.7 Diagram applicability

END OF CHAPTER

Chapter 10

Outline guide to UML notation

10.1. Overview of the diagram set.

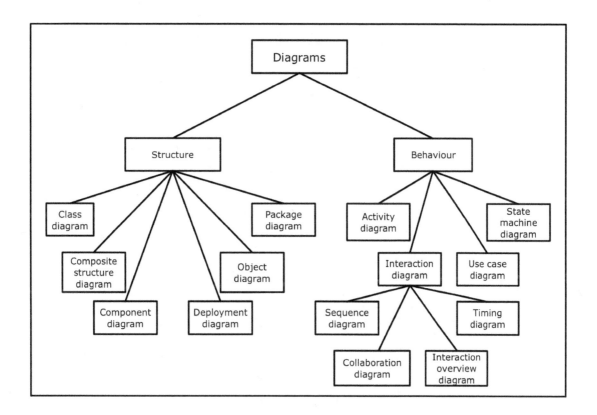

Figure 10.1 UML 2 diagrams as specified in the UML superstructure document

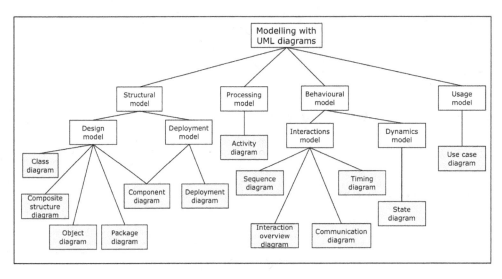

Figure 10.2 UML 2 diagrams - an application-based view

10.2. Activity diagrams.

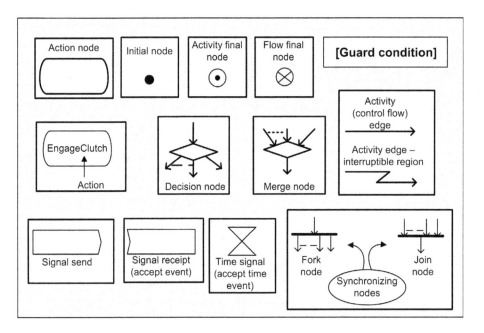

Figure 10.3 Activity diagram symbols (basic)

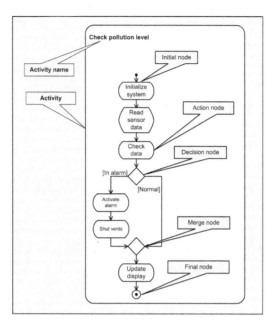

Figure 10.4 Simple activity diagram example

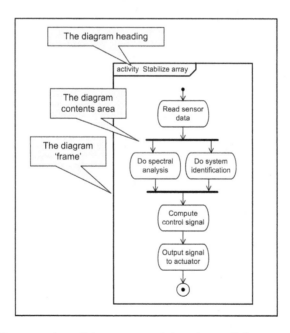

Figure 10.5 Activity diagram describing sequential and parallel processing

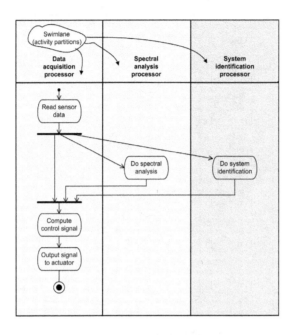

Figure 10.6 Activity diagram swimlanes (activity partitions)

10.3. Artifacts.

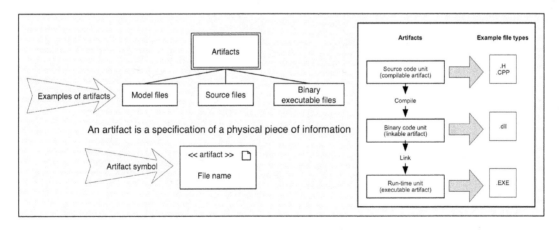

Figure 10.7 Examples of artifacts

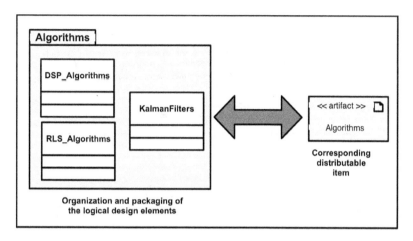

Figure 10.8 A package and its corresponding artifact

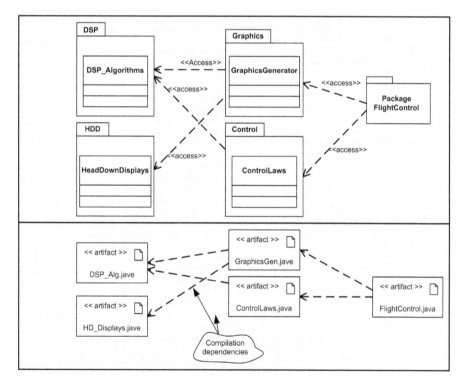

Figure 10.9 Relating packages, artifacts and dependencies

10.4. Class diagrams.

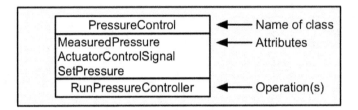

Figure 10.10 Class symbol

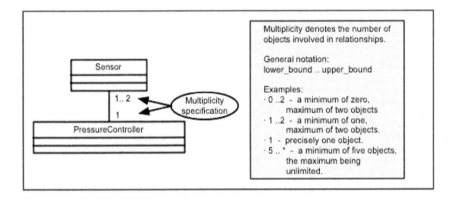

Figure 10.11 Associations and multiplicity

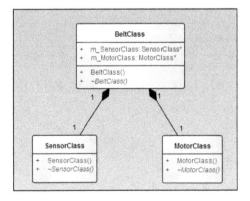

Figure 10.12 Composite aggregation example

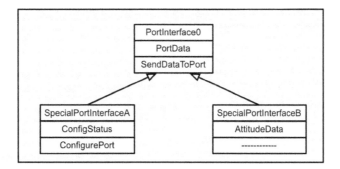

Figure 10.13 Inheritance example

10.5. Component diagrams

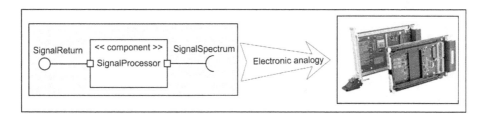

Figure 10.14 The component - external view

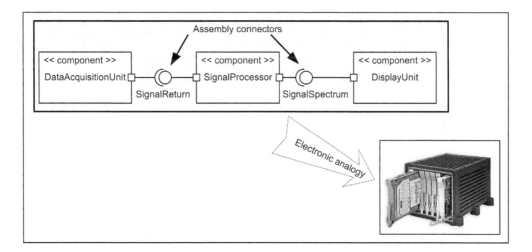

Figure 10.15 Wiring components together using assembly connectors

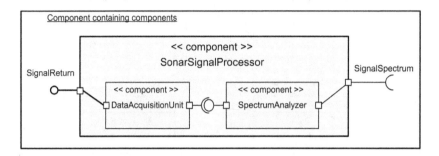

Figure 10.16 Component containing components

10.6. Deployment diagrams.

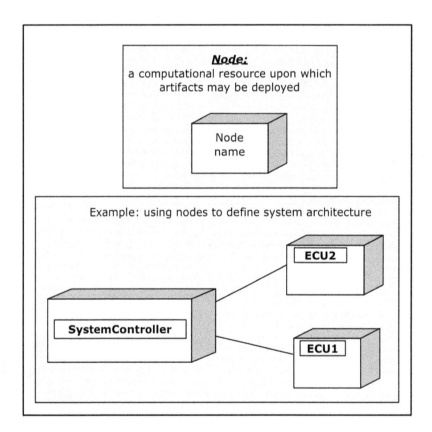

Figure 10.17 Nodes and system architecture

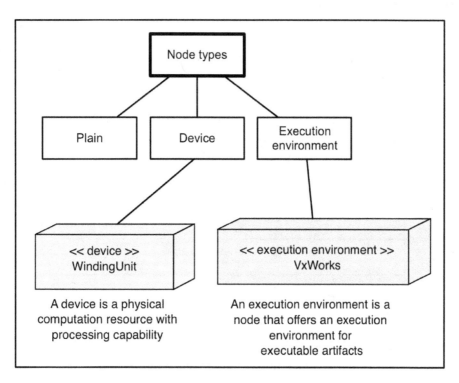

Figure 10.18 Example node types

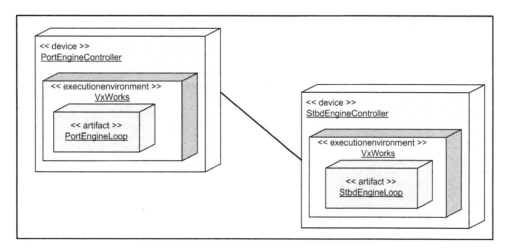

Figure 10.19 Example deployment diagram

10.7. Interaction diagrams.

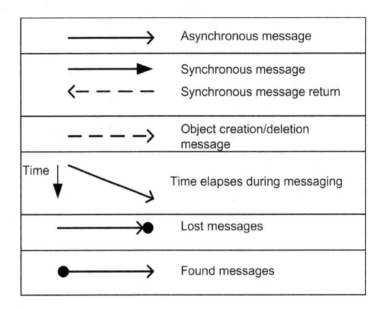

Figure 10.20 UML message notations

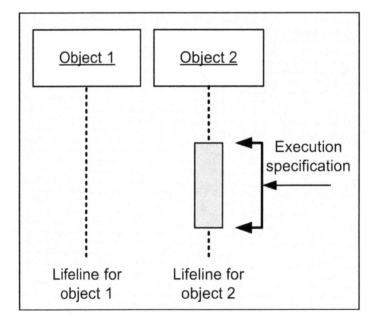

Figure 10.21 UML sequence diagrams and object lifelines

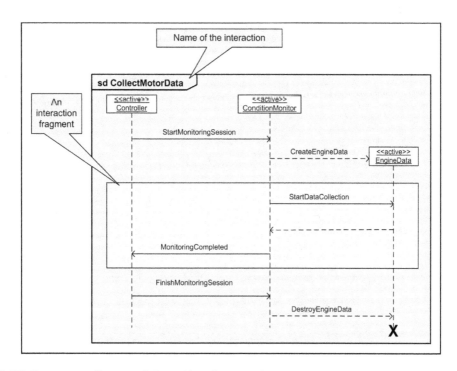

Figure 10.22 Sequence diagram interaction fragment

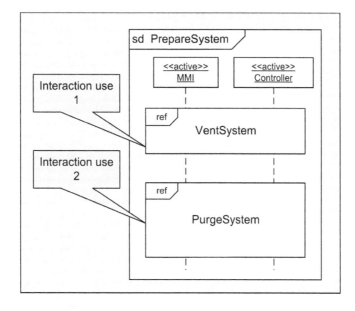

Figure 10.23 Interaction overview diagram

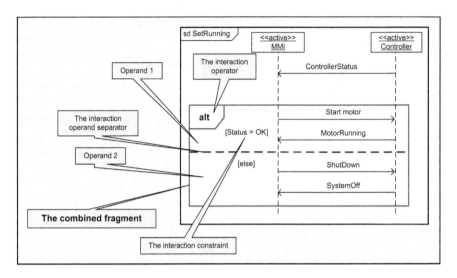

Figure 10.24 Combined fragment specifying alternative courses of action

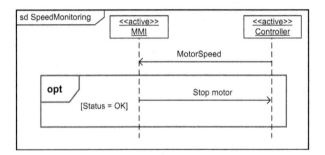

Figure 10.25 Combined fragment specifying optional actions

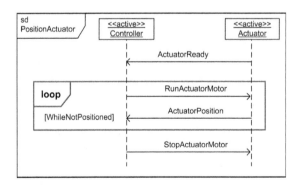

Figure 10.26 Combined fragment specifying a loop

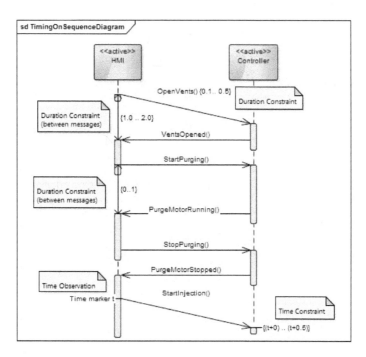

Figure 10.27 Sequence diagram - example timing information

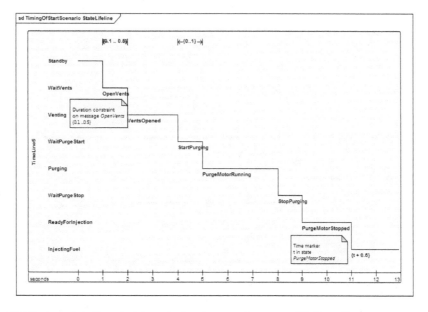

Figure 10.28 Timing details of object behaviour - the state lifeline diagram

10.8. Object diagrams.

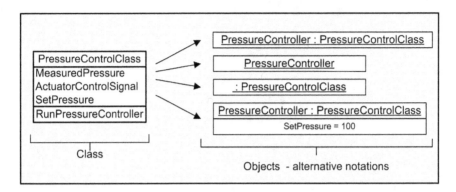

Figure 10.29 Example class and object notation - single class

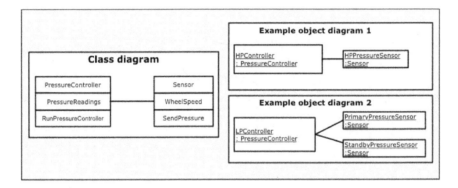

Figure 10.30 Example object and class diagram - multiple classes

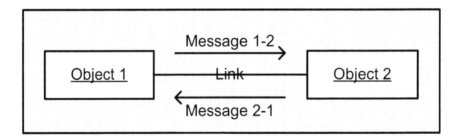

Figure 10.31 Object communication diagram

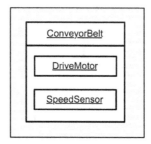

Figure 10.32 Composite object

10.9. Composite structure diagrams.

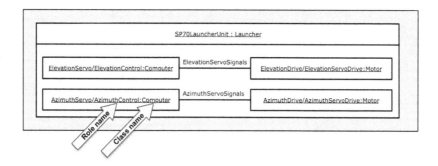

Figure 10.33 Composite object diagram showing roles

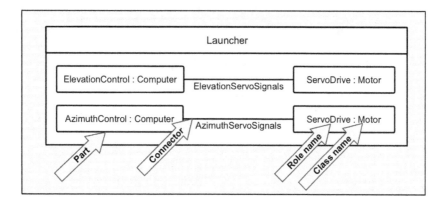

Figure 10.34 Composite structure diagram

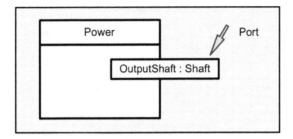

Figure 10.35 Composite structure diagrams and ports

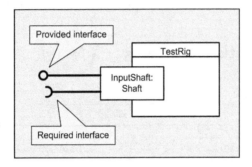

Figure 10.36 Interfaces on ports

10.10. Package diagrams.

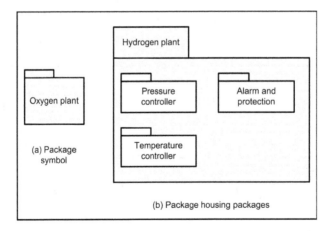

Figure 10.37 Basic package diagrams

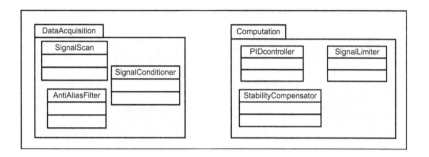

Figure 10.38 Packaging classes

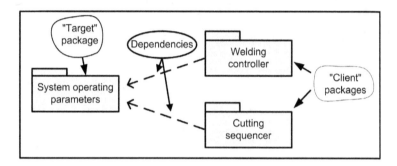

Figure 10.39 Package dependencies

10.11. State diagrams.

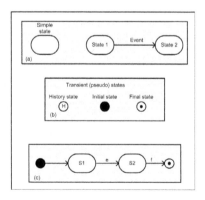

Figure 10.40 Basic UML notation for state machines

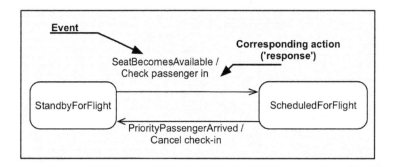

Figure 10.41 Events and responses

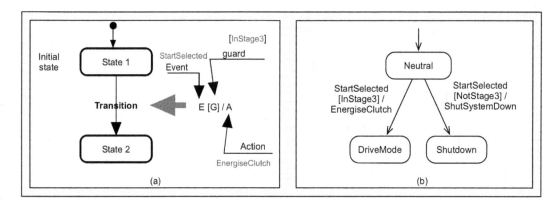

Figure 10.42 State diagrams and guards

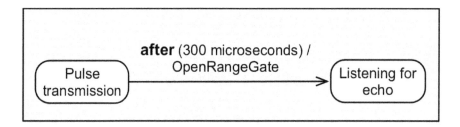

Figure 10.43 Transition caused by time elapse

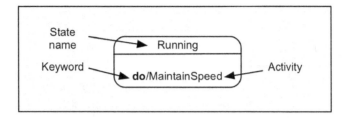

Figure 10.44 Do activity within a state

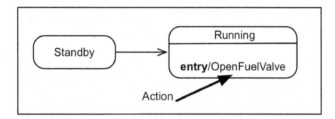

Figure 10.45 Entry action

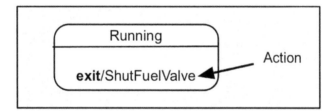

Figure 10.46 Exit action

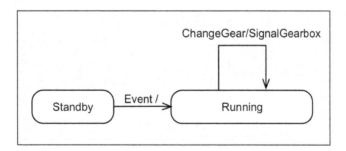

Figure 10.47 State machine - self-transitions

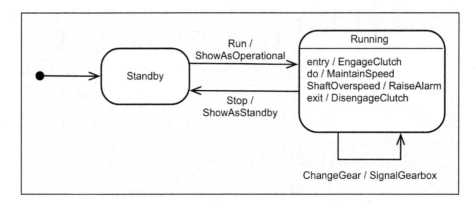

Figure 10.48 Combined transition and state related behaviour

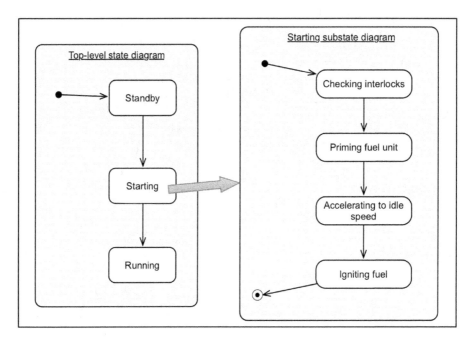

Figure 10.49 Refinement and substates

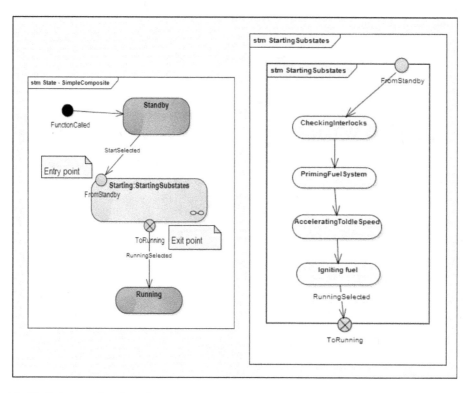

Figure 10.50 Entry and exit points

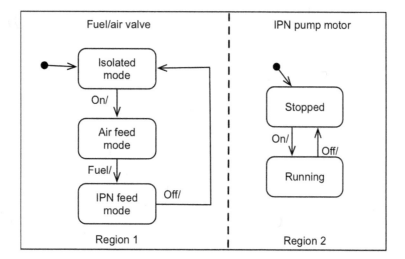

Figure 10.51 Concurrent state modelling in UML

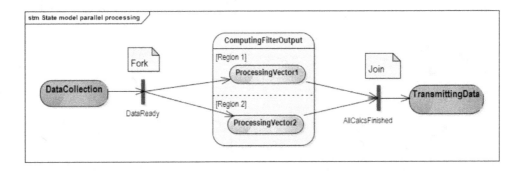

Figure 10.52 State model of parallel processing

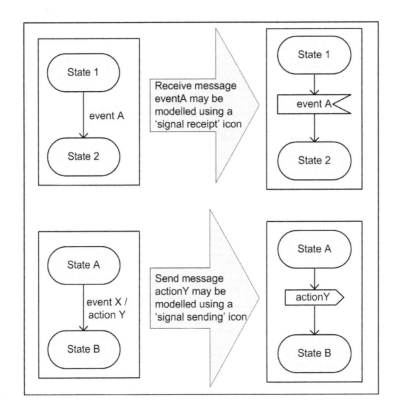

Figure 10.53 Receive and send signals

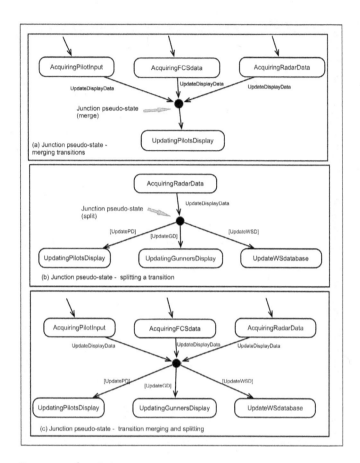

Figure 10.54 Junction pseudo-states

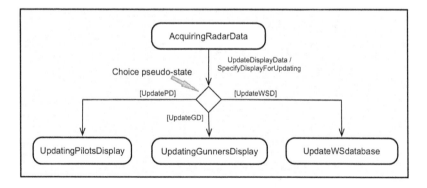

Figure 10.55 Choice pseudo-state

10.12. Use case diagrams.

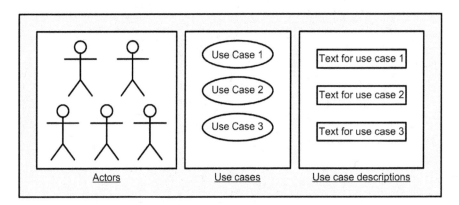

Figure 10.56 The components of the use case model

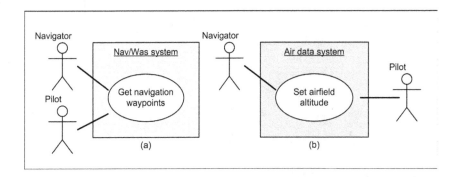

Figure 10.57 Example use case diagrams

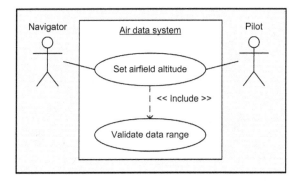

Figure 10.58 The include relationship

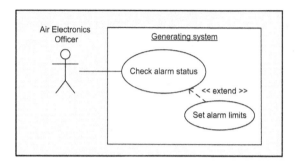

Figure 10.59 The extend relationship

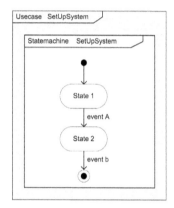

Figure 10.60 Use case behaviour - state machine description

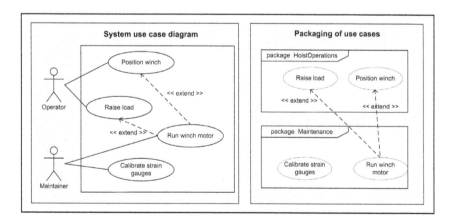

Figure 10.61 Use cases and packages

END OF CHAPTER

References, further reading and bibliography

1. Papers.

T.R.G.Green: *Pictures of programs and other processes, or how to do things with lines,,* Behaviour and Information Technology, Vol.1, No.1, pp3-36, 1982.

G.A.Miller: *The magical number seven, plus or minus two,* Psychological Review, 63(2), pp 81-87, 1956.

N.M.Rothon: *Design structure diagrams: a new standard in flow diagrams,* Computer Bulletin, series 2, no.19, pp 4-6, 1979.

B. Henderson-Sellers; C. Gonzalez-Perez (2006): "Uses and Abuses of the Stereotype Mechanism in UML 1.x and 2.0". in: *Model Driven Engineering Languages and Systems.* Springer Berlin / Heidelberg.

===

2. Books.

Jim Cooling: Real-Time Operating Systems.
Available as an ebook from Amazon:
UK: www.amazon.co.uk/dp/B00GO6VSGE
USA: www.amazon.com/dp/B00GO6VSGE

Jim Cooling: Software Engineering for Real-Time Systems.
UK: www.amazon.co.uk/dp/B00L1FXOCY
USA: www.amazon.com/dp/B00L1FXOCY

Miro Samek: Practical Statecharts in C/C++, cmpBooks, ISBN 1-57820-110-1

===

3. Useful web references.

Architecture Analysis & Design Language (AADL):
http://standards.sae.org/as5506a/

Source code analysis tools:
1. Understand (https://scitools.com)
2. Polyspace (mathworks.com/products/polyspace/)

Systems Modelling Language SysML:
http://www.omgsysml.org/

Tri-Pacific Software Inc: RapidRMA for IBM Rational Rhapsody: The Art of Modeling Real-Time Systems in UML:
http://www.tripac.com/html/prod-fact-rry.html

Unified Modeling Language documents:
    http://www.omg.org/spec/UML/2.3.
    http://www.omg.org/spec/UML/2.3/Infrastructure
    http://www.omg.org/spec/UML/2.3/Superstructure
    http://www.omg.org/spec/UML/2.5/Beta1/

    UML Profile for MARTE:
    http://www.omg.org/spec/MARTE/1.0

Enterprise Architect CASE tool:
http://www.sparxsystems.com/resources/uml2_tutorial/).

Discussion papers:
1. Conrad Bock (http://www.jot.fm/issues/issue_2004_11/column5/)
2. Steve Cook (http://blogs.msdn.com/b/stevecook/archive/2009/06/17/uml-structured-classes-part-1.aspx)

The Index

A

Acivity diagrams - action nodes 177
Acivity diagrams - as program structure diagrams 183
Acivity diagrams - control nodes 177
Acivity diagrams - decision nodes 177
Acivity diagrams - exception handler activity 181
Acivity diagrams - exception handling 181
Acivity diagrams - final flow node 182
Acivity diagrams - fork and join nodes 178
Acivity diagrams - formalizing written specifications 185
Acivity diagrams - guards 177
Acivity diagrams - merge nodes 177
Acivity diagrams - partitions and swimlanes 179
Acivity diagrams - protected node 183
Acivity diagrams - send and receive signals 177
Acivity diagrams - showing sequential and parallel actions 179
Acivity diagrams - time signal 181
Acivity diagrams - time signal as a trigger 181
Acivity diagrams - wait time action 181
Active objects 114
Activity diagram example 178
Activity diagram symbols 177
Activity diagram symbols on interaction overview diagrams 189
Activity diagrams - activities and actions 177
Activity diagrams - and structured programming 190
Activity diagrams - decomposition symbol 188
Activity diagrams - mapping to pseudo-code 190
Activity diagrams - mapping to source code 192
Activity diagrams - structured activity and sub-activities 188
Activity diagrams - structuring and decomposing (general) 187
Artifact example 107
Attribute values 106

B

Ball and socket notation 92

C

Class - abstract 84
Class - active 115
Class - base 79
Class - denoting private and public items 58
Class - introduction 55
Class - operations 56
Class associations 63
Class attributes 55
Class diagram and multiplicity 65
Class symbol 56
Classes - concrete 84
Client-server relationship - basics 61
Coding aspects - client-server relationships 66
Coding aspects - explicit wiring functions 70
Coding aspects and bi-directional associations 70
Coding aspects and peer-to-peer relationships 70
Coding aspects and uni-directional associations 66
Coding aspects of composite aggregation 73
Coding aspects of interface inheritance 84
Coding example - implementation inheritance 72
Coding example of modular construction 74
Communication diagram - object 76
Component - basics 100
Component - external view 97
Component - UML definition 96
Component interfaces 99
Component object - informal notation 100
Components - internal structures 101
Composite objects - whole and parts 72
Composite aggregation 73
Composite classes - design example 93
Composite diagrams and connectors 91
Composite object diagram 93
Composite structure and class design 95
Composite structure diagram 94
Composite structure diagrams and ports 92
Composite structures and parts 90
Composition and composite objects 72
Context diagram 53
CORBA IDL 104
CORBA IDL module 102

D

Deployment diagrams 112
Diagrams - a communication vehicle 23
Diagrams - high and low-level views 32
Diagrams - key qualities 23

Diagrams and post-design work 23
Diagrams and the two-stage design process 23
Diagrams as a design tool 29
Diagrams for documenting designs 30

H
Hidden object - 'main' 63

I
Implementation inheritance 78
Inheritance - general aspects 78
Inheritance and dynamic polymorphism 87
Inheritance and interfaces 83
Inheritance and polymorphism 86
Inheritance and static polymorphism 86
Inheritance and subclasses 79
Inheritance and subclassing 79
Inheritance and superclasses 79
Inheritance structures 80
Inheritance vs adaption 81
Interface inheritance 83
Interfaces - required and provided 61

M
Message - asynchronous 117
Message - synchronous 117
Methods and messages - concepts 62
Model definition 1
Modelling as a specification method 5
Modelling for analysis 3
Modelling for performance improvement 4
Modelling for prediction 3
Modelling qualities - Dynamic behaviour 13
Modelling qualities - Interactions 10
Modelling qualities - Processing 10
modelling qualities - structure 8
Modelling qualities - Usage 14
Modelling reality with diagrams 25
Modular construction - basics 72

N
Node types 112
Nodes 112

O

Object - active 53
Object - alternative notations 57
Object - global view 54
Object communication diagram 60
Object icon 53
Object model - flat 61
OO design - the simple model 52
OO design techniques - basics 211
OO models - broad perspective 18
OO programming design techniques - basics 212
OOD method definition 212
OOP design method 211

P

Package and artifact diagram relationship 107
Package dependencies 107
Passive objects 115
Peer-to-peer relationships 64
Ports as a connecting mechanism 91
Process models- typical applications 173
Processing modelling and examples 174

R

Real-time CORBA 104
Relationships - uni and bi-directional 64

S

Sequence diagram - active object interactions 118
Sequence diagram - alt interaction operator 129
Sequence diagram - assert interaction operator 133
Sequence diagram - break interaction operator 132
Sequence diagram - combined fragments 129
Sequence diagram - concurrent operations 118
Sequence diagram - consider interaction operator 133
Sequence diagram - critical interaction operator 121
Sequence diagram - duration constraint 135
Sequence diagram - duration observation 135
Sequence diagram - dynamic object creation 123
Sequence diagram - dynamic object deletion 123
Sequence diagram - execution specification 118
Sequence diagram - focus of control 118
Sequence diagram - found message 123
Sequence diagram - fundamentals 116
Sequence diagram - gates 128

Sequence diagram - ignore interaction operator 131
Sequence diagram - interaction constraint 129
Sequence diagram - interaction fragments 124
Sequence diagram - interaction occurrence 126
Sequence diagram - interaction operand 129
Sequence diagram - interaction operand separator 129
Sequence diagram - interaction operator 129
Sequence diagram - interaction overview diagram 126
Sequence diagram - interaction use 126
Sequence diagram - loop interaction operator 130
Sequence diagram - lost message 123
Sequence diagram - maintenance 123
Sequence diagram - navigation 124
Sequence diagram - neg interaction operator 133
Sequence diagram - opt interaction operator 130
Sequence diagram - overview of timing information 142
Sequence diagram - par interaction operator 132
Sequence diagram - passive object interactions 120
Sequence diagram - seq interaction operator 133
Sequence diagram - sequential operations 119
Sequence diagram - strict interaction operator 133
Sequence diagram - time constraint 135
Sequence diagram - time observation 135
Sequence diagram - timing information 135
Sequence diagram lifelines 118
Sequence diagrams - message types 117
Software - application-level 209
Software - logical design model 105
Software - physical design model 105
Software - service-level 209
Software development - independent design and build 208
Software machine - defined 17
Software machine and the object 17
Software machines - essentials 17
Software object - template 55
State and value lifelines - combined view 137
State lifeline diagram 137
State machine - event 147
State machine - transition 147
State machine diagram - basic UML notation 147
State machine diagram - core constructs 145
State machines - actions and effects 149
State machines - activities within a state 164
State machines - after keyword 153
State machines - behavioural state machines 150
State machines - choice pseudostate 168
State machines - combining state models 162
State machines - composite state machine 158
State machines - compound events 152

State machines - concurrent machines 160
State machines - concurrent state modelling 160
State machines - controller code for generalized state machine 170
State machines - decomposition indicator 158
State machines - deep history 166
State machines - do keyword 154
State machines - entry action 154
State machines - entry and exit point pseudo-states 158
State machines - event attributes 154
State machines - exit action 155
State machines - for a composite unit 160
State machines - fork pseudo-state 162
State machines - generalized state machine 169
State machines - guards 151
State machines - history pseudostate 164
State machines - history pseudostate icon 165
State machines - join pseudo-state 162
State machines - junction pseudostates 167
State machines - Mealy machine 149
State machines - merge junction 167
State machines - merge/split junction 167
State machines - Moore machine 149
State machines - multiple events 152
State machines - multiple responses 153
State machines - protocol state machine 150
State machines - pseudo states 147
State machines - responses 151
State machines - self-transition 156
State machines - shallow history 165
State machines - signal receive icon 163
State machines - signal send icon 163
State machines - split junction 167
State machines - state controller 170
State machines - state-related behaviour 154
State machines - sub-state model 157
State machines - transient states 147
State machines - transition-related behaviour 150
State machines - triggers and events 147
State machines - when keyword 152
State modelling - simple example 149
Structured classifiers 92

U
UML - overview 44
UML artifacts - examples 107
UML diagram set - overview diagram 20
UML in real-time systems 49
UML origins 43

UML package 103
Use case - the base use case 201
Use case analysis - overview 195
Use case definition 199
Use case diagrams - actors 197
Use case diagrams - basics 197
Use case diagrams - notation for devices as actors 204
Use case diagrams - roles 196
Use case extend relationship 202
Use case flow chart description 200
Use case goal 199
Use case include relationship 202
Use case model - component parts 197
Use case models and text descriptions 197
Use case packaging 204
Use case scenario types 201
Use case scenarios 199
Use case state machine description 201
Use case symbol 197
Use cases - definition 197
Use cases - external systems as actors 203
Use cases - include vs extend relationships 203

V
Value lifeline diagram 137

W
Wiring components using assembly connectors 98
Wiring objects at declaration time 68
Wiring objects together - intro 66